FOOD SAFARI

Glorious Adventures through a World of Cuisines

MAEVE O'MEARA

Photography by Sharyn Cairns

hardie grant books
MELBOURNE · LONDON

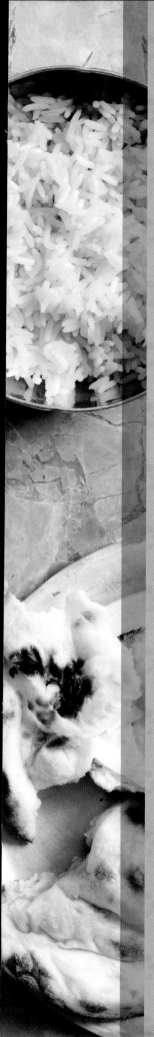

CONTENTS

To my lovely Toufic and
my family – Conor, Kitty
and Scarlett, my mum
Maev and my late father
John, brother Matt and
family – who have all
made the journey so
much fun and who have
(almost) always revelled
in my delicious new finds.

Baklawa

Preface

Welcome to the culinary United Nations ...

This beautiful book aims to lead you by the hand through some of the most delicious and intriguing foods around the world. With its help you can become the food-savvy companion others turn to and ask, 'How much *za'atar* should I buy at one time?', 'What sort of chilli do I need for my Thai red curry?' and 'What the hell do I do with okra?!'

In these pages lie some of the secrets behind thirty-four different cuisines that are all represented in Australia's rich and diverse society. They include mouth-watering descriptions of traditional herbs and spices, seasonal vegetables, favourite drinks and snacks as well as tips on key ingredients and cooking implements. The recipes are simple, delicious and will always work – and will impress your family and friends. They have been gathered from talented cooks and chefs who have grown up learning from their mothers and grandmothers – their kitchen wisdom brings each cuisine alive.

So how did this exciting food adventure start? Well, many years ago I realised that my culinary boundaries growing up in a meat-and-three-veg Irish–Australian family were fairly limited. I was always keen to explore more exotic flavours so I've gradually discovered and been welcomed into a world full of big, boisterous families and tables groaning under amazing food. It has been an honour to be included at the table of so many warm and welcoming new friends and I've enjoyed a delicious adventure at the same time.

I hope you'll love all of these new tastes and flavours and I wish you many delicious adventures of your own.

Maeve O'Meara

AFRICA

What an incredible mix of cooking styles, unusual ingredients and delicious surprises are found in this vast continent. Having travelled in the north and south of Africa, I have a keen interest in African food and have been lucky enough to have taken part in preparing it many times. Yet I was still blown away by the discoveries I've recently made closer to home. The marvellous spice mixes, deeply satisfying dishes, unusual serving arrangements and the sheer warmth and generosity of the African people I've met have been overwhelming – where one dish was enough, a whole feast would appear just because I showed an interest. Such generosity from people who come from a continent so often beset with natural and man-made disasters ... It says something about the human spirit that dishes that have evolved in Africa are not just sustaining but truly magnificent.

The West

West Africans love chilli and spices and will use these to add a little heat and extra flavour to many of their dishes. Ghanaians have developed a hot chilli and smoked fish accompaniment called *shitto* (yes, really!). It is an intensely smelly, wonderfully hot and salty paste that they use readily, even enjoying it simply with plain rice.

Red palm-fruit oil is the oil of choice in West Africa, and when it's heated, magic happens. The oil melts to the most wonderful, deep-ruby colour and it adds a golden crispiness to anything cooked in it. One of my great finds has been disks of plantain (green banana) fried in palm-fruit oil, like chunky potato chips – divine! This oil is often confused with its infamous, trans-fatty cousin made from the kernels of the palm oil tree. Palm-fruit oil comes from the fruit, which is pressed with the same technique used to make virgin olive oil, without any heat or solvents. As a result, the palm-fruit oil is high in betacarotene and antioxidants and is actually good for you.

The Horn

Ethiopia, Eritrea and Somalia are home to *injera*, a wonderfully spongy, fermented bread that is a cross between a crumpet and a pancake and the size of a wide circular tray. It's baked on a large, flat griddle and almost every meal is served on it, the round flatbread working as an edible plate – the diner breaks off pieces of the bread to scoop up meat or vegetable stews.

AFRICAN BASIL

A herb with a warm, sweet, camphor-like scent and a gentle taste with a hint of clove. This is used in many recipes from the Horn of Africa. The dried leaves and seeds are ground for use in spice mixes.

AFRICAN MINT (*EFIRI*)

Found in some plant nurseries and easy to cultivate, this has a distinctive fresh flavour.

BERBERE

A hot chilli and spice mix used widely in stews and sprinkled on top of many dishes for garnish and extra kick. Brick-red in colour, the mix usually includes red chillies, *timiz* (long peppers), cardamom, cumin, fenu-greek, ginger, cloves, nutmeg, corian-der, allspice, rue berries and ajowan (a spice known as bishop's weed). Freshly ground then sun dried, *berbere* is best stored in an airtight container and used within six weeks. For Ethio-pians and Eritreans, this is red gold! It is sold in African grocery stores and specialty spice shops.

BROWN CARDAMOM

Larger and more fibrous than green cardamom, these pods have a camphor-like aroma and smoky flavour. They are used in stews and spice mixes in the Horn of Africa.

NIGELLA SEEDS

When crushed these little black seeds smell a little like oregano. Their slight bitterness and fragrant aroma is useful in stews.

NITER KIBBEH

Spiced clarified butter that is usually made in large quantities and kept for daily use. Ingredients include cardamom, fenugreek and nigella seeds. Some recipes also add garlic, ginger, finely chopped onion, turmeric, nutmeg, cloves, cinnamon sticks, fennel seeds and *korseret* (a herb native to Ethiopia with a minty thyme flavour). While often homemade, *niter kibbeh* can be purchased from African grocery stores.

RED PALM-FRUIT OIL

Oil extracted from the fruit of the African oil palm. Not to be confused with palm-kernel oil. Native to Africa, red palm-fruit oil has long been appreciated as an excellent base for cooking.

One of the dishes I love is an Ethiopian slow-cooked stew called a *wat*. It starts with many kilograms of diced onions (chopping these is a tear-jerker!) that are slowly cooked in a heavy-based pot for more than an hour. No oil or fat is used to start the cooking process and what you end up with is a sweet, dark base of onion to which lots of the popular *berbere* spice is added, as well as other spices and meat or vegetables. The resulting stew is spicy and delicious, especially served with *injera*.

Another great Ethiopian tradition is the coffee ceremony, which is a crucial part of social and cultural life there – this is fitting, perhaps, as coffee was first discovered growing wild in Ethiopia centuries ago. Surprisingly, the green coffee beans are only roasted just before they're used. Enough beans for each pot are poured into a small metal pannier and roasted over a flame, then the beans are ground and water is added. The resulting brew has a deliciously soft flavour, which is sometimes intensified by the addition of spices, including kibbled ginger. The coffee ceremony involves the serving of three rounds of coffee accompanied by the burning of frankincense. It's a heady feast for the senses and takes at least an hour – very different from the Italian espresso you gulp while standing up in a coffee bar! No coffee ceremony is complete without popcorn and sometimes dates and a sweet, soft bread called *himbasha* are also served.

The East

Along the Swahili Coast of Kenya and Tanzania you find a wonderful culinary fusion of African, Indian, Arabic and British flavours, a legacy of spice trading in the area. Local produce such as fish, bananas and coconuts feature prominently and these are mixed with the more exotic tastes of curries, pickles, saffron, nutmeg and pomegranate. The Portuguese also had an impact on the cuisine of the region, as seen in the marinating and barbecuing techniques used there.

Further inland, cattle-breeding tribes like the Maasai live on a meat- and milk-based diet, although maize meal, rice, potatoes and cabbage are becoming popular. In Uganda staple foods are steamed plantains called *matoke*, cassava, sweet potatoes, peanuts and beans. Simple and delicious food.

Making *Fufu*

In Africa, no meal is complete without a starchy porridge called *fufu* (also known as *ugali*, *pap*, *iwisa*, *sadza* or *mealie meal*). This is made from yams and sometimes plantains, cassava or maize and African people say they don't feel full unless they've had their *fufu*.

Making *fufu* to the required consistency takes some energy. Dried, pounded meal is mixed with water in a saucepan, which is placed over a fire or gas flame. As the *fufu* heats and thickens, the cook uses a large wooden spoon to stir it vigourously in a circular motion. It takes a good ten minutes to get the *fufu* just right – thick and smooth. When cooked it is scooped by the cupful into a bowl and, with a few spoonfuls of warm water added, is shaken back and forth until it forms a ball. It's then served with a little meat or some vegetables in a rich sauce on the side.

It takes practice to eat *fufu* with your hands. You pinch off a ball with your right hand, making an indentation with your thumb and at the same time not letting it touch the palm of your hand. You then deftly scoop up a small amount of the accompanying stew and eat. Let's say it's a delightful, tactile learning experience!

'Don't entrust money to a man with a flat stomach.'

Mahindi Ya Naz
Corn in Coconut Sauce
from Shukri Abdi

This is a typical dish of the Swahili Coast, with its Arabic and Indian influences, and it makes a delicious meal when served with lamb *suqaar* and the cardamom-spiced bread *mahamri*. *Suqaar* is a traditional Somalian stir-fry, which can use beef, chicken or lamb. *Mahamri* are known as 'Swahili buns' and are eaten plain for breakfast or used to slurp up sauce at dinnertime – you vary the amount of sugar in the recipe depending on what you're going to serve them with.

MAHAMRI

450 g (3 cups) plain flour

1 cup coconut milk powder

55–110 g (¼–½) cup sugar

1 teaspoon ground cardamom

1 tablespoon dried yeast

250 ml milk

oil for deep-frying

CORN

6 corn cobs, cut into 10 cm pieces

1 cup coconut milk powder

500 ml water

1 large onion, diced

3 tablespoons tomato puree

1 teaspoon turmeric

salt

SUQAAR

1 tablespoon olive oil

500 g lamb, finely diced

1 onion, diced

½ red capsicum, finely diced

2 tablespoons tomato puree

pinch of salt

To make the *mahamri*, mix the flour, coconut milk powder, sugar, cardamom and yeast in a large bowl. Add the milk and combine well to form a dough. Cover the bowl and set aside in a warm place until the dough rises.

To make the coconut corn, put the corn pieces in a large saucepan. Mix the remaining ingredients together and pour over the corn. Cook over low heat for 10–15 minutes.

Once the *mahamri* dough has risen, form the dough into balls (about the size of tennis balls), roll out to ½ cm thick and cut into quarters.

Heat the oil for the *mahamri* in a deep, heavy-based frying pan. When the oil is hot, add the pieces of dough carefully, a few at a time, and fry until they puff up and turn golden. Remove with a slotted spoon and drain on paper towel.

Heat the olive oil for the *suqaar* in a frying pan over medium heat. Add the remaining ingredients and stir-fry for a few minutes until the meat is cooked. Remove from the heat and serve alongside the *mahamri* and coconut corn.

Serves 6–8

Doro Wat
Ethiopian Red Chicken Stew
from Karim Degal

A *wat* is a stew that uses the marvellous red *berbere* spice mix and a rich base of onion. A vast quantity of onions is used so it is a good idea to finely dice these in a food processor. If six tablespoons of *berbere* sound like a lot (it contains plenty of chilli powder), reduce the amount when you first cook this recipe – you can always make it hotter next time! For a healthier alternative you can replace the *niter kibbeh* with more olive oil. If you can't find African basil (it is not readily available in Australia), simply leave it out.

This dish is traditionally served on top of *injera* bread. It is best left to sit overnight so that the flavours infuse – then eat it the following day at room temperature.

3 kg onions, finely diced

1 large chicken, preferably free-range

100 ml white vinegar

juice of 1 lemon

100 ml olive oil

3 tablespoons *niter kibbeh* (see recipe on page 11)

6 tablespoons *berbere*

12 eggs, hard-boiled

MIXED SPICES

2 tablespoons cardamom seeds

2 tablespoons nigella seeds

2 tablespoons ajowan or fennel seeds

1 tablespoon dried African basil (optional)

2 teaspoons black peppercorns

2 tablespoons salt

Place the onion in a large, heavy-based pot, cover with a lid and cook over low–medium heat, stirring occasionally. Do not add any oil or liquid. Cook for about 1 hour, until the onion has reduced.

While the onion is cooking, remove the skin from the chicken and cut into portions, trimming off any fat. (In Ethiopia, they cut it into 21 portions.) Mix the vinegar and lemon juice together and sit the chicken pieces in the liquid for 10–15 minutes, then drain.

Combine the ingredients for the mixed spices in a mortar and grind to a powder.

When the onion has reduced add the olive oil, *niter kibbeh* and *berbere* and stir well. Add the chicken. Bring the mixture to the boil, then reduce the heat to a simmer. Stir the spices into the stew and add extra salt if needed. Simmer until the chicken is cooked through, making sure the onion does not stick to the bottom of the pot. Spoon out some of the excess oil that settles on top.

Cut vertical grooves into the hard-boiled eggs to ensure the flavour seeps in. When the stew is cooked, add the eggs and turn off the heat. The *doro wat* can be served immediately with *injera* but is even better the following day when the spices have worked their magic.

Serves 8

'The heart that does not
eat chilli is a feeble one.'

Jollof Rice

from Kunle Adesua

Jollof rice, or *ceebu jen* as it's known in Senegal, is perhaps the best known West African dish because it's delicious, colourful and easy to prepare. It is a little like an African paella made from parboiled long-grain rice, vegetables and meat but without any butter or wine added. It is delicious served hot with fried plantain slices.

The recipe calls for African mint (*efiri*), which you can buy in some plant nurseries – if you can't get it, simply leave it out of the recipe. If you prefer a milder dish, remove some of the seeds from the chillies.

OBE ATA SAUCE

5 tomatoes, chopped

3 red capsicums, chopped

6 small red chillies

100 ml red palm-fruit oil

1 onion, finely chopped

3 shallots, finely chopped

3 spring onions, finely chopped

1 celery stalk, chopped

handful of African mint (optional)

pinch of salt

FISH AND RICE

1 kg firm fish fillets such as marlin, cut into large cubes

25 g chilli flakes mixed with 1 teaspoon salt

2½ red palm-fruit oil

2 medium carrots, chopped

1 red capsicum, chopped

1 green capsicum, chopped

2 tomatoes, chopped

2 zucchini (or 2 celery stalks with leaves), chopped

pinch of salt

250 ml water

2 cups parboiled long-grain rice

To make the *obe ata*, use a hand-held blender to process the chopped tomato in a bowl. Blend the capsicum and chilli in a separate bowl.

Heat the oil in a saucepan and add the onion, shallots, spring onion, celery, African mint and salt and sauté, stirring well, until the onions are translucent. Add the tomato and the capsicum and chilli and cook over moderate heat for 10 minutes.

To make the fish and rice, sprinkle the fish cubes with the chilli flakes and salt and set aside.

Heat the oil in a large saucepan and add the carrot, capsicum, tomato and zucchini (or celery) and salt. Cook over moderate heat for 10 minutes until softened a little. Add the fish, water and rice and the *obe ata* sauce. Gently mix together and bring to the boil. Cover the saucepan and simmer for approximately 45 minutes, until the rice and vegetables are cooked.

Serves 10

Akara with Red *Kosayi*
Black-eyed Bean Fritters
with Dipping Sauce
from Bathie Dia

Protein-rich and widely available, black-eyed beans are a popular ingredient throughout Africa and *akara*, or black-eyed bean fritters, are the national snack food of Senegal and Nigeria. These fritters are great for vegetarians and vegans and are especially delicious with the *kosayi* dipping sauce.

A good red *kosayi* shouldn't be too hot – you should just be able to feel the heat. The sauce will keep for about six months in the refrigerator and the older it gets the better it tastes. This recipe recommends you make the sauce at least two days before you want to use it.

RED *KOSAYI*

9 small red capsicums

3 long red chillies

7 small red chillies

2 tablespoons vegetable oil

75 g (⅓ cup) sugar

75 ml white vinegar

1 teaspoon salt

olive oil

AKARA

500 g black-eyed beans

salt and pepper

handful of fresh herbs such as flat-leaf parsley or coriander, chopped (optional)

1 teaspoon baking powder (optional)

oil for frying

To make the *kosayi*, place the whole capsicums and chillies in a large saucepan of cold water and bring to the boil. Simmer for 25 minutes or until the capsicums are soft. Remove from the heat, cover with a lid and set aside until cool.

When cooled, dry the capsicums and chillies and remove the seeds. Peel the capsicums. Place the capsicums and chillies in a food processor and blend to a paste. Press the mixture through a fine sieve to remove any remaining skin.

Add the oil, sugar, vinegar and salt and mix together well. Pour the mixture into a sterilised jar with a thin layer of olive oil on top and leave in the refrigerator for at least 2 days to mature.

To make the *akara*, bring a large saucepan of water to the boil, add the beans and boil for 2 minutes. Drain the beans and spread them out on a clean tea towel. Cover with a second tea towel and roll the beans back and forth between the towels using the palms of your hands. After a few minutes the beans will have shed their skins. Remove any skins that remain attached to individual beans by rubbing the bean between your thumb and forefinger. To separate the beans from the skins, tip them back into the saucepan, add lots of water and swirl around in a circular motion until the skins have risen to the top. Scoop out the skins and leave the beans to soak for 2 hours.

In a food processor blend the beans to a very fine paste. Knead the paste for 2–3 minutes, until the starch is released, then divide in half.

Place one half in a bowl over a saucepan of simmering water and stir continuously with a rubber spatula or wooden spoon until the mixture comes together like a dough. Take great care that the mixture does not cook or curdle. If necessary, briefly lift the bowl away from the heat from time to time. Then mix in the remaining paste and continue stirring over the simmering water for about 1 minute, so the dough comes together. Take the bowl off the heat and continue to stir until the dough has cooled to room temperature.

Season the bean dough and add herbs if using. Add the baking powder if you want a lighter texture. Shape into fritters roughly the size of eggs and shallow-fry in oil. (You can deep-fry the fritters if you prefer or wrap them in banana leaves and steam them.) Serve the fritters warm or cold with a dipping bowl of *kosayi*.

Makes about 25 fritters

Kulwha
Eritrean Stir-fry

from Rahel Ogbaghiorghis

Fast, fresh, simple and delicious, *kulwha* is an Eritrean stir-fry that uses the spiced clarified butter called *niter kibbeh*. This recipe makes more *niter kibbeh* than you need, but it can be refrigerated for up to three months and used in other recipes. For a healthier alternative you can replace the *niter kibbeh* with more olive oil.

NITER KIBBEH

500 g unsalted butter

½ teaspoon ground cardamom

½ teaspoon ground fenugreek

½ teaspoon nigella seeds, ground

KULWHA

1 tablespoon *niter kibbeh*

1 tablespoon olive oil

1 onion, sliced

1 long green chilli, chopped

2 tomatoes, diced

500 g lamb fillet, diced into small cubes

pinch of salt

1 tablespoon *berbere*

To make the *niter kibbeh*, heat the butter in a small saucepan over low–medium heat until it has begun to simmer gently. Simmer for about 30 minutes, skimming the foam off the surface, until the top layer of butter is completely clear. Strain the butter through a fine sieve over a bowl, leaving the milk solids in the bottom of the pan. Stir in the spices. Allow to cool then transfer to an airtight container, reserving 1 tablespoon for the *kulwha*.

To make the *kulwha*, put the *niter kibbeh*, oil, onion, chilli, half the tomato, the lamb and salt into a large frying pan and place over high heat. Stir-fry until the meat is cooked through (about 3 minutes) then add the *berbere* and the remaining tomato. Serve with *injera* or rice.

Serves 4

'Do not eat alone – you will enjoy your food more when you share it with people.'

BRAZIL

Brazilian food is an exuberant, colourful mix of Portuguese, African and native Amazonian flavours and in Australia we've embraced it wholeheartedly. We love the easy Brazilian lifestyle that mirrors our own, especially when it includes the *churrasco* barbecues, the fresh lime and sugarcane cocktails (*caipirinha*) and the tasty little cheese breads (*pão de queijo*) that are starting to be sold here.

Brazilians are people who like intensity and when they love a particular food, they eat it a lot – lots of salt, sugar, caffeine and chilli. The national dish is *feijoada*, a slow-cooked, dark mixture of black turtle beans, cured meats and *chouriço* (spicy sausage). It is so popular that Brazilians eat it twice a week – on Wednesdays and again on Saturdays. This dish originated with African slaves who were brought to Brazil to work on plantations developed by Portuguese settlers. Beans were cheap and the air-dried beef and pork off-cuts were the least attractive and most affordable parts of the animal. The resulting dish was simple but also rich, comforting and satisfying and has been treasured ever since.

The Africans also brought to Brazil red palm-fruit or *dende* oil, coconuts, plantains and okra. The Portuguese, who were able to sustain themselves on large voyages of discovery due to their salted cod, brought with them this useful fish as well as a love of cooking with onions and garlic and a love of rich desserts made with many eggs and sugar. These elements were combined with the ancient foods of the native Indian inhabitants of Brazil, such as the Amazon forest berry called *açaí* (pronounced 'ah-sah-ee'), which contains loads of antioxidants and vitamins; guarana, another forest berry; hearts of palm, which are a terrible waste of a beautiful tree but very delicious; and cassava, a long tuber with pinkish-brown skin and milky white flesh that is now a staple of Brazilian cooking.

To add further to this mingling of cuisines, western European and Arab immigrants to coffee plantations in the southern part of Brazil brought with them the skills for cheese making and preserving meat. They also contributed to the diverse cuisine that is centred around the Minas Gerais region. Cheese became the basis for one of Brazil's most popular savoury snacks, the *pão de queijo*, which is a bite-sized cheese bread made with cassava flour. *Salgadinhos*, or snacks, in Brazil are always taken with strong, black coffee or the lime-based *caipirinha* cocktails.

CARNE SECA
Literally translates as 'dried meat' and describes varying cuts of beef that are salted, cured then rehydrated to make *feijoada*.

CORIANDER
In the northeastern region of Brazil, Bahia, fresh coriander leaves are a common garnish for seafood and poultry dishes.

DRIED SHRIMP
These tiny sun-dried shrimps add depth of flavour to Bahian dishes such as *xinxim de galinha*. They are finely blended to a powder and sometimes soaked first.

LIME
Regularly used in marinades for meat and fish or squeezed over seafood dishes. Lime is the key ingredient in the ubiquitous *caipirinha* cocktail.

MALAGUETA CHILLIES
An extremely hot chilli that is a popular addition to many Brazilian dishes. You can substitute with other hot chillies such as birdseye or jalapeño.

PLANTAIN
From the banana family, plantains are larger, firmer and lower in sugar content than regular bananas. They're used green (and therefore starchy) or ripe (and therefore sweet). When green they can be sliced diagonally and fried to make dense but delicious chips.

One surprise is that the *caipirinha* can be served as early as mid-morning, as I've discovered at a number of Brazilian homes I've visited. And this alcohol is 45 per cent proof! The Brazilian sips cocktails at the same speed that ice melts – very slowly. Two or three cocktails will last them a whole evening.

Another popular Brazilian export is the barbecue called *churrasco*. It originated in the south of Brazil where the *gauchos*, or cowboys, used a cut of meat from the top of the beef rump (in Brazil it's called the *picanha*), rolled it in rock salt and sometimes garlic, and cooked it rotisserie-style over charcoal on long skewers. The fat on the meat bastes it and keeps the meat moist and delicious. *Churrasco* restaurants are becoming increasingly popular, where long skewers of varied meats are ferried from charcoal barbecues straight to the table.

To finish meals, tropical fruit is abundant and eaten across Brazil but sweets are also very popular – and very sweet! Some are flavoured with fruits such as pineapple or with coconut – like *quindim*, which is a deliciously dense coconut custard.

'To compliment the chef
say "*Que comida deliciosa!*"
(What delicious food!)'

Xinxim de Galinha

from Regina Kyztia

An easy and delicious dish of chicken and prawns braised in coconut milk. Dried shrimp, garlic, ginger and crushed cashews add extra crunch and flavour.

1 kg chicken thigh fillets, diced

juice of ½ lime

1 teaspoon crushed garlic

1 teaspoon grated ginger

salt

1 medium onion, finely chopped

1 tablespoon olive oil

200 g tinned diced tomatoes

1 tablespoon red palm-fruit oil

50 g dried shrimp, finely ground in a blender

125 ml coconut milk

½ bunch coriander, leaves picked

2 tablespoons crushed cashews or peanuts

200 g shelled green prawns

chopped chillies (optional)

black pepper

Marinate the chicken in the lime juice, garlic, ginger and salt for 30 minutes.

Sauté the onion in the olive oil then stir in the marinated chicken. Add the tomato and palm-fruit oil and cook for about 10 minutes, then add the ground shrimp and coconut milk and simmer gently for another 10 minutes. Add the coriander, cashews or peanuts and prawns, cover with a lid and continue to simmer for another 5–10 minutes, until the prawns are cooked through. Stir in the chilli if using, add a little black pepper and taste for salt. Serve with rice and salad.

Serves 4

'Always cook with love and passion and everything will taste beautiful.'

Feijoada
from Edna Barzel

This national dish is made from various kinds of beef and pork, which are slow cooked with black beans then served with crunchy *farofa*. The smoked and cured meats are available from Spanish, Portuguese and South American delis. When the *feijoada* is nearly ready, be careful not to use a fork or spoon (or in fact any metal utensil) in the dish. This is said to spoil the flavour and turn the dish sour.

500 g black turtle beans, rinsed

500 g *chouriço* sausage, diced

750 g smoked beef ribs, divided into pieces

thick piece of bacon or speck (about 250 g), diced

400 g smoked pork loin, diced

500 g *carne seca* (dried beef), diced and soaked in cold water for a few hours

small red chillies to taste

2 bay leaves

4 garlic cloves, finely chopped

salt

1 onion, finely chopped

olive oil

sliced orange or pineapple to serve

FAROFA

2 tablespoons butter

1 onion, diced

250 g bacon, diced

500 g toasted cassava (manioc) flour

salt and pepper

3 flat-leaf parsley sprigs, chopped

3 spring onions, chopped

Place the beans, all the meat, chillies, bay leaves and half the garlic in a medium-sized pot (or pressure cooker) and season with salt. Add enough water to just cover. Bring to the boil then simmer, covered with a lid, for about 2 hours.

Sauté the onion and remaining garlic in olive oil in a separate frying pan. Once softened, add to the *feijoada*. Cook for another 15 minutes.

To make the *farofa*, melt the butter in a large frying pan and add the onion and bacon. Cook until the onion is soft, then add the cassava flour a little at a time until incorporated. Taste and season with salt and pepper. Transfer to a serving bowl and garnish with the parsley and spring onion.

Serve the *feijoada* with sliced orange or pineapple and the *farofa* on the side.

Serves 4–6

Feijoada

Moqueca de Peixe

from Patricia Nunes

A marvellous seafood stew with the fresh flavour of lime and the mellow taste of red palm-fruit oil, a Brazilian favourite.

1 kg thick, firm, white fish fillets or cutlets or 1 kg shelled green prawns, or a mixture of both

juice of 2 limes, plus extra to serve

2 garlic cloves, chopped

1 onion, sliced

1 tablespoon grated ginger

5 long red chillies, chopped

1 red capsicum, sliced

5 tomatoes, chopped

olive oil

salt and pepper

250 ml fish or vegetable stock

1 bunch coriander, chopped
(reserve some leaves to garnish)

spring onions, finely sliced, to garnish

120 ml red palm-fruit oil (optional)

Halve the fish fillets or cutlets and marinate in the lime juice with half the garlic for at least 30 minutes. If using prawns, marinate them whole.

In a large saucepan, sauté the remaining garlic, onion, ginger, chilli, capsicum and tomato in olive oil until a sauce is formed. Taste and add salt and pepper. Add the stock and fish and simmer gently until cooked. If using a combination of fish and prawns, add the prawns later as they cook in less time. Taste again for seasoning and stir through the chopped coriander. Place in a serving dish and squeeze over some extra lime juice. Sprinkle with the spring onions and extra coriander leaves and drizzle over the palm-fruit oil, if using. Serve with rice.

Serves 4–6

Quindim

from Doralice Silva

A sweet, dense baked custard flavoured with coconut.

12 egg yolks

440 g (2 cups) sugar

250 ml water

100 g shredded coconut

2 tablespoons butter, melted

1 teaspoon vanilla essence

glucose syrup

Preheat the oven to 180°C. Combine the ingredients other than the glucose syrup in a bowl and mix well.

Spread a thin layer of glucose syrup in the bottom of eight 250 ml individual baking moulds. Add the custard to three-quarters full. Bake the custards in a water bath for around 20 minutes.

Make sure they are cool before turning out. Serve cold.

Serves 8

CHINA

Walk into a Chinese kitchen and you enter a realm of incredible skill. Each part of the kitchen is humming as pastry is made and rolled, dim sum stuffed, rice-flour sheets steamed and folded into *cheong fan*, vegetables chopped with cleavers at incredible speed and little golden pies baked. All around you deep-frying vats bubble, enormous bamboo steamers hiss and a steady stream of waiters and trolleys moves seamlessly in and out of the action. Amongst this the roaring flames under the row of woks sound like an express train. It's intense and fun and leaves you full of admiration for the chefs.

Chinese cuisine is, after all, one of the greatest in the world – complex, ancient and incredibly diverse. It varies throughout China's vast regions from exquisitely refined to deliciously simple and rustic.

As more people from all over China have moved to other countries, the Chinese restaurant scene in our major cities has really diversified, with eateries now specialising in the spicier Sichuan and Shanghai cuisines, the lighter flavoursome Chiu Chow and the robust hearty food of northern China. We're spoiled for choice with places to eat yum cha, the delicious series of steamed and fried snacks taken with tea. This tradition originated in the teahouses of Guangzhou and has spread throughout the world. There are numerous dim sum makers and dumpling houses, tea specialists and tofu makers. Major supermarkets now have most of the ingredients you need for a good stir-fry and many of us probably whip one up in our woks at least once a week.

We've also become familiar with the communal style of eating that is very popular throughout China. Although some remote communities in China still segregate men and women when eating, most Chinese enjoy a shared meal, especially a popular communal dish such as steamboat. With chopsticks and a little wire basket, diners add shaved meats (such as lamb), sliced vegetables and mushrooms, and seafood or poultry to a bubbling pot of stock, which cooks their choice of ingredients in front of them. The waft of fragrant steam as the lid of the steamboat is lifted at the table and the careful arrangement of the ingredients adds to the 'five senses experience', which is central to Chinese culture – eating with the eyes, smelling delicious aromas, and getting the taste buds ready for the tastes and textures to come.

To finish meals, many Chinese people will simply have tea. The hankering for sweets to round out a meal is very much a Western thing. In Shanghai, green tea finishes a meal; in the north it is jasmine tea; while in the south, oolong tea is preferred. Many older Chinese like the smoky taste of *bo lei* tea, which they believe helps to counter the fattiness of food and aids digestion.

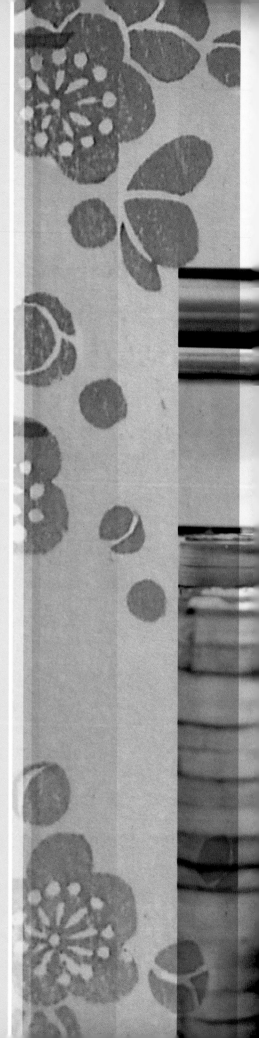

FIVE-SPICE POWDER

A delightful, aromatic spice blend of star anise, Sichuan pepper, cinnamon, cloves and fennel seeds.

OYSTER SAUCE

A rich, thick, dark brown sauce with a pleasant saltiness that is added to marinades or to finish steamed green vegetables.

RICE WINE

Also known as Shaoxing cooking wine, this is like a medium-sweet sherry. It is made from fermenting steamed glutinous rice and is fabulous for marinades and sauces.

SESAME OIL

With a rich, nutty flavour, this oil is extracted from toasted sesame seeds and is used in sauces, stir-fries and marinades.

SOY SAUCE

Made from soybeans that are fermented with roasted grain, water and salt. Light soy sauce is pleasantly salty and used in stir-fries, marinades and as a dipping sauce. Dark soy sauce has been left to ferment further, which develops the flavour and intensity but reduces the saltiness. It is used where a thicker sauce is needed, such as in braised dishes (especially with dark meats like beef) and heartier, spicy stir-fries. It also adds a rich caramel colour to food.

BAMBOO STEAMER

Essential for steaming dim sum, vegetables and fish. Food is placed on a plate or large leaf in the steamer, which sits above a wok or saucepan of simmering water.

CHAN

A versatile tool used to flip and toss ingredients when stir-frying. It is also used to measure sauces and remove cooked food from the wok to a serving plate.

CLEAVER

Extremely useful for chopping through bones when cutting a chicken or duck into portions, and good for chopping vegetables. The flat side easily cracks open garlic cloves ready for mincing.

WOK

Used extensively for stir-fries, steaming and deep-frying.

Beef Stir-fry

Anthony Lui

Here are the secrets to a tasty, healthy, tender beef stir-fry: buy good-quality beef, seek out vegies of many colours and have all the ingredients ready to cook before you fire up the wok. This is an easy and very popular recipe!

400 g beef eye fillet
1½ tablespoons potato starch, plus ½ teaspoon extra
750 ml water
salt
1½ tablespoons peanut oil
6 fresh baby corn, halved diagonally
4 fresh shiitake mushrooms, sliced
60 g snow peas, trimmed
4 yellow squash, sliced
1–1.25 litres oil for deep-frying
1 garlic clove, chopped
½ red capsicum, diced
1 tablespoon oyster sauce
1 teaspoon sugar
1 tablespoon rice wine
1 teaspoon sesame oil

'Toothpicks are frequently used between courses as it is believed that the tastes of one course should not be allowed to mar one's enjoyment of the next course. One hand covers the mouth while the toothpick is used.'

Trim the beef and slice it thinly across the grain. Make a thin paste with the potato starch, 100 ml of the water, ⅔ teaspoon of salt and the peanut oil. Add the beef, stir well to coat and set aside for 30 minutes.

Heat the remaining water in a wok until boiling. Add ½ teaspoon of salt and the baby corn and cook for 30 seconds. Add the mushrooms, snow peas and squash and cook for a further 30 seconds. Drain the blanched vegetables in a colander.

Heat the deep-frying oil in the wok until the surface is shimmering. Add the beef and fry until it just changes colour. Strain out the beef and empty the wok of oil, leaving 1 tablespoon.

Reheat the wok over a high flame and add the garlic, capsicum and beef. Stir-fry for 30 seconds then add the blanched vegetables, oyster sauce, sugar, ½ teaspoon of salt and the extra potato starch. Toss well. Finish with the rice wine and sesame oil for aroma and gloss. Serve immediately.

Serves 2–4

Salt and Pepper Squid

from Ying Tam

I have wanted this recipe for so long that I was delighted when my friend Ying, a legendary restaurateur, graciously shared it. It makes more five-spice mix than you need but you can store the rest in an airtight container for another day.

FIVE-SPICE MIX

1 tablespoon ground ginger

1 tablespoon celery powder

1 tablespoon chicken stock powder

1 tablespoon salt

1 teaspoon five-spice powder

SQUID

500 g fresh whole squid

2 tablespoons self-raising flour

vegetable oil

cornflour

4 spring onions, chopped

2 garlic cloves, chopped

1 red chilli, chopped

½ tablespoon rice wine

'To thank someone for pouring you tea, tap your index and middle fingers twice on the table near the cup.'

Combine the ingredients for the five-spice mix and set aside.

Clean the squid by pulling the tentacles from the body. Wash out the tube and remove the clear 'backbone'. Peel off the skin if desired. Cut the tentacles from the head and discard the head. Cut the tube into triangles, which helps the squid to curl during cooking.

In a bowl, mix the self-raising flour with 1 tablespoon of vegetable oil and a little water to make a paste. Add the squid pieces and tentacles and coat well. Sprinkle and toss with enough cornflour until the pieces are dry.

Heat enough vegetable oil in a wok for deep-frying. Add the squid in batches and cook until golden and crisp. Remove with a wire basket or slotted spoon. When all the squid is cooked, drain most of the oil from the wok.

Add the spring onions, garlic and chilli to the wok. Stir-fry for 30 seconds until aromatic. Return the squid to the wok, add 2–3 teaspoons of five-spice mix and toss well. Add the rice wine, toss and serve immediately.

Serves 4

Shanghai-Style Stir-fried Eggplant

from Chris Yan

The secret to making this eggplant meltingly tender is to gradually add the water as the eggplant is cooking. The result is delicious and I now know why my friend Chris missed this dish so much when he first moved to Australia.

500 g Japanese eggplants
100 ml oil
1 long red chilli, roughly cut into chunks
2 garlic cloves, bruised
200 ml water
3 tablespoons dark soy sauce
1 tablespoon sugar

Cut or snap the eggplants into 5 cm pieces. Heat the oil in a wok until shimmering. Add the chilli and garlic and cook for 20–30 seconds. Remove the chilli and reserve.

Add the eggplant and gently stir-fry. When the eggplant has soaked up all of the oil, add 1 tablespoon of the water. Keep adding water a tablespoon at a time until the eggplant is soft and you have used around half of the water.

Stir in the dark soy sauce and sugar then add the remaining water. Cover with a lid and cook for 1 minute. Remove the lid; the liquid should be absorbed. Return the chilli to the wok, toss for 30 seconds and serve.

Serves 4 as a side dish

Whole Snapper Steamed with Black Beans and Lemon

from Frank Shek

This is always on the menu at Frank Shek's restaurant China Doll, yet it is easy enough to make at home – and it's incredibly healthy! The recipe includes making a simple black-bean paste (briefly frying preserved black beans with garlic), although you may wish to use ready-made black-bean paste instead. Both preserved black beans and black-bean paste can be bought at Asian grocery stores or large supermarkets. Mushroom soy sauce is a type of dark soy flavoured with straw mushrooms.

2½ tablespoons vegetable oil

50 g garlic cloves, finely chopped

100 g Chinese preserved black beans, rinsed and drained

700 g whole snapper, cleaned and scaled

sea salt

1 lemon, sliced, plus extra lemon to squeeze

1 long red chilli, sliced into strips

3 spring onions, thinly sliced on the diagonal

small handful of coriander leaves

1 tablespoon mushroom soy sauce

1 tablespoon peanut oil

Heat the oil in a wok or frying pan and fry the garlic for 2–3 minutes until it just begins to brown. Add the black beans and stir-fry for another 2 minutes. Remove from the heat and allow to cool. Reserve 1 heaped tablespoon of this black-bean paste for the fish, and store the rest in a sterilised jar in the refrigerator for up to 3 months. (You can also use the paste in stir-fries, marinades and braises.)

Rinse the fish and pat dry with paper towel. Lay on a chopping board and use a sharp knife to cut slashes in the flesh where it is thickest – cut them about 3 cm apart crossways as well as lengthways. Turn the fish and do the same on the other side. Season inside and out with sea salt.

Place onto a large plate. Spread with the black-bean paste and arrange the lemon slices over the top. Place the plate into a large bamboo steamer over a wok of simmering water. Cover with a lid and steam for about 12 minutes.

Remove from the steamer and top with the chilli, spring onion and coriander. Drizzle with the mushroom soy sauce and a squeeze of lemon. Heat the peanut oil in a small frying pan until smoking and pour over the fish. This will sizzle the herbs, releasing their aroma. Serve with steamed jasmine rice.

Serves 2

'If something is not to their liking, Chinese people will often say it has too much salt.'

Char Siu Pork

from Jacky Mai

This is the lovely, sticky, red-coated pork you see in Chinese barbecue restaurants – it smells divine as it's cooking and is very easy and yummy. *Char siu* sauce is made from hoisin, rice wine, honey and sugar. It can be bought at most supermarkets or Asian grocery stores.

⅓ cup *char siu* sauce

2 spring onions, chopped

1 teaspoon five-spice powder

1 tablespoon oil

450 g pork fillets, trimmed

1 tablespoon honey

Combine the *char siu* sauce, spring onion, five-spice powder and oil in a large bowl. Add the pork fillets and marinate for at least 30 minutes or for up to 2 hours.

Preheat the oven to 200°C. Line the base of a baking dish with baking paper. Remove the pork fillets from the marinade and lay in the dish. Cook for about 40 minutes, basting occasionally and turning over halfway through the cooking time, until cooked through. Remove from the oven and brush with the honey while still warm. Cover with foil and rest for 5 minutes before slicing.

Serves 2–4

Mango Pudding

from Rosetta Lee

This creamy mango pudding is so yummy that one is never enough!

1½ tablespoons powdered gelatine

165 g (¾ cup) caster sugar

250 ml boiling water

1 litre mango ice cream, softened

75 ml evaporated milk

1 cup crushed ice

1 large mango, flesh diced

Stir the gelatine and sugar into the boiling water until thick and syrupy. Pour into a bowl. Stir in the ice cream, evaporated milk, crushed ice and diced mango. Ladle into serving bowls or glasses and refrigerate for about 2 hours until set.

Serves 6–8

CROATIA

Ask Croatian people about the food they grew up with and their eyes grow moist remembering spit roasts and fish cooked perfectly over charcoal, intensely perfumed summer fruit and luscious cakes, and glorious wines and golden evenings. Their descriptions of this wonderful food make you want to go there ... But even in your own backyard you can summon up the aromas and flavours of Croatia.

The best addition to backyard Croatian cooking is a bell-shaped, metal cooking pot called a *peka*. It's like a barbecue but upside down. The food is placed in a large metal dish with the *peka* placed over the top. Red-hot coals are then heaped onto the *peka* so the food steams slowly in its own juices. Anything on the bone – like pork or turkey – tastes absolutely wonderful, especially when cooked with lashings of garlic and paprika, two of the favourite flavourings of Croatia.

Garlic and paprika star in the beloved smallgoods, which are the start to many Croatian meals. They also make the *sarma* (cabbage rolls) of central Croatia come alive and add flavour to lovely rich sauces and many stews.

It's no wonder the food is good when you see where Croatia lies on a map – right in the centre of Europe and spread along the beautiful Dalmatian Coast. Dotted near the coast are many islands, where the food is heavily influenced by the Mediterranean and dishes like risotto and polenta have been adapted to suit Croatian palates. For instance an Italian-inspired seafood stew called a *brodet* is traditionally served over soft polenta; and a rich, black risotto is made using squid ink. Almost every Croatian we met who had grown up by the sea told us they started fishing almost before they could walk, which is impressive. How they cook their catch is even more so. Seafood is basically a way of life there and even when simply grilled the fish is incredibly delicious.

It's rare to eat by yourself in Croatia – everything is shared. In the spring, whole lambs or pigs are cooked on the spit and everyone gathers for the feast. The smell of roasting meat, often stuffed with garlic and fresh herbs like rosemary, creates a mouth-watering aroma. Then there are the sweets – all throughout Croatia these are luscious, bountiful and beautiful.

My friend Mira makes a whole range of Croatian sweets and would never think of baking just one type of biscuit at a time. Her cakes, dumplings and tortes are filled with seasonal fruits like plums, apricots and apples and her biscuits are bursting with poppy seeds and walnuts. She'll often whip up *palacinke* pancakes too – just in case you have a little more room ... As one inventive Croatian friend put it, you have your stomach and then you have your 'sweets stomach' – that one can always try just one more delicious thing!

Smallgoods

Croatians love smallgoods and have created many of their own special varieties. These include *kulen*, a spicy pure pork and garlic sausage in a natural casing made from pig's appendix; *suha slanina*, a type of speck that is used in soups and cabbage rolls; *csabai*, a sausage that is also found in Hungary and is popular on its own or layered with potato to make the dish *rakott krumpli*; *suha koljenica*, smoked hock used in soups, with cabbages or cooked with dried beans; and *ćevapčići*, a skinless sausage cooked over charcoal.

AJVAR

A relish made from grilled red capsicum, eggplant, garlic and olive oil. Available in hot and mild variations, it is often served with grilled and roasted meat and *ćevapčiči*.

CABBAGE

Eaten raw and finely shredded dressed with a simple vinaigrette in the famous Croatian coleslaw which is a popular accompaniment to grilled meats. Also used as shredded preserved leaves with a distinct sour taste (sauerkraut) and as pickled whole leaves for making cabbage rolls.

GARLIC

Used liberally in many Croatian dishes, garlic adds flavour to everything from soups to homemade sausages. One passionate Croatian cook says it's hard to imagine a single household in all Croatia that doesn't have a large supply of garlic.

PAPRIKA

Available in sweet and hot versions and most commonly used in the inland part of Croatia, close to the Hungarian border.

PROVDL

A beautiful, smooth Croatian spread made from small native plums. *Provdl* is favoured for baking as it tends to keep its shape rather than spreading while cooking.

'You'll never find a single home in Croatia without garlic – it's unthinkable!'

Brodet
Seafood Stew

from Ino Kuvacic

This is the classic, spectacular seafood stew from the Dalmatian Coast. I was amazed to see Ino preparing the eel by running his hand down the length of it to break any small bones. If you're buying eel for the first time, get your fishmonger to show you how this is done – if you can find one that stocks eel! For the recipe you need to use at least three different kinds of fish and some shellfish – white-fleshed reef and rock fish are good choices. Ideally one fish will be for flavour, one for its flesh and one to boost the thickness of the stew. Scampi are great for flavour or you can use Balmain bugs or crabs instead. Serve with soft polenta.

1.5 kg fish such as eel, rockling, coral trout or rock flathead, cleaned and scaled, heads and tails removed, cut into cutlets

100 ml extra-virgin olive oil, plus extra for frying

juice of ½ lemon

20 garlic cloves, minced

½ bunch flat-leaf parsley, chopped

1 large onion, finely chopped

½ cup finely chopped tomatoes

100 ml white wine

salt and pepper

500 ml fish stock or water

12 mussels, cleaned and de-bearded

6 scampi, Balmain bugs or crabs

12 cherry tomatoes

Marinate the fish in the oil, lemon juice, a couple of tablespoons of the minced garlic and most of the parsley (reserve a little for garnish) for a few hours.

Heat some more oil in a large, heavy-based saucepan or claypot and sauté the remaining garlic, adding the onion after a few seconds. When the onion is lightly coloured, add the chopped tomato and cook for 1 minute. Add the wine and cook for about 20 minutes, until it loses its acidity.

Season the marinated fish with salt and pepper, making sure you get each piece. Add to the pan and stir well, then add the fish stock or water to just cover the fish. Bring to the boil over high heat then continue cooking rapidly for 20 minutes. Don't stir but carefully shake the pan instead to avoid breaking up the fish. Add the mussels, scampi (or Balmain bugs or crabs) and cherry tomatoes in the last 5 minutes.

Serve the stew with soft polenta. Garnish with parsley.

Serves 6

Punjeni Artichoke
Stuffed Artichokes
from Dennis Valcich

A dish that celebrates this delicious vegetable, which is only available fresh for a limited time in spring each year. My friend Dennis is a masterful chef and this recipe is a true favourite. It works well either as a main dish or an accompaniment.

5 large, tender globe artichokes

1 cup fresh breadcrumbs

3 garlic cloves, finely chopped

½ tablespoon chopped flat-leaf parsley

pepper

500 g baby new potatoes

100 g freshly shelled peas

100 g freshly shelled broad beans

salt

250 ml olive oil

Remove any old and loose leaves from the artichokes. With a sharp knife, cut off the stalks, reserving them for later. Slice about 2 cm off the top of each artichoke. Remove the choke by scooping it out with a teaspoon.

Make the stuffing by mixing the breadcrumbs, garlic, parsley and pepper. Gently open the leaves of each artichoke with your thumbs and add stuffing between the leaves.

Place the artichokes upright in the centre of a large saucepan. Add the potatoes around the artichokes. Scatter the peas, broad beans and artichoke stalks on top and sprinkle with any remaining stuffing. Season with salt and pepper. Drizzle with the olive oil and add enough water to cover the artichokes. Bring to the boil then reduce the heat to low and cook uncovered for about 1 hour. Don't stir; just shake the pan occasionally.

Serve the artichokes warm with crusty bread.

Serves 2 as main course, 4–5 as an accompaniment

Barbecued Rack of Lamb
from Tonci Farac

A lovely, simple way of cooking lamb on a spit-roast barbecue. Tonci's tip on ageing the meat first is brilliant – it gives a richer, more flavoursome result. Afterwards, take the meat out of the fridge half an hour before cooking so it doesn't suddenly leap from the cold of the fridge to the extreme heat of the barbie.

1 lamb rack with outer layer of fat intact
(be sure the butcher doesn't remove it)

rosemary sprigs, broken into short pieces

sea salt

Place the lamb on a wire rack and refrigerate uncovered for a couple of days to age the meat.

Make shallow cuts all over the outer layer of fat and stud with rosemary sprigs, leaving some of the leaves exposed. Rub liberally with sea salt.

Spit-roast over high heat to seal. Reduce the heat and continue to cook to your liking. Slice into cutlets and serve with roasted vegetables.

Serves 3–4

Sarma
Cabbage Rolls

from Branka Roncevic

A delicious recipe that is bursting with flavour. It is best served in the traditional Croatian way with lashings of creamy mashed potato. You can prepare the meat stock in advance (dried pork ribs are available from European delis). Note that whole pickled cabbage leaves come in jars from European delis and some butchers.

STOCK

500 g chicken wings

250 g beef oxtail

1 piece of dried pork rib

2 celery stalks, roughly chopped

2 carrots, chopped

1 vegetable stock cube

salt and pepper

ROLLS

125 ml vegetable oil

8 shallots, diced

3 garlic cloves, crushed

250 g speck, finely chopped

2 tablespoons sweet paprika

500 g minced beef topside

500 g minced pork neck

1 vegetable stock cube, crumbled

1 teaspoon mustard powder

1 teaspoon freshly ground black pepper

250 g arborio rice

2 eggs, beaten

½ cup chopped flat-leaf parsley

20 pickled cabbage leaves (large leaves can be cut in half to make 2 leaves)

TO COOK

200 g sauerkraut

500 g speck, cut into 3 × 5 cm pieces

3 tablespoons vegetable oil

2 garlic cloves, crushed

2 shallots, diced

2 teaspoons mustard powder

2 tablespoons plain flour

1–2 vegetable stock cubes

1 tablespoon sweet paprika

Place the stock ingredients in a large pot. Cover with water, bring to the boil and simmer for 1 hour. Strain and cool before using, skimming the fat from the surface if necessary.

To make the rolls, heat the oil in a frying pan and fry the shallots, garlic and speck for a few minutes, then stir in the paprika. Remove from the heat and leave to cool. Combine with the minced meat, stock cube, mustard powder and pepper. Stir in the rice, egg and parsley. Mix well with your hands.

Place the cabbage leaves on a board and add 3 tablespoons of the mixture to each one. Shape the stuffing into a sausage and roll up inside the leaves, tucking the ends of the leaves back into the rolls.

To cook the rolls, lay the sauerkraut over the base of a large pot. Add the rolls, tucking the speck pieces in between. There will be 2–3 layers in the pot. Pour over the cooled stock and gently bring to the boil. Simmer for 1½ hours.

Heat the vegetable oil in a frying pan and add the garlic, shallots, mustard powder, flour, stock cubes and paprika. Stir to a thick paste then add a small amount of stock from the simmering rolls to make a smooth sauce. Pour over the rolls and stir through. Simmer the rolls for a further 30 minutes.

Serve with mashed potato.

Serves 8–10

Plum Jam Biscuits

from Mira Valcich

Delicious melting biscuits from the queen of sweets, my friend Mira. Make sure you find *provdl*, which is favoured for baking as it tends to keep its shape rather than spreading while cooking – it comes in jars and is found in European delis and some supermarkets.

250 g unsalted butter, softened
300 ml cream
2 tablespoons vanilla sugar
1½ teaspoons baking powder
400 g (2⅔ cups) plain flour
provdl plum jam
caster sugar

Mix the butter, cream, vanilla sugar and baking powder. Slowly add the flour to make a soft, stretchy dough. Knead for 5 minutes. Roll the dough out thinly and cut into 15 cm triangles with a pizza cutter or sharp knife. Place a triangle in front of you with a wide edge facing you. Add 1 teaspoon of jam at the wide edge and roll the triangle up over the jam. Form the roll into a U shape. Repeat with the rest of the triangles.

Bake the biscuits at 200°C until golden. Roll in caster sugar while still warm.

Makes 24 biscuits

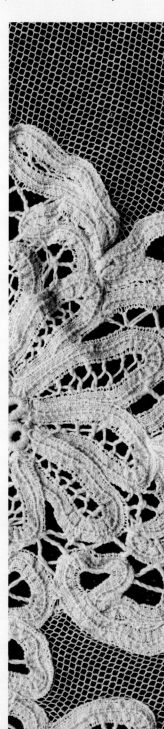

'To compliment a meal say *"Odlično!"* (Excellent/Delicious!)'

EGYPT

The amazing thing about Egyptian food is that dishes that were popular in the days of the pharaohs are still being enjoyed today. Some crops have been cultivated on the Nile River's fertile flood plain for thousands of years and are still being prepared and eaten in much the same way. As one of the world's most ancient civilisations, Egypt certainly got its recipes right from the very start!

Then, as now, pulses and beans are the centre of the Egyptian diet for both rich and poor. They're used extensively and creatively – as a source of protein and fibre and for comfort. *Ful medames* (slow-cooked fava beans with lentils) makes a great breakfast and is described as a 'stone in the stomach', capable of sustaining a worker all day. Egyptian expatriates say the *ful medames* sold on the streets of Cairo is unsurpassed – there's a flavour imparted from cooking such large quantities that apparently can't be equalled at home. An ingenious system of pulleys and baskets allows apartment dwellers high above the streets to lower a basket and get their '*ful* fix', a cumin-scented bowl of warm *ful medames* to eat with bread and fresh herbs. I've only eaten this in Sydney, without the vibrance of Cairo around me, but it was still delicious ... and sustaining.

The other national dish revered above all others is *molokhia* soup. This tall, leafy vegetable has been cultivated for centuries. It has the highest amount of protein and folic acid of any green leafy vegetable and is also rich in betacarotene, iron, calcium and vitamin C. When cooked, *molokhia* develops a wonderfully mucilaginous quality loved by Egyptians – who also believe it has aphrodisiac powers.

While *molokhia* is still an Egyptian secret, another Egyptian mainstay has been readily embraced. This food is dukkah, a fragrant mix of whole spices toasted and mixed with nuts and seeds.

The traditional bread of Egypt is a flatbread called *eish baladi* – *eish* means 'life' or 'survival'. It's dipped into oil then dukkah and eaten. And, as in the Middle East, the flatbread is used as plate, cutlery and napkin and is an essential part of every meal.

Meat is still a luxury for many in Egypt and many dishes make a little go a long way. You can smell meat cooking on the streets – tantalising aromas from juicy marinated skewers cooking over hot charcoal or tagines of lamb slowly cooking with spices and vegetables.

Fresh fruit is the healthy conclusion to most Egyptian meals, along with strong coffee, black tea or the delicious, refreshing red tea called *karkade*, made from dried hibiscus flowers and said to reduce high blood pressure.

Preparing a New Tagine

Tagine (pronounced 'tar-gen' in Egypt) are shallow terracotta plates with conical lids that are used for slow-cooking. To prepare a new tagine before cooking, first soak it overnight in water. The next day fill it with fresh water, add some salt and a few bay leaves and cardamom pods. Heat over a low gas flame until boiling to infuse the herbs into the porous terracotta. If your tagine is used regularly this won't need to be redone. Tagines can be used on the barbecue, charcoal or low gas flame but are not recommended for electric cook tops or in the oven.

Dukkah

from Morris Mansour

This is a dry mix of toasted nuts, seeds and spices. Traditionally dukkah is eaten by dipping bread into olive oil and then into the mixture but it is also used as a versatile seasoning in Egyptian cooking.

Combine half a cup each of pine nuts and coriander seeds in a large frying pan and place over medium-high heat, stirring regularly. When these start to colour, add ¾ cup of sesame seeds and continue to toast until golden brown.

Tip the mixture into a food processor. Add half a teaspoon each of cumin, baharat, chilli powder and salt. Blend together.

BAHARAT

Arabic for 'spice mix'. This all-purpose blend is popular for enhancing the flavour of fish, chicken, beef, vegetables – particularly *bamya* (okra) – tomato sauces and soups. To make Egyptian *baharat* mix equal quantities of ground white pepper and cinnamon with half quantities of black pepper, nutmeg and cloves.

CORIANDER

Coriander leaves and coriander seeds feature prominently in Egyptian cooking. The seeds (whole or ground) are used to make dukkah and are also a key ingredient in one of the national dishes of Egypt, *molokhia* soup.

CUMIN

This is the most popular spice in Egypt. It is bought weekly and used liberally in *ful* (beans), seafood dishes, marinades and dukkah.

FAVA BEANS

Dried fava beans, or broad beans, are hugely popular in Egypt. This ancient staple is eaten for breakfast as *ful medames* and split fava beans are used in Egypt's version of falafel called *tameya*.

MOLOKHIA

Molokhia is a leafy green vegetable with a slippery consistency much like okra, and it is available fresh for just a few weeks at the height of summer. The taste of the famous *molokhia* soup varies according to the method of cooking and the stock that is used. It can be made from fresh, frozen, dried or preserved leaves, which are sold in most Middle Eastern emporiums.

Bamya (Okra) with Lamb

from Nadia Fawzi

This thick stew of tender lamb and baby okra is a common dish in Egypt – okra is the edible fruit pod of a plant related to the hibiscus and is used in many dishes for its thickening properties. Lamb backstrap or fillet is lean and quick and easy to use, although other cuts of lamb would work – the meat from the leg or shoulder is lovely too. The secret to this dish is the long, slow simmering that brings the flavours gently together.

1 tablespoon clarified butter (ghee)

1 medium onion, diced

2 garlic cloves, finely chopped

500 g lamb backstrap, cut into thick pieces

2 × 400 g tins pureed tomatoes

1 tablespoon tomato paste

salt and pepper

250 ml stock or water (optional)

500 g baby okra, topped and tailed

juice of 1 lemon

Melt the ghee in a saucepan and sauté the onion until soft, then add the garlic. Fry for a couple of minutes then add the lamb and toss until sealed and lightly browned.

Add the tomato puree and paste and season to taste with salt and pepper. If you think more liquid is needed, add the stock or water. Cover and simmer for 30–35 minutes.

Add the okra and cook for another 5–10 minutes. Add the lemon juice and remove from the heat. Serve with rice.

Serves 4–6

Ful Medames
Slow-cooked Fava Beans with Lentils

from Alice Ibrahim

This national dish is cooked very slowly, traditionally overnight in a copper pot so it is ready for a hearty breakfast. It is typically eaten with Egyptian bread as a tasty and filling start to the day, particularly during Ramadan when Muslims fast during daylight hours. It goes beautifully with many spicy, crunchy treats such as the bright-pink pickled turnips (coloured with beetroot) and crunchy pickled cucumbers that are sold in Middle Eastern food stores.

2 cups dried fava beans (broad beans), rinsed and soaked overnight

1 cup red lentils, rinsed and soaked overnight

salt and pepper

ground cumin

lemon juice

olive oil

Drain the soaked beans and lentils and rinse again. Place them in a large saucepan and cover with 750 ml of water. Boil over high heat until frothy. Skim the froth as it accumulates then cover the saucepan and simmer on the lowest heat for up to 5 hours or until the beans are very soft and the liquid has reduced. The *ful* thickens as it cools, so be careful not to reduce the liquid too much.

Add salt, pepper, a generous amount of cumin and lemon juice to taste. Drizzle a liberal amount of olive oil over the top.

For a sandwich-style snack, serve the *ful* in a pocket of flatbread with fresh salad, tahini, pickles and banana chillies. Or simply scoop the warm *ful* up with bread.

Serves 6

'If you share bread and salt,
you're a friend for life.'

Kushari

from Therese Shehata

Kushari is a delicious dish made from green
lentils, macaroni and rice mixed together
with caramelised onions. It is served with
a tomato-based sauce and finished with a
crispy onion garnish and is best accompanied
by a garden salad.

CRISPY ONIONS

oil for deep-frying

2 onions, finely sliced

SAUCE

2 tablespoons olive oil

1 small onion, finely diced

2 garlic cloves, crushed

250 g tomato paste

1 teaspoon *baharat*

salt and pepper

chilli flakes (optional)

250 ml water

RICE, MACARONI AND LENTILS

olive oil

1 cup medium-grain rice

salt

1 cup green lentils, rinsed until the water runs clear

2 cups small macaroni

2 large onions, finely sliced

1 teaspoon *baharat*

Prepare the onion garnish by heating sufficient
oil in a saucepan, adding the onions and deep-
frying until dark brown. Remove from the oil
and drain on paper towel. Leave to cool.

To make the sauce, place a saucepan over
moderate heat and add the oil and onion. Cook
until the onion is soft. Add the garlic and fry
to pale brown. Stir in the tomato paste and
baharat and add salt, pepper and chilli flakes
(if using) to taste. Add the water and simmer
for 15–20 minutes or until the sauce has reduced
by half. Remove from the heat.

Heat 2 tablespoons of olive oil in a separate
saucepan over moderate heat. Add the rice and
1 teaspoon of salt and fry for 2 minutes, then add
500 ml of water. Stir well and bring to the boil.
Once boiling, lower the heat, cover and simmer
for 15 minutes until the rice is cooked.

Meanwhile, place the lentils in another
saucepan with 500 ml of water and simmer until
tender then drain. In another saucepan boil the
macaroni with a little salt until al dente then
drain. Heat 80 ml of olive oil in a frying pan
and cook the onions until soft and caramelised.

To serve, reheat the tomato sauce. Place the
hot macaroni in a large serving dish and coat
with a little extra olive oil. Add the hot rice,
lentils and caramelised onions and mix through.
Sprinkle with the *baharat* and pour over the
desired amount of tomato sauce. Garnish with
the crispy onions.

Serves 4–6

'In Egypt the worst thing you can do as a host is to eat with your guests – you must make sure they have the best of everything!'

Fish Tagine

from Ramy Megalaa

The Egyptian tagine is much like the better-known Moroccan tajine – the conical-topped clay cooking pot that cooks spicy stews to perfection. This recipe uses barramundi instead of the traditional Nile perch, but the squid and prawns are authentic, being fruits of Egypt's Mediterranean coastline and its famous river.

MARINATED FISH

1 barramundi fillet, cut into 2 cm pieces

1 squid tube, sliced

250 g green prawns, shelled and de-veined

½ tablespoon olive oil

1 tablespoon crushed garlic

juice of ½ lime (or lemon)

1 teaspoon ground cumin

½ cup roughly chopped coriander

salt and pepper

SAUCE

1 red capsicum, roasted and peeled

3 tomatoes, chopped

1 cup chopped celery

1 teaspoon ground cumin

2 tablespoons olive oil

1 red onion, sliced

1 tablespoon tomato paste

small handful of coriander leaves

salt and pepper

Place the barramundi, squid and prawns in a mixing bowl and add the remaining marinade ingredients. Mix well and marinate for 4 hours.

To make the sauce, use a hand-held blender or food processor to blend the capsicum (including its seeds) with the tomato, celery and cumin.

Heat the olive oil in a large frying pan over high heat and fry the red onion until soft. Add the blended sauce and bring to a high simmer. Stir in the tomato paste, coriander and salt and pepper to taste.

Preheat the oven to 180°C. Cover the base of the tagine with some of the sauce, add the sea-food, then cover with the remaining sauce. Place the tagine on the stove over medium heat for a few minutes to start the cooking process. Transfer to the oven and cook for 40–45 minutes.

Serve with fresh bread, couscous or rice.

Serves 3

Molokhia and Chicken Soup

from Ramy Megalaa

If you are using frozen *molokhia*, add it to the soup without thawing it, don't over-stir it and make sure it never reaches boiling point other-wise it can split from the stock. *Molokhia* can also be made with duck, beef or rabbit. With rabbit it is said to be the meal of the pharaohs as only the wealthy could indulge in it.

1 large chicken, preferably free-range

1 large onion, halved

5 garlic cloves, 2 left whole, 3 finely chopped

3 bay leaves

salt and pepper

clarified butter (ghee) or butter

500 g fresh *molohkia* leaves, very finely sliced

1 tablespoon ground coriander

Place the chicken in a pot and add the onion, whole garlic, bay leaves and salt and pepper. Cover with boiling water and bring to a simmer. Cook until the chicken is tender. Remove the chicken and strain the stock.

Cut the chicken into pieces and fry them in ghee or butter.

Meanwhile, bring 1 litre of the stock back to the boil, reduce the heat and add the *molokhia*. Simmer uncovered for 10 minutes. The soup should be thick and sticky; if it seems too thick, add more stock.

The next stage is known as preparing the *tasha*. Heat a frying pan and fry the chopped garlic in a little ghee or butter until light brown. Add the coriander then stir the mixture into the hot soup. Leave the soup to sit for 2 minutes, then serve with the fried chicken and with steamed rice.

Serves 4

Basbousa

from Amira Georgy

This sweet semolina cake topped with a rose-water and lemon syrup is incredibly easy to make.

2½ cups coarse semolina

1 cup desiccated coconut

220 g (1 cup) caster sugar

75 g (½ cup) self-raising flour

200 g thick yoghurt

200 g unsalted butter, melted

1 teaspoon vanilla extract

25–30 blanched almonds

milk if needed

SYRUP

330 g (1½ cups) sugar

250 ml water

1 teaspoon lemon juice

1 teaspoon rosewater

Preheat the oven to 190°C. Mix the semolina, coconut, sugar, flour, yoghurt, melted butter and vanilla in a bowl. If the mixture seems too thick, add a little milk – but it should still be fairly stiff. Spread the mixture with your hands in a buttered 30 × 25 × 5 cm baking tray. Cut it into diamond shapes, pressing hard. Place an almond in the centre of each diamond. Bake for 35–40 minutes until golden brown.

Meanwhile, make the syrup. Place the sugar and water in a saucepan and bring to the boil, stirring until the sugar dissolves. Simmer for 5 minutes without stirring. Stir in the lemon juice and rosewater and remove from the heat. Leave to cool.

Pour the syrup over the cake while the cake is still hot. Cool to serve.

Makes 25–30 pieces

Basbousa

ENGLAND

The author W. Somerset Maugham once remarked that the only way to eat well in England was to have breakfast three times a day! Another wit decided that the British zeal for colonising the world was motivated by their longing for a decent meal. That said, English food is popular and can rise above its reputation – often thought of as simple comfort food, there is still much pleasure in it and much to learn.

The ingenuity of English food interests me – using up stale bread, clever ways with secondary cuts of meat, turning unwanted fish into something so yummy it is now popular throughout the world … The story of fish and chips goes like this: When the English fishermen in the North Sea adopted the use of long-haul nets in the nineteenth century, they found they were landing a huge by-catch as well as the prized fish they were after. So as not to waste good food, the poorer quality fish was sent along the newly built rail networks to every town and village throughout the country. The fish was filleted, fried in batter and served with another cheap staple, potatoes, which were sliced into chips and also fried. The chippie or chipper was born and the tradition is still going strong in the English-speaking world – as are many other age-old English recipes and ingredients.

As I write in the middle of summer, my twelve-year-old daughter has insisted that I buy punnets of all sorts of berries so she can make the lovely summer pudding recipe on page 51. A celebration of red, purple and black berries, it is easy enough for a child to make. I'm delighted as the pudding she made was delicious and I'm always keen to encourage my children to cook!

Sauces

Horseradish Sauce

Derived from the root of the horseradish plant. This sharp relish is served as a condiment alongside traditional roast beef.

Mint Sauce

A condiment served with joints of lamb for the Sunday roast. The clean, fresh flavour of the mint beautifully cuts through the richness of the lamb.

Worcestershire Sauce

Inspired by a visit to India in the 1800s, this now classic English sauce is said to have tamarind as its secret ingredient.

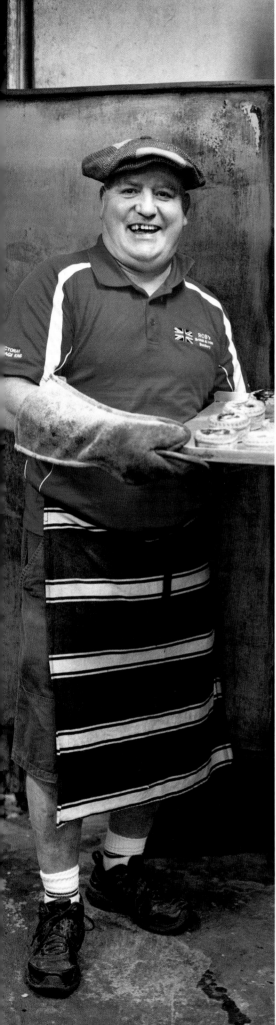

Essential flavours

CHEESE

While there are many cheap, commercial versions of traditional English cheeses around, there are still a number of farmhouse dairies that make the old favourites the original way. Cheddar and cheshire are the heart of a ploughman's lunch. Stilton is the classic English blue-vein cheese.

HADDOCK

A member of the cod family, generally fished in the North Atlantic. Smoked haddock is the most common fish used to make kedgeree, a breakfast dish that was popular among British colonials in India and later found favour in England. Haddock is also frequently the fish of choice for fish and chips.

MALT VINEGAR

Made by malting barley, and traditionally light brown in colour. It is served with fish and chips at the traditional 'chippie'. A cheaper synthetic alternative, labelled as a 'non-brewed condiment', is popular in northern England.

MEAT AND OFFAL

British beef is a traditional favourite however English cooking also uses many cheaper, tougher cuts of meat for slow cooking like ears, tongues and cheeks. Kidneys and lamb's fry, or liver, are breakfast staples. Kidneys are celebrated in steak and kidney pie. The making of smallgoods is an art form and there are numerous local sausages that differ from region to region, as well as cured cuts of pork, gammon, and the famous black pudding or blood sausage.

PICKLES

Pickling fish or vegetables is a tasty way of preserving fresh produce to eat throughout the year. Rollmops are pickled fish fillets that are often wrapped around a pickled cucumber or onion. Pickled onions are common in a ploughman's lunch and served with strong cheddar cheese. Branston Pickle is a popular commercial relish of pickled cooked vegetables in a dark, tangy chutney.

'Never make pastry
after the sun comes up.'

Whiting Rollmops
with Beetroot Compote

from Jeremy Strode

Traditionally a rollmop is a pickled herring that is rolled around a pickled cucumber or onion, secured with a toothpick and eaten as an appetiser or as part of a light meal. This recipe is light and delicious and with the beetroot and watercress it looks great too.

PICKLED FISH

1 litre water

1 litre white-wine vinegar

1 kg sugar

2 tablespoons fennel seeds

2 tablespoons mustard seeds

6 thyme sprigs

6 bay leaves

12 small king george whiting fillets

DRESSING

2 egg yolks

2 teaspoons grain mustard

1 teaspoon white-wine vinegar

200 ml extra-virgin olive oil

200 ml olive oil

2½ tablespoons cream

salt and pepper

BEETROOT COMPOTE

4 onions, finely diced

4 garlic cloves, finely chopped

olive oil

salt and pepper

6 medium beetroots, peeled and cut into small cubes

200 ml white-wine vinegar

2 tablespoons mustard seeds

watercress sprigs to serve

To make the pickled fish, place the water, vinegar, sugar, seeds and herbs in a large saucepan and bring to the boil. Remove from the heat and leave to cool (to speed the cooling process you could pour the liquid into a large bowl).

To prepare the fish, trim the edges if needed so the fillets are more or less an even width. Place the fish skin-side down and roll up from the tail end. Pierce each roll with a sturdy toothpick to hold it in place and add to the cool pickling liquid. Leave the fish to pickle in the refrigerator for 1–2 days.

To make the dressing, whisk the egg yolks, mustard and vinegar in a bowl and gradually whisk in the oils as if making a mayonnaise. Thin out with a little pickling liquid if necessary. Finally whisk in the cream and season to taste.

To make the beetroot compote, sweat the onions and garlic in a little olive oil, seasoning well. When very soft and starting to colour, add the beetroot, vinegar and mustard seeds. Cook until the beetroot is al dente. Use more oil as required to prevent sticking. Leave to cool.

Serve the rollmops with the beetroot compote, dressing and fresh watercress.

Serves 6

Classic English Fish and Chips

from Sue Pearson

This is a nice crispy batter that helps to steam the fish – make sure you buy firm, thick, white fillets such as flathead. The secret of the best chips is in the double cooking! It is also a good idea to use a variety of potato that has a low water content.

300 g (2 cups) plain flour, plus extra for dusting

375–500 ml dark beer

1 tablespoon dried yeast

salt

1 teaspoon olive oil

6–8 potatoes such as Dutch cream

canola oil for deep-frying

8 flathead fillets

Place the flour in a large mixing bowl. Make a well in the centre and pour the beer into it. Start whisking the flour with the beer and, if necessary, adding water into the mix little by little to avoid lumps forming. Keep whisking until all the flour is incorporated and the batter is smooth. Whisk in the yeast and salt to taste. Leave the batter in a warm place for 1–1½ hours. Just before using add the olive oil, which adds gloss to the batter.

Peel and slice the potatoes, pat dry and cut into chips 1.5 cm wide. Heat sufficient oil in a deep saucepan and fry the chips for 5 minutes. Remove from the oil with a slotted spoon and leave to cool and drain on a wire rack for 10 minutes.

Reheat the oil and cook the chips again for 7–10 minutes until golden with a crunchy outer layer. Season with salt.

Dust the fish in flour and lightly coat in batter. Add to the hot oil and cook for up to 3 minutes, turning regularly. Drain on paper towel, season with salt and serve with the chips.

Serves 4

Roast Beef and Yorkshire Puddings

from Sean Connolly

Sean's recipe for this classic dish is just lovely – the meat becomes tender and full of flavour and the puddings act as little cups for the gravy, which is made with a good pinot. Yorkshire puddings were traditionally served as a filler before the main roast but they make an excellent accompaniment. The secret of the puddings is to make sure the fat in the muffin tins is smoking before pouring in the batter. If you don't have any dripping on hand, speak to your butcher who could give you some beef fat to render down.

2 teaspoons plain flour

2 teaspoons mustard powder

freshly ground black pepper

2 kg wagyu rump or scotch fillet

rosemary sprigs

2–3 tablespoons olive oil

4 red onions, halved

4 large carrots, halved

8 garlic cloves

thyme sprigs

sea salt

1 litre beef stock

½ bottle good pinot noir

YORKSHIRE PUDDINGS

200 g (1⅓ cups) plain flour

10 g salt

4 eggs

450 ml full-cream milk

beef dripping or duck or goose fat

Combine the flour, mustard powder and pepper and dust over the surface of the meat. Stud the meat with rosemary. Do not season with salt as it has a tendency to draw the moisture out.

Preheat the oven to 180°C. Heat some of the oil in a frying pan and seal the beef on all sides, allowing it to caramelise a little. In a large roasting tray add the remaining oil and the onion, carrot and garlic and place the beef on top. Sprinkle with thyme and salt and roast for 1½ hours until medium–rare.

Meanwhile, prepare the puddings. Sift the flour into a bowl and stir in the salt. Beat the eggs and milk together in a separate bowl. Make a well in the centre of the flour and add the egg and milk mixture one-third at a time, whisking vigorously to incorporate. Once the batter is smooth, rest it in the refrigerator. Warm a muffin tray in the oven during the last 15 minutes of cooking the beef.

Transfer the beef to a warm plate and rest covered in foil for 30 minutes. The meat juices will pool on the plate to be used in the gravy. Remove the vegetables from the tray and keep warm (or you can pop them back in the oven for 10 minutes prior to serving). Keep the roasting tray aside for the gravy.

Turn the oven up to 220°C. Melt the dripping or fat in a saucepan and pour 1 cm into the base of each mould in the warm muffin tray. Place in the oven until the fat is smoking. Pour the batter into each mould to three-quarters full. Bake in the oven for 15–20 minutes until crisp and golden brown.

Meanwhile, make the gravy. Heat the beef stock in a saucepan. Warm the roasting tray gently over low heat loosening the sediment at the bottom with a wooden spoon. Pour in the pinot and boil until reduced by half. Add the juices from the beef plate and the hot stock and reduce once more. If you prefer your gravy on the thick side, you can make a cold paste of 2 teaspoons of butter with 2 teaspoons of plain flour and whisk this into the gravy, simmering over low heat for 8–10 minutes.

Slice the beef and serve with the vegetables and puddings. Pour on the gravy.

Serves 8–10

Shepherd's Pie

from Alice Parsons

This dish is a wonderful way of using up leftover meat. Alice's version has a few additions to add extra flavour, like a dash of soy sauce for saltiness, cider for a little sweetness and lemon zest for a slight tang. As well as leftover meat, Alice says you can add other leftovers from the fridge such as peas, gravy and leeks. Topped with creamy mashed potato that forms a crispy crust when baked, this dish is delicious at any time of the day.

500 g cooked lamb (or whatever meat you have left over)

8–10 medium potatoes such as desiree

2 tablespoons olive oil

1 onion, finely chopped

2–3 celery stalks, diced

2 carrots, finely diced

salt and freshly ground black pepper

2–3 teaspoons plain flour

2 teaspoons mustard powder

about 125 ml stock (chicken, beef or vegetable)

dash of soy sauce

generous splash of Worcestershire sauce

3 pinches of ground mace

grated zest of 1 lemon

125 ml apple cider

2 bay leaves

½ bunch flat-leaf parsley, chopped

1 tablespoon butter, plus extra for glazing

warm milk

1 egg, lightly beaten

grated cheese (optional)

Mince the lamb in an old-fashioned mincer or in a food processor. Put the potatoes in a large pot of water and boil until soft.

Meanwhile heat the olive oil in a large frying pan and add the onion and celery. Fry until the onion is translucent then add the carrot. Cook over medium heat for 3–5 minutes, stirring occasionally. Season with salt and pepper.

Stir in the lamb, then add the flour and mustard powder along with the stock for moisture. Stir well. Add the soy sauce, Worcestershire, mace, lemon zest and apple cider – the mixture should be gooey but not sloppy. Add the bay leaves and parsley and take off the heat.

Once the potatoes are soft, drain and mash with the butter and warm milk. Season to taste and stir in the egg.

Butter a large baking dish and add the meat mixture. Top with a thick layer of mashed potato. Sprinkle with grated cheese if you wish. Glaze the mash with some extra melted butter.

Bake in a moderate oven for 20 minutes or until the potato is golden on top.

Serves 8–10

Summer Pudding

from Matthew Kemp

This traditional English pudding is a favourite – it is easy, uses up stale bread and makes the most of the bright colours and tangy flavours of fresh summer berries.

BLACKCURRANT COULIS

250 ml water

250 g (1 cup) sugar

250 g blackcurrants (or mixed berries)

1 mint sprig

PUDDING

1 day-old loaf of sliced white bread

200 g small strawberries, hulled and quartered

100 g blackberries or mulberries

100 g blueberries

100 g raspberries for garnish

To make the syrup, boil the water and sugar together in a saucepan for 5 minutes. Transfer to a bowl and return 125 ml of the syrup to the pan and add the berries and mint (refrigerate the remaining syrup for another use). Cook until the fruit is soft. Discard the mint then puree the coulis in a food processor or rub through a sieve.

'Always wait till Wednesday to make scouse.' (Scouse is a Liverpool dish made up from leftovers of Sunday's lamb roast dinner – the flavours would be stronger and the meat more tender later in the week.)

Cut the bread into circles (leaving the crusts behind) to fit inside 8 large ramekins – you will need 3 circles per ramekin. Dip the bread circles into the coulis and lay out on a tray. Set aside.

Reheat the remaining coulis in a medium saucepan and bring to the boil over moderate heat. Add the strawberries, blackberries (or mulberries) and blueberries. Bring back to the boil then immediately remove from the heat. Drain off one-third of the coulis and reserve, and transfer the remaining fruit and coulis to a bowl to cool.

Place a soaked bread circle in the bottom of each ramekin followed by 1 tablespoon of the fruit, another circle of bread and more fruit. Top with a final circle of bread and a small amount of coulis. Press down firmly. Chill and set in the refrigerator for 4 hours or more.

Run a knife around the inside of the ramekins and turn the puddings out onto serving plates. Garnish with the raspberries and drizzle with reserved coulis. Serve with luscious thick cream if desired.

Serves 6–8

FRANCE

From all the different cuisines that I've sampled, I'd have to say that the dishes I went up a dress size after were the French ones! France is simply gastronomic heaven. There the people love food and really focus on it – there are few places on earth where so much attention is paid to what people are going to eat and how they then eat it. Those of you who have experienced the pure joy of a freshly baked baguette with its warm, golden crust, or a small wedge of one of the thousands of French cheeses, or a spoonful of something as simple and rustic as French onion soup will know what I mean.

It has been so interesting visiting both restaurants and homes to see how this exquisite food comes together and what French people simply will not compromise on in the kitchen – good butter, fresh seasonal vegetables and fruits, the best oil and vinegar to dress salads, and good-quality meat, cheese and wine.

This refined cuisine is the result of many years of evolution. It was fostered at the royal court centuries ago and gradually spread once the subsequent revolution removed many class barriers and people became more prosperous. In professional kitchens there was a strict hierarchy and a rigorous chef's apprentice system which rewarded excellence. Add to this local farmers and suppliers who are proud of the quality of their ingredients and an adoring, food-obsessed audience and you have the right climate for flavours and dishes to really become perfected.

This focus on food has elevated French chefs to almost godlike status, as has the coveted Michelin star system that rates top chefs and restaurants. In 1900, the Michelin tyre company first sponsored the now-famous *Michelin Guide* in an effort to encourage people to explore France by road. For more than a century, this guide has awarded stars to a select number of European restaurants of outstanding quality – these stars are recognised and renowned worldwide.

The recognition of quality is also behind the French movement to certify regional products – from cheese and butter to salt and wine – with the label AOC (Appellation d'Origine Contrôlée). Across France, the origin of produce is of critical importance and this labelling guarantees authenticity and quality – French shoppers will always seek out the best. With an abundance of local produce markets, they are spoiled for choice and many people shop every day to source the freshest food. Some even visit the baker twice a day to get baguettes that are just out of the oven and most bakers continue baking through the day to satisfy their exacting customers.

Cheese

France produces the greatest number of cheeses in the world and cheese is always enjoyed at the end of a French meal. The cheese trolley is often regarded as a mark of a restaurant's quality. When tasting cheeses, begin with the mildest in flavour and work your way up to the strongest.

BASIC CATEGORIES OF CHEESE

Blue vein: roquefort, *fourme d'ambert*

Chèvre (goat's milk cheese): *cabécou, pouligny saint-pierre, crottin de chavignol*

Hard: gruyère, *beaufort*

Medium–firm: *saint-nectaire, morbier, cantal*

White and red mould (washed rind): *brie de meaux, camembert, livarot, munster-géromé*

BUTTER

A churned cream that is washed to remove leftover buttermilk, which improves the texture and flavour. The addition of salt improves the shelf life. French butter is often slightly fermented for an extra depth of flavour. It is essential to many traditional sauces, for sautéing, for baking, for making pastry and of course to spread on crusty French bread.

CHARCUTERIE

A collectived term meaning 'cooked meat', including *rillettes* and pâtés, terrines, confit and various types of *saucisson* (sausage).

DIJON MUSTARD

Pale yellow in colour with a creamy, smooth consistency and mild flavour, dijon mustard is used in sauces, rubbed on roasts and whisked in the classic vinaigrette dressing.

HERBS

Herbs are to French cooking as spices are to Asian cuisine and a large range are used including basil, chervil, mint, marjoram, parsley, rosemary, tarragon, thyme, sage and savory.

SHALLOTS

These small bulbs are a type of onion but have a sweeter, more delicate and less pungent flavour. They are very typical in French cooking.

TRUFFLES

A finely veined tuber formed in a magical underground exchange by the bonding of its filaments with the roots of certain types of trees, most traditionally oak. Season, climate, soil conditions and an element of great mystery surround the cultivation process, making the truffle a highly prized and expensive ingredient.

TURNIP

Believed to have first been cultivated in 2000 BC, turnips are picked young at the beginning of summer when they are small and sweet. The French love them pureed, pan-fried, steamed or paired with duck in the classic *canard aux navets* or in lamb navarin.

Soup à l'oignon
French Onion Soup
from France Vidal

The secret of this classic dish is to buy the best onions – they should be really fresh with papery skins – and the best gruyère and a fresh, crusty baguette. I am amazed at the depth of flavour of this simple, lovely soup.

60 g unsalted butter

4–5 onions, finely sliced

50 g (⅓ cup) plain flour

2 litres water

200 ml white wine

salt and pepper

100 g good-quality gruyère,
½ cut into cubes and ½ grated

1 baguette

Melt the butter in a heavy saucepan and add the onion. Sauté for 25 minutes, stirring from time to time, until deep golden brown and beginning to caramelise.

Add the flour and stir for 2 minutes then add the water and wine and season with salt and pepper. Stir in the cubes of cheese and bring to the boil, then reduce the heat, cover and simmer for 20–25 minutes. Check the seasoning.

Slice the baguette and sprinkle the slices with the grated cheese. Grill until the cheese melts.

Ladle the soup into bowls and serve with slices of cheese baguette on top.

Serves 6

Snapper Grenobloise
from Meyjitte Bourgenhout

It's the simplicity of this traditional fish dish from the city of Grenoble in the French Alps that is so seductive – it takes less than 15 minutes to cook and looks and tastes sensational.

4 × 150 g thick snapper fillets, skin on

sea salt and pepper

250 ml fish stock

2 large potatoes, peeled and cut into thick slices

1 cinnamon stick

1 star anise

2 tablespoons olive oil

2 bunches young spinach, trimmed

1 tablespoon butter

3 tablespoons croutons made from sourdough

2 tablespoons slivered almonds

2 teaspoons capers

2 tablespoons chopped flat-leaf parsley

2 tablespoons semi-dried tomatoes

Score the snapper fillets with a couple of shallow cuts on the flesh side and season the flesh with salt and pepper.

Bring the fish stock to a simmer and add the potatoes, cinnamon and star anise. Cover and cook until just soft then set aside.

Heat 1 tablespoon of the olive oil in a frying pan and fry the snapper skin-side down until crispy, for approximately 3–4 minutes. Turn the fish over, turn the heat down to low and cook for another 5 minutes. Remove from the pan.

Add the remaining oil to the pan and quickly wilt the spinach, adding salt and a dash of fish stock from the potatoes. Remove from the pan.

Add the butter to the pan along with the remaining ingredients and 1 tablespoon of the fish stock. Warm briefly, seasoning to taste.

Place slices of potato in the middle of each plate followed by the spinach and then the fish. Top with the ingredients from the frying pan.

Serves 4

Beef Bourguignon

from Guillaume Brahimi

A lovely dish with tender beef cooked to perfection. The speck adds a delicious smoky pork flavour and the carrot puree stirred through towards the end adds colour and sweetness. Serve with fresh sourdough.

125 ml extra-virgin olive oil

1 kg beef (preferably wagyu but any braising beef such as rump, topside or chuck steak is fine), cut into large chunks

2 carrots, halved lengthwise and sliced

2 celery stalks with leaves, halved lengthwise and sliced

1 leek, halved lengthwise and sliced

1 onion, chopped

5 shallots, halved

10 thyme sprigs

7 bay leaves

300 g speck, diced

500 ml red wine, boiled briefly to reduce acidity

salt and pepper

300 g button mushrooms

1 bunch flat-leaf parsley, chopped

CARROT PUREE

5 carrots, chopped

salt

MASHED POTATOES

6 large desiree potatoes

salt

200 ml milk

100 g butter

Heat the oil in a large heavy-based saucepan over medium–high heat. Brown the beef in batches. Remove the final batch of beef from the pan, leaving the oil, and add the carrot, celery, leek, onion and shallots. Sauté for 5–8 minutes.

Place the beef and vegetables in a large casserole pot. Stir in the thyme, bay leaves and speck. Pour over the red wine, season with salt and pepper and cover with a lid. Bring to the boil then reduce the heat to very low and cook for 40 minutes.

Meanwhile, prepare the carrot puree by boiling the carrots with salt until just soft. Puree.

To make the mashed potatoes, boil them whole with salt until soft. Peel, return them to the saucepan and mash finely. Stir the mash over medium heat for 3–5 minutes to remove excess water (this will also add air to the potatoes, making them light and fluffy). Warm the milk in a separate saucepan and gradually add to the mash. Stir in the butter. Cover the mash with a lid or plastic wrap and keep warm.

Add the mushrooms and carrot puree to the bourguignon and cook for a further 10 minutes. Sprinkle with the parsley.

Serve the bourguignon with the mashed potatoes and with sourdough.

Serves 6–8

Soufflé au Fromage
Cheese Soufflé

from Marie Helene Clauson

Everything you'd want from a good soufflé –
it's light and full of lovely creaminess. Serve
straight away!

60 g butter
60 g plain flour
500 ml milk
200 g good-quality gruyère cheese, grated
salt and pepper
grated nutmeg
6 eggs, separated

Preheat the oven to 200°C. Butter a large
soufflé dish.

To make a roux, melt the butter in a heavy-
based saucepan over low heat and add the flour,
stirring with a wooden spoon until the mixture
foams. Add the milk in small amounts and
heat, stirring, until smooth and thick. Add the
cheese and season to taste with salt, pepper and
nutmeg. Remove from the heat and stir in the
egg yolks.

In a large bowl, beat the egg whites with a
pinch of salt to stiff peaks – they should be firm
but not dry. With a large metal spoon gently
fold a little cheese mixture into the egg whites.
Once incorporated, pour in the remaining
cheese mixture and mix gently.

Pour into the soufflé dish and smooth the top.
Bake in the centre of the oven for 10 minutes.
Turn the oven down to 180°C and cook for
another 25–30 minutes until well risen and
golden brown. Serve immediately.

Serves 4–6

'French food rule
number one –
only buy what is
in season.'

'A lunch that does not finish with cheese is like a beautiful woman with only one eye.'

Coeur à la Crème d'Anjou
Cream Heart from Anjou

from Gabriel Gaté

This delicate dessert, made with a fresh soft cheese called *fromage blanc* (smooth quark), is a speciality of Gabriel's native region of Anjou in France. The *coeur* or 'heart' is moulded in a special heart-shaped porcelain dish that is perforated with holes to drain off the excess moisture of the cheese. A colander can be used as an alternative, although you won't end up with the same heart shape). Here it is served with fresh raspberries.

2 egg whites

pinch of cream of tartar

110 g (½ cup) caster sugar

200 ml whipping cream

250 g smooth quark

juice of 1½ lemons

600 g raspberries

juice of 1 orange

icing sugar

Beat the egg whites and cream of tartar until stiff peaks form. Add one-third of the sugar and continue beating until smooth.

Beat the cream in a separate bowl until it just starts to stiffen.

Beat the quark in a separate bowl with another third of the sugar and one-third of the lemon juice. Fold in the whipped cream then gently fold in the beaten egg whites.

Place the heart-shaped mould on a tray. Line the mould with damp muslin cloth then fill it with the cream mixture. Cover with the muslin and drain in the refrigerator for at least 4–5 hours or overnight.

Puree half the raspberries with the remaining sugar, lemon juice and orange juice. Pass through a sieve to remove the seeds. Refrigerate until 10 minutes before serving.

Carefully turn the heart out onto a serving plate. Top with the remaining whole raspberries and dust with icing sugar. Serve with the raspberry sauce.

Serves 6–8

Crepes Suzette

from Laurent Branover

Crepes are a delightful way to start the day – as many French families do every Sunday.

250 g (1⅔ cups) plain flour	
50 g (¼ cup) caster sugar	
pinch of salt	
3 eggs	
500 ml milk	
2 tablespoons citrus-flavoured liqueur such as Cointreau, Grand Marnier or curaçao	
butter	

SUZETTE BUTTER

150 g butter, softened	
180 g caster sugar	
4 sugar cubes	
1 orange	
1 lemon	
2 tablespoons cognac	
2 tablespoons citrus-flavoured liqueur	

TO FLAME

2 tablespoons cognac	
2 tablespoons citrus-flavoured liqueur	
1 tablespoon caster sugar	

Place the flour, sugar and salt in a large bowl and make a well in the centre. Add the eggs and combine with a whisk. Slowly add the milk and whisk until smooth. Add the liqueur and leave to rest for 1 hour.

To make the suzette butter, cream the butter and three-quarters of the caster sugar.

Rub 3 of the sugar cubes against the orange skin and 1 against the lemon to absorb the flavour. Place the cubes in a bowl with the remaining caster sugar and add the juice of half the orange. Crush the sugar with a fork then stir into the butter mixture. Add the cognac and liqueur.

Heat a crepe pan and brush it with butter. Add a ladleful of crepe batter, tilting the pan to coat evenly. Cook the crepe until golden at the edges and turn to cook the other side. Continue cooking crepes until you have used all the batter.

Add a knob of suzette butter to the pan and when it melts (without colouring), place a crepe in the pan. Spread more butter over the top of the crepe and fold it in half and in half again to a triangular shape. Keep the crepe warm (at the side of your pan if you have room) and continue with the rest of the crepes.

To flame the crepes, return all the crepes to the pan and pour on the cognac and liqueur. Carefully flame by tilting the pan towards the stove flame or by setting a match to it. Sprinkle the sugar on the flame and serve.

If you are cooking crepes for a number of people, you may prefer to flame each serve individually.

Makes 10–16 crepes

GERMANY

Here's a country that's serious about its food. Germans do nothing by halves – their love of food and their cold climate mean that they delight in big, hearty servings of well-cooked dishes. Think of pork knuckle with crunchy, golden crackling served with potatoes, sauerkraut and apple sauce … They also enjoy many varieties of delicious sausages, hams and cheeses; dense, seed-rich breads; and pretzels dusted with salt. These foods are all delicious but the culinary tradition I love most is that the whole country stops at 4 pm for coffee and cake – and serious cake at that, with liqueur-laced layers, rich toppings and cream … And they do this every day!

One fond memory I have of travelling to Germany is of the groaning breakfast buffets, full of sliced hams and *wursts* (sausages), different types of cheese including the beloved quark, six different sorts of bread, roll-mops and pickles and still more tables laden with yoghurts, cake and muesli. Breakfast is a real showcase of the best this rich farming country has to offer.

And how many sausages come from this one country! There are hun-dreds of variations on three main types: sausages similar to frankfurters come under the heading *brühwurst,* which means a parboiled sausage made from finely chopped meat; then there's *rohwurst,* which is a raw sausage made from cured meat; and also *leberwurst,* which is a fully cooked sausage. Sausages make great snack food between meals and are sold at street stalls in a bun with lashings of mustard.

As in most European countries, local wines and artisan beers are always accompanied by food. In Bavaria, bar food might consist of a salty pretzel, elsewhere you might get a smoked sausage or a selection of cold cuts, known as *aufschnitt*. German beer is dear to many hearts and the 1200 breweries around the country have firmly supported local purity laws, which stipulate that only hops, barley, yeast and water can be used to make their beer.

Back to those cakes – one of the most popular recipes included here is my friend Martin's show-stopping black forest cake, known in Germany as *schwarzwälder kirschtorte*. This cake was originally created in the late sixteenth century in the Black Forest region of Baden-Württemberg, known for its sour cherries and *kirschwasser* (or kirsch, a double-distilled, clear brandy made from the sour morello cherry). Cherries combined with layers of chocolate cake and cream, topped with little shavings of choco-late to represent the bark of trees … this is a seriously good cake. I'd stop every day at 4 pm for a slice of this!

CABBAGE

Both the white and red cabbage are used extensively in German cooking. Sauerkraut is the most popular dish, where the cabbage is finely shredded and pickled. Red cabbage is slightly sweeter and sometimes cooked with apple.

JUNIPER BERRIES

Naturally occurring in the evergreen forests of Germany, juniper berries are commonly used to flavour game dishes such as rabbit, goose and duck. They have a clean, sharp flavour that is a bit spicy or savoury. They are considered an essential ingredient in sauerkraut.

MUSTARD

The mustard plant is native to Europe and is therefore a very cheap spice, widely used in European cooking. The seeds of the mustard plant are ground into a paste, which in Germany is a distinctive dark colour and is used as an essential accompaniment to *wursts* (sausages).

QUARK

A fresh curd cheese made from skim milk. With its neutral flavour, quark accounts for approximately half of all the cheese consumed in Germany. It can be used in sweet and savoury dishes.

Lentil Soup

from Michael Vieh

Smoked pork belly or hock is the basis of the stock used to make this hearty soup. Celery, carrot and parsnip are also used, although any other good stock vegetables can be included. Traditionally eaten during the autumn harvest in the wine region of Germany, this soup recipe can be stretched depending on how many people you're feeding – this version feeds six people. You can happily make more than you need as the soup keeps well and gets better with time – simply freeze or store in the refrigerator for up to five days.

1 smoked pork belly or hock

2 celery stalks, roughly chopped

2 carrots, roughly chopped

1 parsnip, roughly chopped

2–3 litres water

salt

4 cups green lentils, soaked for 2 hours

3 large, waxy potatoes, cut into cubes

1 tablespoon lard

1 tablespoon plain flour

Place the belly or hock, celery, carrot and parsnip in a large pot and cover with the water. Add 2 teaspoons salt (or less if the pork is very salty) and bring to the boil. Simmer gently for a couple of hours.

Remove the pork and strain the stock, discarding the vegetables. Bring the stock back to a simmer and add the lentils. Cook for 10 minutes.

Cut the pork into rough smallish chunks and add back to the pot. Simmer for a few more minutes then add the potato. Cook for another 15–20 minutes.

Melt the lard in a frying pan and add the flour and brown lightly. Add to the soup being careful not to let it splash and burn; as the flour cooks it will thicken the soup.

Serves 6

Sauerbraten with Napkin Dumplings and Sautéed Cabbage

from Detlef Haupt

Sauerbraten (sour roast) is said to be Germany's national dish. It's a long-marinated meat dish that uses some of the great flavours of German cooking – juniper berries, allspice and red wine. Detlef likes to use star anise and the red-currant jelly, sour cream and sultanas are added for a slightly sweet finish. This recipe is very yummy and the bread dumplings are worth the work!

200 ml red wine

200 ml red-wine vinegar

500 ml water

6 juniper berries (or more to taste)

a few star anise or whole allspice berries

a few peppercorns

2 bay leaves

1 kg piece of beef brisket or rump

2 carrots, roughly chopped

2 celery stalks, roughly chopped

1 onion, roughly chopped

1 leek, roughly chopped

a few flat-leaf parsley stalks

salt and pepper

olive oil

butter

60 g gingerbread from last Christmas, crumbled (optional)

2 tablespoons sour cream

100 g red-currant jelly

150 g sultanas or raisins

DUMPLINGS

1 large good-quality, day-old vienna loaf, crusts discarded and cut into chunky cubes

150 ml milk

1 onion, diced

100 g speck, diced

duck fat or lard

4–6 eggs

½ bunch flat-leaf parsley, finely chopped

a little freshly grated nutmeg

salt and pepper

fresh breadcrumbs if needed

butter (optional)

CABBAGE

1 onion, diced

100 g speck, diced

1 tablespoon duck fat or lard

½ cabbage, finely sliced

1 teaspoon caraway seeds

salt

Bring the red wine, vinegar and water to the boil. Add the spices and bay leaves and allow to cool. Place the beef, vegetables and parsley in a deep bowl and pour over the red-wine marinade. Marinate in a cool place (or in the refrigerator) for a minimum of 2 days, turning the beef frequently.

Take the beef out of the marinade and pat dry with paper towel. Rub the beef generously with salt and pepper. Heat some olive oil and a knob of butter in a heavy-based ovenproof pot and quickly seal the meat, browning well all over. Add the vegetables from the marinade and sauté with the beef.

Pour over the marinade liquid and add the gingerbread if using. Bring almost to the boil then reduce the heat, cover and braise the beef over low heat for 1½–2 hours or until the meat is tender. Add more water if necessary to keep the beef covered while it cooks.

Meanwhile, make the dumplings. Place the bread pieces in a bowl. Heat the milk and pour it over the bread. Sauté the onion and speck in a little duck fat or lard until the onion is glossy and the speck is cooked and add to the bread. Add 4 eggs, one at a time, mixing well with a wooden spoon. Add the parsley and nutmeg and season well with salt and pepper. If the mixture seems too dry you may need to add another egg

or two. If it appears too wet, add a handful of breadcrumbs. Turn the mixture onto a piece of muslin cloth and shape into a large sausage. Roll up inside the cloth and tie the ends tightly with butcher's string.

Carefully slide the dumpling into a saucepan of boiling salted water and cook for about 40 minutes. Remove from the water and let it cool a little before unwrapping and cutting into slices 2 fingers thick. You can serve the dumplings like this, or pan-fry the slices in butter to add a bit of extra flavour and crunchiness.

When the beef is cooked, remove it and keep warm. Strain the liquid, discarding the vegetables, and return it to the pot to reduce a little and form a sauce. Whisk in the sour cream and red-currant jelly and season well. Rinse the sultanas or raisins under warm water and add to the sauce. Keep simmering at very low heat.

To make the cabbage, sauté the onion and speck in the duck fat or lard until the onion is glossy and the speck is cooked. Add the cabbage and sauté for 2–3 minutes. Add the caraway seeds and a little salt.

Slice the beef and arrange on a warm plate. Dress with the sauce and serve with the hot dumplings and cabbage.

Serves 8

'There is nothing better than the joy of eating *sauerbraten* and all the trimmings with a few generations together around a big dinner table.'

Pork Knuckle with Potato Dumplings and Braised Red Cabbage

from Max Dietz

A favourite all over Germany, these pork knuckles (otherwise known as hocks) are the perfect mix of crunchy crackling and tender meat – and they're so easy to cook. Here they're infused with garlic and caraway and served with delicious potato dumplings and slow-cooked red cabbage. For a really deluxe meal, add some fried onion rings and apple sauce. Start the dumplings and cabbage the day before. A perfect dish to prepare on lazy winter days.

POTATO DUMPLINGS

500 g potatoes

100 g (⅔ cup) plain flour

1 egg

1 bunch chives, finely chopped

salt and pepper

freshly grated nutmeg

RED CABBAGE

2 red cabbages, finely sliced

2 apples, peeled, cored and finely sliced

1 onion, finely sliced

2 juniper berries

2 cloves

2 bay leaves

2 tablespoons sugar

salt and pepper

250 ml red wine, plus a splash extra

2 bacon rashers, finely sliced

1 tablespoon butter

PORK KNUCKLE

1 kg pork hocks (2 pieces)

2 tablespoons salt

finely chopped garlic

olive oil

caraway seeds

The day before, boil the potatoes for the dumplings in their skins until soft. Leave to cool. For the red cabbage, combine the cabbage, apple, half the onion, the spices, bay leaves, sugar, salt, pepper and wine and leave to marinate overnight.

The next day, preheat the oven to 180°C. Rub the skin of the pork hocks with generous amounts of salt, garlic and oil. Sprinkle with the caraway seeds. Place in a baking dish with 2 cm of water and roast for 2 hours.

To make the potato dumplings, peel the cooked potatoes and mash them. Incorporate with the flour, egg, chives, salt, pepper and nutmeg. Roll into a long sausage and cut into pieces about the size of golf balls. Roll into balls.

To cook the red cabbage, fry the remaining onion and bacon in the butter. Add a splash of red wine, then add the marinated cabbage mixture. Cover and braise for 20 minutes over low heat until soft. Season to taste.

Cook the dumplings in salted boiling water until they float (around 2 minutes) then drain.

Arrange the roast pork with the dumplings and red cabbage on a serving plate and carve at the table.

Serves 4–6

Black Forest Cake
from Martin Boetz

I'm ordering this for every birthday – Martin's version of the classic cake makes your knees go weak. He uses a chocolate mousse recipe from Heston Blumenthal's book *In Search of Perfection* (but any basic mousse recipe is fine) and likes to garnish the cake with fresh cherries that have been marinated in kirsch for one week.

BUTTER CAKE

300 g butter

300 g caster sugar

6 eggs

300 g (2 cups) plain flour

1½ teaspoons baking powder

CHOCOLATE CAKE

250 g chocolate, chopped

180 g butter

6 eggs

250 g caster sugar

225 g (1½ cups) plain flour

CHOCOLATE MOUSSE

4 egg yolks (combined weight of 80 g)

200 g caster sugar

100 ml full-cream milk

150 g top-quality dark chocolate, chopped

generous pinch of salt

200 ml whipping cream

CHOCOLATE GANACHE

95 ml whipping cream

1 teaspoon glucose syrup

pinch of salt

95 g top-quality dark chocolate, chopped

20 g unsalted butter

CHERRIES

680 g jar sour (morello) cherries

1 vanilla bean, split

1 tablespoon sugar

Continued over page …

'If you don't sweat in
the kitchen while you
cook, the food will
taste only half as good!'

TO ASSEMBLE

kirsch

whipped cream

shards of dark or milk chocolate

10 whole fresh cherries
(preferably soaked in kirsch for 1 week)

To make the butter cake, preheat the oven to 180°C and butter a cake tin. Cream the butter and sugar. Beat in the eggs one at a time then fold in the flour and baking powder. Pour into the tin and bake for 55 minutes. Leave to cool.

Butter another cake tin of the same size for the chocolate cake. Melt the chocolate and butter together in a bowl set over a saucepan of simmering water then leave to cool. Beat the eggs and sugar together. Fold in the melted chocolate then the flour. Pour into the tin and bake for 1 hour. Leave to cool.

To make the chocolate mousse, beat the egg yolks with the sugar for 5 minutes or until stiff. Gently warm the milk in a saucepan then remove from the heat. Stir in the egg yolks and return to medium heat. Cook for 2–3 minutes, stirring frequently. Use a digital probe to monitor when the temperature of the mixture reaches 80°C and remove from the heat.

Place the chocolate in a mixing bowl and pour over the warm milk and egg mixture, stirring until the chocolate has melted. Add the salt and leave to cool.

Whip the cream until soft peaks form then fold into the cooled chocolate mixture. Spoon into a piping bag and refrigerate to stiffen.

To make the chocolate ganache, gently heat the cream, glucose syrup and salt. Place the chocolate in a bowl and add the warm cream, stirring until the chocolate melts. Add the butter and stir until it melts.

Strain the cherry juice into a saucepan. Add the vanilla bean and sugar and simmer until reduced to a syrup.

Carefully cut each cake into three slices. Place a layer of butter cake on a flat plate and splash with a little kirsch. Pipe a rim of mousse around the top of the cake to form a wall to keep in the cherries. Fill with some cherries then top with a layer of chocolate cake. Spread with whipped cream. Repeat the layers but instead of topping the cake with cream, spread with ganache. Allow it to run down the sides of the cake or if preferred, use a spatula to smooth the ganache around the sides of the cake. Sprinkle with chocolate shards (to resemble the bark of trees in a forest) and garnish with whole cherries. Leave the cake to set for 3–6 hours – in the refrigerator if necessary but take it out at least 1 hour before serving.

Serves 16

Black Forest Cake

GREECE

Thank God they came! When the Greeks began emigrating in large numbers in the 1950s and '60s, our culinary landscape started to change for the better.

Greek households transplanted their native flavours and grew much of what they needed in their own gardens – a pot of basil at the back door to ward off the evil eye, and healthy rows of herbs and vegetables as well as fruit trees in the backyard. Often there was an extra kitchen installed in a big double garage or cellar where some of the 'heavy duty' cooking was done, such as the preserving of sweets in heavy syrup. Called spoon sweets, these intense little treats are served on a glass saucer with a small teaspoon and a glass of icy-cold water as soon as a visitor is two steps inside the house.

Since their arrival we've embraced the Greeks and their approach to food wholeheartedly: fetta, a wide range of olive varieties, olive oil, taramasalata is a word most people recognise and vine leaves are used in dishes around the country. We also readily cook with filo pastry and add oregano and garlic to our lamb roasts.

And we love the fact that Greek food is so damned good for us. Much of what is preached as ideal eating in the food pages of magazines is integral to Greek cuisine – simplicity, seasonality and freshness. Bunches of spinach and silverbeet so fresh they almost squeak, ripe tomatoes that really do taste like tomatoes, very fresh cucumber with its sweetness and crunch, thick creamy Greek yoghurt and olive oil ... (Although the oil isn't used quite as liberally as one would in Greece. My friend George laughs that his grandmother would hold a whole conversation as she upended the olive oil in whatever dish she was making!)

The key to Greek cuisine is the power of the *yia yia* (usually the grand-mother and sometimes extended to include the aunties). She is the keeper of recipes and traditions, the one who knows whether moussaka has the right amount of salt just from smelling it, who knows exactly how hot the oil should be for *loukoumades*, and whose oven never quite cools down in the huge baking frenzy that happens in the run-up to Greek Easter.

My friend Peter, a great chef, says the focus on food is unwavering: 'Greek women chase you round with a spoon from the minute you open your eyes in the morning. It's all about the food!' There was a time not long ago when no self-respecting Greek would be seen in a Greek restaurant. Firstly, Greek cooking is generally so good at home that you'd never go out and eat an inferior version of what your Mum could make, and then there's the public humiliation – 'Our mothers would kill us if they thought we were eating Greek food away from home. What if someone saw? Everyone would think Mum couldn't cook!'

Pastries and Biscuits

Greek pastries and biscuits are wickedly addictive – from the first satisfying crunch of baklava filled with crushed nuts and bathed in syrup to a large forkful of a creamy, custardy wonder still warm from the oven ... you'll be enchanted for life.

Amigdalota: Almond swirl biscuits that are chewy inside and crunchy outside.

Baklava: A symphony of filo pastry, ground nuts (usually almond or cashew) and syrup traditionally cut into a diamond shape.

Galaktoboureko: Thick custard between crunchy filo pastry served warm with syrup – an experience that will make your eyelids flutter.

Kataifi: A shredded pastry that replaces filo to make pastries filled with nuts and drenched in sugar syrup. It is extra crunchy and looks amazing too.

Kourambiedes: The most heavenly, melting shortbread crescents made with toasted almonds and smothered in icing sugar.

Melamakarona: Honey and orange biscuits shaped in a lozenge, topped with crushed walnuts and with a wonderful cinnamon aroma.

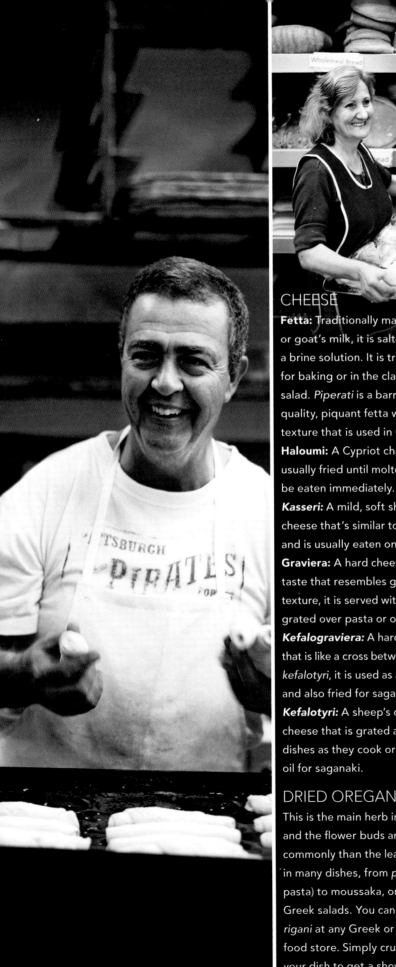

CHEESE

Fetta: Traditionally made from sheep's or goat's milk, it is salted and cured in a brine solution. It is traditionally used for baking or in the classic Greek salad. *Piperati* is a barrel-aged, high-quality, piquant fetta with a creamy texture that is used in Greek salads.

Haloumi: A Cypriot cheese that is usually fried until molten – it must be eaten immediately.

Kasseri: A mild, soft sheep's milk cheese that's similar to cheddar and is usually eaten on its own.

Graviera: A hard cheese with a mild taste that resembles gruyère in texture, it is served with meals or used grated over pasta or other dishes.

Kefalograviera: A hard, salty cheese that is like a cross between *graviera* and *kefalotyri*, it is used as a grating cheese and also fried for saganaki recipes.

Kefalotyri: A sheep's or goat's milk cheese that is grated and added to dishes as they cook or fried in olive oil for saganaki.

DRIED OREGANO (*RIGANI*)

This is the main herb in Greek cooking and the flower buds are used more commonly than the leaves. It is used in many dishes, from *pastitsio* (baked pasta) to moussaka, or sprinkled over Greek salads. You can buy bunches of *rigani* at any Greek or Mediterranean food store. Simply crush the buds over your dish to get a shower of this fragrant dried herb.

MASTIC

A gum resin from trees that grow only on the Greek island of Chios. It is used in the making of ice cream, sweets, chewing gum and liqueur and also has medicinal and pharmaceutical properties. It has an earthy, musky, vanilla-like flavour.

MEZEDES

In Greece you rarely drink without eating and a whole tradition of small snacks (*mezedes*) surround what you take as an aperitif. *Mezedes* (plural for 'meze') include anchovy fillets, salted fish, *pastourma* (dried and spiced meat – originally camel but now commonly beef), yellow cheese, dips such as taramasalata, *melitzanosalata* (eggplant dip) and tzatziki, as well as *kafteri* (spicy fetta), calamari, octopus (either grilled or braised in various ways), *tiropita* (cheese pastries), zucchini patties, *keftedes* (meat balls), fried haloumi and *loukanika* (spicy Greek sausages), and let's not forget olives and pickled peppers.

OLIVES

Kalamata: These strong, salty olives range in size from small, mammoth and colossal to super colossal.

Throumbes: From the island of Thasos, these sun-dried olives have a raisin-like flavour.

'The ultimate compliment
for a Greek cook is
"Yia sta heria!"
(I kiss your hands!)'

Spanakopita

from Dimitra Alfred

Such a fabulous combination of flavours –
spinach, dill and spring onions with a creamy
mix of cheeses. My daughter is always cooking
this at home. The spinach can be prepared a day
ahead – it must be as dry as possible to ensure
the spanakopita doesn't become soggy.

1 bunch spinach or silverbeet

300 g fetta

100 g ricotta

40 g (½ cup) finely grated hard cheese such
as *kefalograviera*, parmesan or pecorino

5 eggs

2 tablespoons dry breadcrumbs

¼ teaspoon ground nutmeg

½ teaspoon freshly ground black pepper

3 tablespoons olive oil

2 dill sprigs, chopped

4 spring onions, chopped

375 g fresh (not frozen) filo pastry

125 g butter, melted

Trim the roots from the spinach or if using
silverbeet, cut out the stems. Wash leaves and
drain well. Coarsely shred and set aside.

Place the fetta in a large bowl and roughly
mash with a fork. Add the ricotta, hard cheese,
eggs, breadcrumbs, nutmeg, pepper, oil, dill and
spring onions. Mix with the fork to combine.
Place the spinach or silverbeet on top.

Preheat the oven to 180°C. Lightly oil or
butter a 20 × 30 × 5 cm baking dish. Lay the filo
out on a work surface. Line the dish with a sheet
of filo and brush it with butter. Top with another
sheet of filo brushed with butter and continue
until about half the filo is used. When not using
the filo, cover it with a dry tea towel and then
a damp one to keep it from drying out.

Use your hand or a large metal spoon to
gently mix the spinach filling until thoroughly
combined. Tip into the filo base and spread out
evenly. Layer with the remaining sheets of filo
brushed with butter, ensuring the final sheet is
well buttered. Trim off any overhanging pastry
and tuck in the sides.

Use a sharp knife to score the pastry into dia-
monds. Pierce the pastry once or twice to allow
air to escape during baking. Sprinkle lightly with
water and bake in the oven for 45–60 minutes
or until well browned. Gently shake the baking
dish; the spanakopita should slide easily when it
is cooked. Cover with foil if it is over-browning.
Cool on a rack for 15 minutes before cutting to
serve.

Serves 8–10

Spanakopita

Greek Salad

from George Calombaris

When cucumbers and tomatoes are at their summer best, there is nothing to match this fresh-tasting salad. Seek out the best fetta you can find.

½ ciabatta loaf, crusts discarded

2 Lebanese cucumbers, peeled, quartered lengthwise, diced

2 vine-ripened tomatoes, diced

handful of kalamata olives

3 shallots, finely sliced

1 teaspoon *rigani* (dried Greek oregano)

100 g fetta, crumbled

5 dill sprigs, leaves picked

100 ml olive oil

2½ tablespoons brown vinegar

salt

Break the bread into rough pieces and bake in the oven until golden brown. Set aside to cool.

Combine the cucumber, tomato, olives, shallots, *rigani*, fetta and dill in a bowl. Drizzle over the oil and vinegar and season with salt. Add the bread and toss. Serve immediately.

Serves 4

Greek Lamb with Fennel and Parsley

from George Calombaris

This lamb is tenderised by the yoghurt and honey and is full of classic Greek flavour. It is cooked on the barbie to a perfect caramelised finish.

500 g boneless lamb neck

sea salt

olive oil

1 onion, roughly chopped

6 shallots, roughly chopped

2 garlic cloves, sliced

grated zest of 1 lemon

1 tablespoon *rigani* (dried Greek oregano)

250 ml white wine

200 g natural yoghurt

1 tablespoon honey

1 fennel bulb, finely sliced

6 flat-leaf parsley sprigs, leaves picked

Preheat the oven to 160°C. Season the lamb with salt. Place 100 ml of olive oil in a deep ovenproof pot and seal the lamb until golden brown on all sides. Add the onion, shallots, garlic, lemon zest, *rigani* and white wine to the pot. Cover the lamb with the yoghurt and drizzle with honey. Cover and bake for 1½ hours.

Remove the lamb from the pot and leave to cool. Refrigerate for at least 1 hour.

Strain the vegetables from the pot and place in a bowl. Add the fennel and parsley. Season to taste and drizzle with oil.

Slice the lamb into thin strips. Place the strips on a barbecue and grill on both sides. Serve with the fennel salad.

Serves 4

'To raise a toast say *"Stini yamas!"* (To your health!)'

Bean Skordalia

from George Calombaris

Skordalia is a sauce or dip usually made from potato and flavoured with garlic, olive oil, lemon juice and parsley. This white bean version is fast and delicious.

400 g tin cannellini beans, drained
juice of 1 lemon
2 garlic cloves, roughly chopped
3 tablespoons olive oil

Puree the cannellini beans with the lemon juice, garlic and olive oil until smooth.

Makes 2 cups

Fig *Loukoumades* with Raspberry Syrup

from Peter Conistis

Is there anything sexier than a fresh fig – ripe, heavy in its skin, luscious and honeyed inside? This recipe combines the classic *loukoumades* (fried doughnuts) with gorgeous figs. Simply divine!

BATTER

150 g (1 cup) plain flour
2 teaspoons dried yeast
pinch of sea salt
2 tablespoons sugar
water

SYRUP

440 g (2 cups) sugar
500 ml water
juice of 1 lemon
1 cup raspberries (fresh or frozen)
1 teaspoon rosewater

oil for deep-frying
12 green figs
2 tablespoons plain flour for dusting

To make the batter, place the dry ingredients in a bowl and whisk in enough water to make a smooth batter with the consistency of thick pouring cream. Set aside for 15 minutes.

To make the syrup, place the sugar, water and lemon juice in a saucepan and bring to the boil, stirring until the sugar dissolves. Turn the heat back to a simmer and add the raspberries and rosewater, stirring to loosen the raspberries. Bring back to a simmer then remove from the heat.

Heat the oil in a saucepan. Dust the figs in flour then skewer each one with a fork to dip them into the batter, rolling them around to coat them evenly. Drop the figs into the hot oil and cook until golden brown. Drain on paper towel then arrange on a serving platter. Spoon over the raspberry syrup.

Serves 4–6

Greek Coffee

from Liz Kaydos

There is an art to getting the foamy crema, or *kaimaki,* on top just right when you brew coffee in a *briki* (a Greek coffee pot that is like a small saucepan). If you perfect it, then you're deemed to be marriageable!

water
pulverised Greek coffee
sugar

Measure an espresso cup of water per person into the *briki*. Add 1 heaped tablespoon of coffee per person and 1 teaspoon of sugar if desired and stir briefly. Place over high heat. When the coffee just comes to the boil and there is a thick layer of foam (*kaimaki*) on top, remove from the heat and let stand for about 15 seconds for the foam to settle. Pour or spoon some foam into each cup, then carefully pour in the coffee keeping the foam on the surface.

HUNGARY

I'm always intrigued by the beloved family cooking pots and pans that make the long journey to their new homes from far away. For my Hungarian friend Stephen (Istvan), it was a heavy witch's cauldron called a *bogrács* that could not be left behind. In this he makes the superb dish that's synonymous with Hungary – *gulyas* (goulash). A stew of tender chunks of meat in a rich paprika-laced sauce, *gulyas* has been made since the nomadic tribes rode the Great Plain (although paprika came to be included later). The name *gulyas* actually means 'herdsmen'.

Over centuries *gulyas* came to be eaten by all Hungarians and rose to the heights of a national symbol when Hungary took a stand to protect its distinctive language, culture and gastronomy. That was 200 years ago. *Gulyas* and its variations – *paprikas*, *tokany* and *porkolt* – are still adored and cooked all the time.

During the summer months groups of Hungarian men and sometimes women hold cook-off competitions in central Hungary, gathering in the countryside to vie for the title of best *bogrács gulyas* (kettle goulash). This title is treasured and respected – recipes are carefully guarded and getting everything right is paramount.

The key ingredient in *gulyas* and many other Hungarian dishes is paprika. Paprika was introduced by the Bulgarians and Turks in the six-teenth and seventeenth centuries and is used in Hungary in its powdered form as well as in pastes. Stephen says that when the oil, onion and paprika are starting to cook for *gulyas*, the heart and soul of the dish is born. Each Hungarian dish calls for different types of paprika, ranging from 'exquisitely delicate' through to hot. The paprika pastes are held so dear to people's hearts that they actually have nicknames – *edes anna* ('Gentle Anna') is mild while *eros pista* ('Strong Stephen') is hot and fiery. This is truly a fascinating spice!

Also fascinating and a world unto themselves are Hungarian sweets. These were elevated to an art form in the days of the Austro–Hungarian Empire when many delectable confections were created and celebrated – strudels filled with apple, sour or sweet cherries, cream cheese, poppy seeds and walnuts; elaborate layered cakes like the magnificent *dobostorta*, with its mahogany toffee topping; the light, yeasty *kugelhoph* cake; the sweet, festive *beigli* pastries and many more delights. I fell completely under the spell of these Hungarian cakes and – true confession here – I polished off an entire *kugelhoph* by myself over a day or two. How could I resist this delicious yeast cake with its seam of pure chocolate … It was exceptional!

CARAWAY SEEDS

Thought to be one of the oldest spices in Europe, they have an anise-like flavour and aroma and are a key ingredient in *liptauer* (a spicy cheese spread), some meat stews such as *gulyas*, soups and breads.

MORELLO CHERRIES

A variety of griotte or dark sour cherry. They are grown extensively in Hungary and used in both sweet and savoury dishes, including *hideg meggyleves* (sour cherry soup) and strudels.

PAPRIKA

Paprika comes in seven categories including special, mild, delicate, sweet, semi-sweet, rose and hot. For fiery-hot, look for paprika that is labelled '*eros*'. Any paprika labelled 'sweet' or '*edesnemes*' is more mild than hot. It is usually available in dried or paste form.

POPPY SEEDS

Blue-grey in colour and slightly nutty in flavour, poppy seeds are sprinkled over pasta and used extensively in Hungarian baking – in strudels, tortes and the festive *beigli*.

SAUERKRAUT

A fermented cabbage. Sauerkraut is an excellent source of vitamin C and is commonly eaten with Hungarian *kolbas*, salami or *csabai* sausages. Sauerkraut is generally consumed as part of a traditional dish such as stuffed cabbage or *székely gulyas*.

SOUR CREAM

Traditionally made by leaving cream to sour naturally, it's now made by pasteurising and homogenising single cream and adding a pure form of bacteria that grows until the desired tartness and consistency is reached. Sour cream is used liberally in Hungarian cooking, in both savoury and sweet dishes.

77

'"Jo etvagyat, barataim!" (Enjoy your meals, my friends!)'

Porkolt with *Nokedli* and Cucumber Salad

from Stephen (Istvan) Orosvari

Porkolt is a beautiful casserole of tender veal cooked with paprika and garlic. Beef can be used instead (cuts such as chuck steak or gravy beef), as can pork (neck or leg). Traditionally this is served with *nokedli* – quick homemade pasta served with lashings of butter.

CUCUMBER SALAD

1.5 kg long cucumbers, peeled and finely sliced

2½ tablespoons white vinegar

80 g sugar

pinch of salt and pepper

1 garlic clove, crushed

paprika (optional)

PORKOLT

1 large onion, finely chopped

100 ml oil

20 g sweet paprika

200 ml stock or water

1.4 kg veal leg or shoulder, diced into 2 cm cubes

5 g salt

3 garlic cloves, crushed

1 teaspoon hot paprika paste (*eros pista*)

3 banana chillies (mild Hungarian capsicums), roughly chopped

1 large tomato, roughly chopped

NOKEDLI

salt

4 eggs

650 ml water

800 g plain flour

butter or oil

To make the cucumber salad, mix the ingredients other than the paprika in a bowl and refrigerate for a couple of hours for the flavours to develop. Sprinkle with paprika before serving, if using; it will not change the taste but make the dish more attractive.

To make the *porkolt*, sauté the onion in the oil until golden. Remove from the heat and add the paprika (removing from the heat ensures the colour and flavour is released without burning). Stir for a minute then add the stock or water and return to the heat. Simmer until slightly reduced. Add the meat, salt, garlic and paprika paste and stir well. Simmer until the meat is halfway tender (30–60 minutes depending on the meat). Add the banana chilli and tomato and continue to cook until the meat is tender. Taste for seasoning.

While the *porkolt* is cooking, make the *nokedli*. Bring a large pot (5 litres) of water to the boil and add 20 g of salt. Meanwhile, beat the eggs with the water. Sift the flour and a pinch of salt into a bowl and lightly mix in the egg and water. (Be careful not to over-mix, which will make the dough unworkable.) Push the dough through a *nokedli* maker or *spatzle* press into the boiling water. Cook until the *nokedli* rise to the surface then remove with a slotted spoon. Toss in butter or oil.

Serve the *porkolt* on the *nokedli* alongside the cucumber salad.

Serves 8

Chicken Schnitzel

from Csaba Cserfalvi

This recipe creates tender chicken with a lovely golden coating and it is delicious with mashed, boiled or fried potatoes. We make it at home at least every couple of weeks and love the simple recipe.

2 large chicken breasts

150 g (1 cup) plain flour

salt and pepper

1 egg

1 tablespoon water

2 cups dry breadcrumbs

500 ml vegetable oil

Place the chicken breasts on a chopping board and use a sharp knife to slice horizontally through the breasts to create 2 or 3 (depending on the thickness) thin, even slices per breast. Flatten the slices with a meat mallet.

Lay out 3 wide bowls. Put the flour in one and season it with salt and pepper. In another, beat the egg with the water. Place the breadcrumbs in the other.

Using one hand, lightly coat each piece of chicken in the flour, shaking off the excess. Dip into the egg then coat with breadcrumbs.

Heat a deep frying pan with the oil and fry the schnitzels 1 or 2 at a time, cooking until golden brown on each side. When cooked, stand upright in a deep bowl lined with paper towel to drain. Cook the remaining schnitzels.

Serve with mashed, boiled or fried potatoes.

Serves 4—6

'It is not all sour cream down to the bottom.' (That is, it is not all as good as it seems.)

Nan's Cherry and Cream Cheese Strudel

from Janelle Bloom

A luscious mixture of cherries and cheese encased in golden flaky pastry from a great cook, my friend Janelle. If time allows, drain the ricotta in the fridge for 1–2 hours before making the filling.

125 g full-cream ricotta, drained for 1–2 hours

125 g cream cheese, softened

3 tablespoons caster sugar

1 teaspoon vanilla extract

1 egg

5 filo pastry sheets

80 g clarified butter (ghee), melted

2 tablespoons dry breadcrumbs

680 g jar sour (morello) cherries, drained

1 tablespoon flaked almonds, toasted

icing sugar

Preheat the oven to 200°C and line a baking tray with baking paper.

Combine the ricotta, cream cheese, sugar and vanilla and beat until smooth and creamy. Add the egg and beat well.

Lay a sheet of filo on a work surface and brush with melted clarified butter. Top with another sheet brushed with butter. Repeat until you have used all the sheets (there should be some butter remaining).

Sprinkle the breadcrumbs evenly over the pastry. Spoon the cheese mixture along one long edge, leaving a small border. Top with the cherries and sprinkle with the almonds. Fold in the ends of the pastry and roll up, enclosing the filling. Brush the edge with butter to stick it down. Place on the tray and brush the top with the remaining butter.

Bake for 15 minutes then reduce the oven temperature to 180°C and bake for a further 5 minutes, until the pastry is crisp and deep golden. Allow to cool for 30 minutes before dusting heavily with icing sugar, slicing and serving.

Serves 8–10

INDIA

In a country of extremes – of intense colour, of incredible architecture, of rich and poor – you know that the food is never going to be dull. And given this country stretches from the tropics almost to the world's highest mountain, it is not surprising that there's an amazing range of cooking styles and ingredients used.

When investigating Indian cuisine I was struck by the enormous difference between an Indian kitchen and one you'd find in the 'white-bread' suburbs. An Indian home has a lovely aroma of spice in the air as if these magic ingredients have a life of their own, even when they're not being used for cooking. The other big difference is that the cooking essentials are all within reach. Whether in a kitchen of gleaming, uncluttered bench tops or that of a more compact apartment, every Indian cook has the same glass-topped pannier of spices kept by the stove. Like an artist's palate, this array of six or seven key spices is used to colour and flavour all of their dishes. There is no fiddling with spice canisters in cupboards, instead they're to hand and spooned in with confidence. After years of intense training Indian cooks know how a dish should look and smell so there is no checking of recipes.

And what wonderful spices they are. Some are used whole and toasted in a dry pan then ground, others are pre-ground, others are fresh ... Each recipe calls for a variety and it's this clever blending of spices that creates the depth of flavour in great Indian dishes. Devotees of Indian food can easily pick the difference between regional dishes, particularly those of the north and south – the north favours richer food with lots of ghee, meat and wheat; the south is full of intense tropical flavours, coconut milk and rice.

In just over a generation, we have become a nation that knows its korma from its tandoori – in the UK, where Indian cuisine reigns supreme, vindaloo is almost the national dish. Indian cuisine certainly deserves to be studied and enjoyed as it has made our multicultural tapestry even richer and more fabulous.

KADHAI

A round-bottomed cooking pan similar to a wok. Because of its shape it uses less oil and is especially good for cooking ingredients in their own juices. It's a versatile pan used for everything from deep-frying, stir-frying, steaming and of course making curries.

SPICE GRINDER

Another handy gadget is a spice grinder (you can use a coffee-bean grinder if you reserve it specifically for this purpose). Spices always taste better when freshly ground and you don't need to double up on both whole and ground varieties.

SPICE TRAY OR BOX

There are many different spices used in Indian cooking so most Indian cooks keep a tray of spices in small bowls or a special glass-topped pannier near the stove ready for use. A spice box with compartments for a variety of spices was once a part of a young girls' dowry.

BLACK MUSTARD SEEDS

These add a nice pungent heat to dhal and a tangy pop when cooked in hot oil at the start of many dishes.

CORIANDER SEEDS

Essential in all masala mixes. The lighter coloured seeds have a lemony aroma and taste while the green Indian seeds taste more like the fresh herb.

CUMIN

Used in many dishes including curries, rice dishes, breads and chutney for its warm, earthy flavour.

DAL

Whole or split beans, peas and lentils are referred to as 'dal' and become 'dhal' when cooked. They are a staple of Indian cooking and are high in both protein and fibre. There are many varieties of dal including *urid*, *mung*, *toor* and *masoor* to name just a few.

GARAM MASALA

Meaning 'spice blend', this always includes green cardamom, cloves and cassia, among other spices. It is widely used as part of the harmony of spices that makes up many Indian dishes, and also as a natural medicine due to its antiseptic properties. It can be bought at Indian food stores or made at home by grinding toasted whole spices in a mortar or spice grinder.

TURMERIC

Used widely in many curries to give them their distinctive warm, yellow colour.

Palak Paneer
Firm Cottage Cheese in Spinach Puree
from Daisy Rajan

I was delighted to learn the secret of this beautiful green dish – and how to keep it green as well (by blanching the spinach, pureeing it and then cooking it only briefly in the finished dish). Instead of pureeing the spinach, you can chop it to achieve a more textured dish typically served in Indian homes. You can also substitute frozen spinach for fresh – and that's already chopped! *Paneer* (firm Indian cottage cheese) is now available in supermarkets.

2 bunches spinach, leaves picked

2 tablespoons vegetable oil

1 teaspoon cumin seeds

2 cm piece of ginger, crushed

6 garlic cloves, crushed

1 medium onion, finely chopped

200 g chopped tomatoes (fresh or tinned)

salt

225 g *paneer*, cubed

1 teaspoon dried fenugreek leaves

pinch of garam masala

1 tablespoon thickened cream

Blanch the spinach in boiling water for 3–4 minutes then refresh in cold water, drain and squeeze out the excess water. Puree until smooth.

Heat the oil in a heavy-based saucepan. Add the cumin seeds, ginger, garlic and onion and fry until golden brown. Add the tomatoes and cook until they become a soft paste. Stir in the spinach puree and season with salt. Add the *paneer* and heat through. To finish, add the dried fenugreek leaves, garam masala and cream.

Serves 4

Gujarati Potatoes
from Daisy Rajan

For potato lovers who like a hint of spice, this is the best thing in the world. The snap, crackle and pop as you fry the spices is part of the joy.

400 g pontiac or other waxy potatoes, peeled

1 teaspoon ground cumin

1 teaspoon ground coriander

1 teaspoon turmeric

½ teaspoon chilli powder

salt

2 tablespoons vegetable oil

1 teaspoon black mustard seeds

1 teaspoon cumin seeds

5–6 fenugreek seeds

1 tablespoon desiccated coconut

2 teaspoons sesame seeds

3–4 coriander sprigs, chopped

Boil the potatoes until soft, then cut into cubes.

Place the potato, ground cumin, coriander, turmeric and chilli in a bowl and season with salt. Toss to coat the potatoes evenly.

In a heavy-based pan or *kadhai*, heat the oil and add the mustard, cumin and fenugreek seeds and cook until sizzling (this is called tempering the spices). Add the potato and stir gently to coat in the oil. Stir in the coconut, sesame seeds and chopped coriander and serve with Indian bread.

Serves 4

'Always add a pinch of salt when cooking your onions. It will prevent them from burning.'

Hyderabadi Chicken

from Ajoy Joshi

Is there anything better than tender spiced chicken? My friend Ajoy has an unusual technique for cooking this dish, which involves covering the saucepan with a bowl with a little water inside it instead of a lid. As the chicken cooks in its own juices, it creates steam that holds the bowl in place, sealing in all the delicious flavours. The result is amazingly tender – as if the chicken has been steamed. Ajoy is also a master at blending spices.

1 kg chicken thigh fillets

1 heaped tablespoon sesame seeds

50 g peanuts

milk

80 ml oil

1 onion, sliced

salt

1 tablespoon crushed ginger

1 tablespoon crushed garlic

1½ tablespoons crushed green chilli

pinch of turmeric

1½ cups natural yoghurt

1 teaspoon garam masala

¼ teaspoon black cumin seeds

1 tablespoon lemon juice

Cut the chicken into large cubes without trimming off the fat, as this keeps it moist.

Toast the sesame seeds and peanuts in a dry frying pan then grind to a paste. Mix the paste with a little milk. This paste will thicken and bind the sauce for the chicken.

Heat the oil in a heavy-based saucepan and add the onion and 2 pinches of salt. Cook over medium–high heat until caramelised and golden brown (about 5 minutes). Remove from the heat.

Place the peanut paste, ginger, garlic, chilli, turmeric, yoghurt, garam masala, cumin seeds and a pinch of salt in a large bowl and mix together. Stir in the fried onion and then the chicken. Leave to marinate for 10 minutes (the acidity of the yoghurt will help to tenderise the chicken, but if left for longer, too much moisture will be drawn out of the meat).

Put the chicken and marinade in the saucepan used for the onions and set a large stainless-steel bowl over the top so that it seals around the rim. Add ¼ cup of water to the bowl. The heat of the saucepan will cause suction and hold the bowl in place, creating steam and improvising a pressure cooker. Cook the chicken over medium heat for 30–40 minutes – when the water in the bowl has evaporated you'll know the chicken is cooked. Just before serving add the lemon juice.

Serves 4–6

'Anha daata sukhi bhava.' (Old Sanskrit for 'Thank the giver for this wonderful meal.' It is a pun in the sense that you not only thank the person who has made the food but also the Lord.)

Rogan Josh

from Kumar Mahadevan

Kumar's recipe for this famous Kashmiri dish is a winner. The lamb becomes meltingly tender and the spices smell enticing as you're cooking them. The choice of saucepan is very important – the ingredients should fill no more than a quarter of its depth, so you need quite a deep pan with a heavy base to retain an even temperature.

3 tablespoons vegetable oil

3 bay leaves

2 teaspoons cloves

3 brown cardamom pods

1 tablespoon green cardamom pods

piece of cassia bark

1 teaspoon fennel seeds

4 small dried chillies

1 kg red onions, sliced

salt

½ tablespoon crushed ginger

½ tablespoon crushed garlic

1 teaspoon turmeric

1 teaspoon chilli powder

3 teaspoons ground coriander

1 tablespoon crushed fresh chilli

2 tomatoes, chopped

1 tablespoon tomato puree

1 kg cubed lamb (from a leg or shoulder)

2 tablespoons chopped coriander leaves

Heat the oil in a large, heavy-based saucepan until almost smoking. Add the bay leaves, cloves, brown and green cardamom pods, cassia, fennel seeds and dried chillies and cook until sizzling (the brown cardamom is the most fun – it always explodes and all its flavours go into the oil). Add the onion and ½ teaspoon of salt and fry until the onion is brown and sweet.

Stir in the crushed ginger and garlic and then the turmeric, chilli powder and ground coriander. Stir in the crushed fresh chilli and add a little water to stop the spices from burning. Add the tomato, tomato puree and a good pinch of salt and stir well to combine. Turn the heat up to high and add the meat, searing all over and coating in the flavours. Add a little more water. Cover with a lid and cook for 35–40 minutes.

Remove from the heat and add the chopped coriander. Garnish with tomato wedges, julienned ginger and coriander sprigs.

Serves 4–6

'Food is cooked with hands, but the taste comes from the heart.'

Toor Dal Tadka

from Daisy Rajan

Dhal is a simple meal of cooked, spiced beans, peas or lentils. It is high in protein and fibre. This version uses *toor* dal, or yellow split peas, but other varieties include *urid, mung* and *masoor* to name just a few. To me this recipe redefines dhal – it is so yummy that you can have it for dinner on its own, although it is perfect served with steamed rice or Indian bread. The fresh tomatoes and coriander give it real freshness and the asafoetida is worth seeking out to counter the gassy effects of the split peas – it is available from most Indian food stores.

250 g *toor* dal (yellow split peas), washed and drained

1 teaspoon turmeric

1 litre water

6 garlic cloves

1 cm piece of ginger

salt

2 tablespoons vegetable oil

1 teaspoon black mustard seeds

2 teaspoons cumin seeds

2–3 dried chillies

8–10 curry leaves

1–2 teaspoons chilli powder

pinch of asafoetida powder

200 g chopped tomatoes

coriander leaves

Put the *toor* dal, turmeric and water into a heavy-based saucepan and boil for 45–60 minutes, until the peas are soft when pressed between the thumb and index finger.

Meanwhile, pound the garlic, ginger and a good pinch of salt to a paste in a mortar. Heat the oil in a small frying pan over low heat. Add the mustard seeds and allow them to pop. Add the cumin seeds, dried chillies, curry leaves, chilli powder, asafoetida and ginger and garlic paste and fry until fragrant. Stir into the dhal.

Add the chopped tomatoes and simmer for another 10 minutes. Season to taste with salt and garnish with coriander leaves.

Serves 4–6

'You must always eat using all five fingers of the right hand, as each finger represents one of the five senses, all of which are important when eating.'

Coconut Cardamom *Burfi*

from Raini Singh

A simple and quick cheat's version of the reduced-milk sweet *burfi*. This is a lovely end to an Indian feast and is often served at special occasions.

250 g desiccated coconut

395 g tin sweetened condensed milk

10 cardamom pods, husks discarded, seeds ground to a powder

handful of pistachios, roughly crushed

Mix 200 g of the coconut and the remaining ingredients in a bowl.

Heat a non-stick frying pan over low heat and add the mixture to the pan. Stir until the mixture starts to dry and rolls easily into a ball. Remove from the heat and leave for 5–10 minutes until cool enough to handle.

Place the remaining coconut on a plate. Using damp hands, roll the *burfi* mixture into balls and then roll in coconut. The balls can be stored in the refrigerator for up to 1 week.

Makes 15–20 *burfi*

INDONESIA

There's nothing meek and mild about Indonesian food – it's one of the most vibrant cuisines in the world, full of intense, hot flavours and varied textures, and its devotees wouldn't have it any other way. In fact, some say they can't live without chilli at every meal – in hot climates without chilli to kick-start the taste buds 'you simply don't have an appetite,' says my friend Rohanna from North Sumatra. In the exotic Indonesian tropics, chilli is used in spice pastes, in sambals (spicy side dishes), in stir-fries and even children eat it from a young age.

Indonesian kitchens often have just one or two gas burners yet great recipes come together there – woks sizzle and smoke from fresh ingredients that are tossed together with spices and the beloved sweet, thick soy sauce called kecap manis. It's a kind of theatre and is often breathtaking to watch as feasts materialise in a tiny amount of time.

Most cooking starts with the pounding of garlic, onion, chilli, lemongrass and fresh turmeric, which is the basis for many Indonesian spice pastes. These pastes are then cooked in oil, followed by dry spices, meat or fish and vegetables. It's noisy and sometimes smelly, especially when *trassi* (shrimp paste) is toasted over a flame to release its deep magic. When mixed into pastes and sambals, the intensely salty and fishy *trassi* adds a new depth of flavour.

Rice is always being cooked and eaten and is the central part of every Indonesian meal. Polished long-grain rice is most commonly used, particularly in dishes such as nasi goreng. Along with rice they serve sambals based on chilli and garlic to kick-start the palate, pickles for a sour crunch and small portions of meat, seafood or vegetables often in curry form. The variations on this theme are endless across the 6000 islands that make up Indonesia. Rice is also used as a foundation for sweet desserts such as *bubur ketan hitam*, a sticky black rice pudding made with coconut milk.

CANDLENUTS

Similar to macadamia nuts, these have a high oil content and are loved for their creamy texture in sauces. Inedible in their raw state, the candle-nut is a common thickener in curry pastes. They are available from most Asian food stores.

FRESH TURMERIC

A finger-shaped rhizome prized for its vivid yellow colour and fragrance, fresh turmeric is often used in Indone-sian curry pastes.

KECAP MANIS

A dark, sweet soy sauce made with palm sugar – it is much sweeter and thicker than its Chinese or Japanese counterparts. 'Manis' means sweet in Indonesian.

LEMONGRASS

A tall, bulbous grass with a fragrant, creamy centre that has a tangy lemony taste. The outer leaves are peeled off and the interior is finely ground for spice pastes. Alternatively the entire grass is bruised or tied in a knot and added to curries and soups for extra flavour.

PALM SUGAR

Made from the sap of the palm tree, which is boiled down to a concen-trated, moist sugar. It can range from a light honey-coloured shade to a dense dark brown, which is richer and more caramel in flavour. Usually bought as a hard block, it is best grated for easy use.

PETAI

Affectionately known as 'smelly beans', *petai* are seeds from a vine native to Malaysia and Indonesia. Bright green in colour, the seeds are slightly bitter in flavour and used in stir-fries, curries and sambals. In Australia they are available frozen in packets from Asian food stores.

SHRIMP PASTE

Made from fermented, dried shrimp, which is compressed and cut into blocks. Called *trassi* (known as *belachan* in Malay), shrimp paste is a key ingredient in many types of sambal. A small block is commonly wrapped in foil and briefly roasted in the oven or toasted over a flame, then crumbled into dishes to add an intense fishy flavour and smell.

TAMARIND

An acidic fruit, the sour pulp of which is used to balance the salty, sweet and hot flavours in Indonesian dishes. It's used in everything from salads to sauces and is the key flavour note in *assam* fish. It can be used in liquid or block form – soak the block in warm water and remove the seeds before cooking.

TEMPEH

A thin, nutty cake made from fer-mented soybeans, tempeh originates from Indonesia. It is a highly nutritious and versatile ingredient and its firm texture allows it to be cooked in many different ways – marinated, deep-fried, boiled or steamed.

Two foods other than chilli that are adored by Indonesians are tempeh (fermented soybeans made into blocks, which are high in protein and fibre and quite delicious) and *krupuk* (thin, deep-fried crackers made from wheat, rice, potato or cassava flour that is flavoured with prawn, seafood or vegetables; they are eaten at the start of a meal, often with kecap manis as a dipping sauce).

I love the old name for Indonesia – the Spice Islands. It's very romantic-sounding and fitting for a place that grows nutmeg, mace, pepper and cloves, which Indonesians cook with all the time along with other local favourites like coriander seeds, cardamom pods, cinnamon quills and cumin seeds. All of these spices are used in various ways by the melting pot of nationalities who have added their touch to Indonesian food – the Indians, Chinese, Arabs, Portuguese, Spanish, English and Dutch.

As many Indonesians are Muslim, the Islamic code of generosity to the guest means newcomers are welcomed and a banquet prepared. Whether it's a traditional *nasi lemak*, some *lemper* (rice rolls with spicy filling), or a range of fragrant curries, satays or stir-fries, your senses will be working overtime – and loving it!

'If you make lots of noise with your cutlery you will scare away the spirits that bring good luck.' (Parents trying to stop children from making annoying noise at the dinner table.)

Kari Ayam
Chicken Curry

from Alina Lucas

Creamy and vibrant yellow, this chicken curry is something you can throw together on a weeknight or use to really impress friends at a dinner party.

100 g medium–hot red chillies, seeded

100 g shallots, roughly chopped

25 g garlic cloves

5 candlenuts

40 g fresh turmeric, sliced

15 g ginger, sliced

vegetable oil

2 lemongrass stalks, bruised

25 g galangal, roughly chopped

1 litre coconut milk

2 teaspoons ground cumin

2 teaspoons ground coriander

1 teaspoon fennel seeds, toasted and ground

1 cinnamon stick

1 teaspoon grated nutmeg

5 cloves

15 g shrimp paste, roasted and crushed

1 tablespoon salt

75 g (⅓ cup) sugar

1.5 kg chicken thigh fillets, cut into bite-sized pieces

500 g potatoes, peeled and quartered

fried shallots

Blend the chilli, shallots, garlic, candlenuts, turmeric, ginger and 2 tablespoons of oil to a smooth paste.

Heat a little more oil in a frying pan and fry the paste until it darkens in colour. Add the remaining ingredients other than the chicken, potatoes and fried shallots and bring to the boil. Add the chicken and potatoes and simmer gently until the chicken is tender and the potatoes are soft. If the sauce is too thick, thin out with a little water.

Sprinkle with fried shallots and serve.

Serves 8

Udang Belado
Prawns in *Belado* Sauce

from Rohanna Halim

Belado is a magic sauce as it tastes different depending on what you match it with. Its chilli flavour is warm and delicious and makes you feel wonderful. I'll echo its creator and say 'I LOVE the *belado!*' Instead of prawns, you can use other seafood and meat such as squid, fish or chicken, and also vegetables such as eggplant or potatoes, and tempeh, eggs or tofu. If using eggs or tofu, spread the sauce over the top just before serving. All this dish needs is a simple accompaniment such as sliced cucumber.

5–6 shallots, chopped

1 medium tomato, chopped

300 g red chillies, roughly chopped (long and small chillies can be mixed according to desired heat)

3 tablespoons vegetable oil

3 tablespoons sugar

2 tablespoons salt

juice of 1 lime

handful of *petai* ('smelly beans'), optional

oil for deep-frying

1 kg shelled green prawns

Blend the shallots and tomato for 5 seconds in a blender then add the chilli. Continue blending briefly to a coarse paste.

Heat a wok over medium heat and add the oil, chilli paste, sugar and salt. Lower the heat and fry, stirring occasionally, for 10–15 minutes. The chilli will become fragrant, the mixture will thicken a little and the colour will change to deep red. Add lime juice to taste and the *petai*, if using, and remove from the heat.

Heat the oil in a saucepan and briefly deep-fry the prawns then drain on paper towel.

Reheat the *belado* and stir-fry the prawns in the sauce. Serve with sliced cucumber.

Serves 4

'If you don't cry or your eyes don't water when you're chopping onions, you're an unemotional and stubborn person.'

Satay *Sapi*
Beef Satay

from Paul Rast

This is the perfect satay recipe – the cooked meat is tender and perfectly spiced and the peanut sauce (*katjang*) is the best. So fire up the barbie!

1 kg rump steak, cut into bite-sized chunks

1 medium onion, finely chopped

4 large garlic cloves, finely chopped

100 ml kecap manis

2 tablespoons peanut oil

½ teaspoon sea salt

½ tablespoon grated palm sugar

1 teaspoon ground coriander

PEANUT SAUCE

225 g roasted peanuts

200 ml hot water

peanut oil

1 candlenut, finely chopped

1 teaspoon ground coriander

1 medium onion, finely chopped

3 large garlic cloves, finely chopped

2–3 small red chillies, finely chopped

200 ml coconut milk

1 tablespoon kecap manis

juice of ½ lime

salt

grated palm sugar

Combine the ingredients for the skewers, mixing the beef in well. Marinate in the refrigerator for 3–4 hours.

Soak some bamboo skewers in cold water for 1 hour.

To make the sauce, blend the peanuts and hot water to a smooth paste. Heat a wok over medium heat and add a splash of oil. Briefly fry the candlenuts and coriander, then add the onion, garlic and chilli and cook for 2–3 minutes until the onion softens. Add the peanut paste, coconut milk and kecap manis, stirring well until the sauce starts to simmer. Add the lime juice and season with salt and palm sugar to taste.

Thread the beef onto skewers and barbecue over medium heat. Spoon over the warm peanut sauce.

Serves 6

Satay *Daging*

'When you're halfway through eating a whole fish, never overturn it to get to the meat under the bones. Remove the bones first, otherwise it'll bring bad luck if you travel by boat or ship.'

Bebek Betutu
Balinese Barbecued Duck

from Tjok Gde Kerthyasa

A classic Balinese ceremonial dish that's easy enough to cook in your barbecue. It's full of flavour and incredibly moist. My thanks to Tjok Gde, a prince of the Balinese royal family, for the recipe. Serve with rice, steamed snake beans or Chinese greens, and a hot sambal.

1 duck (preferably free-range and organic, just like Balinese ducks!)

1 cm piece of fresh turmeric, sliced

200 g spinach leaves, blanched and roughly shredded

1 cinnamon stick or piece of cassia bark

1 roll of banana leaves (optional)

SEASONING PASTE

10 shallots or 2 medium onions, chopped

cloves from 1 head of garlic

4 candlenuts, crushed

2 teaspoons shrimp paste, roasted

1 cm piece of galangal

1 cm piece of ginger

1 cm piece of fresh turmeric

3 red chillies, roughly chopped (optional)

1 lemongrass stalk, outer leaves discarded, chopped

1 tablespoon grated palm sugar

1 teaspoon black peppercorns, crushed

2 teaspoons coriander seeds, crushed

3 tablespoons lime juice

3 kaffir lime leaves, finely sliced

2 tablespoons peanut oil

2 tablespoons water

3 teaspoons salt

Preheat a barbecue with a hood (a Weber is ideal). Alternatively preheat the oven to 160°C. Wash the duck inside and out in a bowl of water infused with the turmeric.

Place the seasoning paste ingredients in a blender and blend to a chunky paste.

Combine half of the paste with the spinach leaves and set aside. Rub the remaining paste over the duck inside and out. Stuff the cavity of the duck with the spinach mixture and the cinnamon stick or cassia bark. Wrap the duck well in banana leaves or foil. Whether using leaves or foil, wrap the parcel in a final layer of foil. Place the parcel on an oven tray.

Cook the duck in the barbecue for 4 hours. Alternatively cook it in the oven for 2 hours, then turn down the temperature to 120°C and cook for a further 2 hours.

Remove from the barbecue or oven and drain the juices into a saucepan. Simmer until reduced slightly and combine with a little stuffing from the duck. Serve in a bowl alongside the duck.

Serves 8

'If you leave uneaten rice on your plate, your future wife or husband will have lots of pimples.' (Parents trying to get stubborn children to eat.)

Es Cendol

from Benjamin Moechtar

Pronounced 'ess-chen-doll', this is a dessert or aperitif consisting of highly textural 'green worm' noodles called *cendol* that are made of mung bean flour and coloured with pandan essence. (If you can't find mung bean flour then rice flour will suffice but the *cendol* will be mildly different in flavour, more like the Malaysian version than the traditional Indonesian one.) The noodles are accompanied by a selection of fruit that you can vary as you please (this recipe includes tinned toddy palm seeds and jackfruit) and topped with coconut milk, shaved ice and palm sugar syrup.

Yum! If you have something of the child in you and a bit of sweet tooth, this wild confection is just right – and it's so much fun to shave the ice. (Or you can bang ice cubes together in a tea towel until they're crushed … although an ice shaver can be found in Asian emporiums for under $20).

ice

225 g mung bean flour

a few drops of pandan essence

palm sugar

1 tin toddy palm seeds in syrup, drained and cut into small bite-sized pieces

1 tin jackfruit in syrup, drained and cut into small bite-sized pieces

coconut milk

Pour some water into a large bowl and add plenty of ice.

Pour another 100 ml of water into a saucepan and bring to a simmer. Slowly add the mung bean flour, stirring constantly. Once the mixture is thick and paste-like, stir in the pandan essence and remove from the heat. Push the paste through the holes of a colander directly into the ice bath to form short noodles. The noodles will harden in the water and can remain there for a while, but if you are making them in advance, they can be scooped out and stored in a container with some coconut milk in the refrigerator.

Finely shave some palm sugar and stir it into a small amount of hot water to make a dark syrup.

Shave or crush some more ice.

To serve, layer the ingredients in a tall glass, starting with the *cendol* noodles, then the toddy palm seeds and jackfruit. Top with coconut milk and lots of shaved ice and drizzle with a little palm sugar syrup. Serve with a long spoon and straw.

Serves 6

ITALY

Where would we be as a nation without the culinary input from the many Italians who have come to our shores. They have taught us how to appreciate good coffee, good olive oil and the silky joy of fresh pasta. We have discovered that the colours of the Italian flag can be absolutely delicious – the ripe red of tomatoes for pasta sauce and salads; the zingy greens of rocket, rape, zucchini and fragrant basil; and the milky whites of fresh Italian cheeses – ricotta, buffalo mozzarella and bocconcini. (Thankfully we have managed to evolve from a country that believed all cheese was yellow!) Such has been the influence of Italian cuisine that spaghetti bolognaise is almost our adopted national dish.

To enter the Italian realm is to experience generosity, abundance and seasonal food prepared simply and well. The spirit of sharing is one of the things I adore about Italians – from the baskets of home-grown zucchini that would appear on my front doorstep when I lived in an Italian suburb, to Italian shopkeepers wanting you to try something new they thought you'd like, to the kisses on both cheeks and endless stream of food when you spend any time in an Italian home.

One of the things I've learned is that in Italy food is respected. The salami, *coppa* and prosciutto for antipasti are not pre-packaged but are sliced for you onto waxed paper at the deli. The bread is eaten still warm from the bakery and any leftover bread is used to make delicious salads such as *panzanella* or for breadcrumbs and stuffings. The freshest seasonal vegetables and herbs are used for salads, often straight from the garden – a tomato and bocconcini salad is served with basil picked from big pots just outside the back door and tomatoes plucked from the veggie patch.

Pasta is adored. Some families make their own fresh pasta from flour and eggs, which takes little time to cook and is soft and delicate. Of the dried pastas, the best is made from durum wheat, with the surface dusted with a hint of flour. This should be cooked to al dente (see page 102).

BALSAMIC VINEGAR

A dark, thick, syrupy vinegar with a complex, sweet taste, which originated in Modena in the north of Italy. It is much more expensive than common vinegars – check the label to ensure it is authentic balsamic (*aceto balsamico*) and check if it has a star rating (eight stars is top of the range).

BASIL

A leafy herb used to flavour sauces and salads or added to pizza after cooking. It is a central ingredient in the symbolic red, white and green of the *caprese* salad as well as the classic pesto, originally from Liguria – a magic combination of basil, pine nuts, parmesan and olive oil. Basil should be torn not sliced for optimum flavour.

EXTRA-VIRGIN OLIVE OIL

Common to many Mediterranean countries, olive oil is indispensable to Italian cuisine. It is used for dipping bread into, drizzling over salads and other dishes, and for cooking with. Each region has its own olive oil with its own distinctive flavour, ranging from the light Ligurian olive oils to the deep rich greens of some Sicilian oils. Look for cold-pressed extra-virgin olive oil for optimum flavour.

PARMESAN

Known as the 'the king of cheeses', there are two types of parmesan:

Parmigiano reggiano: is matured for 4 years and has crystals throughout the cheese that melt in your mouth, releasing their flavour. It's best served after a meal with fruit and wine.

Grana padano: has been matured for only 18 months. It is freshly grated and sprinkled over pasta to lift the flavour – my friend John describes it as essential to pasta as tomato sauce is to a meat pie.

TOMATOES

Although they came from South America, Italy adopted the tomato as it own, calling it *pomodoro* which translates as golden apple. The perfect combination of acidity and sweetness, it is celebrated fresh in salads, particularly the fleshy ox-heart variety or the sweet san marzano; the roma variety is popular for the classic tomato sugo (sauce) made at the end of summer and preserved in glass bottles.

For the *primi* (first) and *secondi* (main) courses, dishes vary across regions – *fegato alla veneziana*, *ministrone alla milanese*, *minestra di trippa alla piemontese*, *gnocchi alla romana*, *calamaretti alla napoletana* and so on down the country. And each family has its own recipes that have been perfected for generations. Seafood and meat are used cleverly. Sometimes the secondary catch or what would be considered secondary cuts of meat are transformed into masterpieces such as stuffed calamari, braised octopus, delicious fish stews, osso buco, *cima alla genovese* (shoulder of veal stuffed with vegetables, eggs and cheese) and *involtini* (flattened pieces of meat rolled up with delicious fillings such as herbs, minced meat, cheese, breadcrumbs and spices). Other times the best quality meat is stretched to serve many people – *porchetta abruzzese* is a whole roast pig that is usually served with many accompaniments so everyone feels satisfied. Servings of all dishes are usually generous and communal – the worst thing, the unthinkable thing, would be to not have enough food for one's guests.

The selection of *dolci* (sweets) is vast and beguiling and has been a vehicle of creativity for many Italian cooks. At home, women bake several types of biscuits and cakes at one time – a single choice is never enough! Out of the home and in the *pasticcerie* (bakeries), most of the bakers are men and in Australia many of the best *dolci* masters are from Sicily, where sweets are renowned – *cassata*, *cannoli*, gelato …! Whenever sweets are served, as with everything Italian, there are always plenty and they are all delicious.

'"*Butta la pasta*" is the kitchen cry for "The pasta is going into the water." If you arrive late the pasta will be overcooked, which will be your own fault.'

The Golden Rules of Pasta

Pasta is used daily in Italian cooking and is very easy to make but here are a few simple tips to help you make yours even more delicious and in the true Italian style …

1. Fill a large pot with plenty of water, add salt and bring to a rolling boil.

2. Drop the pasta into the water and stir. Fresh pasta is cooked when it rises to the surface – usually after 2–5 minutes; dried pasta should be cooked according to the packet instructions – generally it takes 7–14 minutes.

3. Don't rinse cooked pasta – if you do, the sauce won't cling to it. Drain but leave some of the cooking water still clinging to the pasta (you can also scoop a little pasta water into a cup before draining the pasta, in case you want to thin the sauce later).

4. Don't drown the pasta with sauce – it should be lightly coated, not swimming in it.

'Never use parmigiano reggiano to grate over pasta – it's too expensive and the cheaper grana padano works perfectly well.'

Fettucine Napoletana
from Maurizio Esposito

This dish is so simple, and even better if you know a few tricks – Maurizio shaves his garlic into very thin discs using a mandolin slicer, prefers shallots to onions for their sweetness, mashes up the best-quality Italian tinned tomatoes with his hands, and tears the basil, adding it last so it stays fresh and green. What a delight!

olive oil
2 garlic cloves, finely sliced
2 shallots, finely diced
800 g tin Italian tomatoes
500 g fettuccine
salt
6 large basil leaves

Heat 100 ml of olive oil in a heavy-based saucepan and add the garlic and shallots. Fry briefly and in the meantime, empty the tomatoes into a bowl and crush them with your hands. Add to the pan and simmer for 10–15 minutes.

Cook the pasta in a large pot of salted boiling water according to the packet instructions, then drain and return to the pot. Pour half the sauce over the pasta and fold through, adding more sauce if needed, but be careful not to add too much. The sauce should just coat the pasta.

Tear the basil leaves into the pasta, season to taste, drizzle with a little more olive oil and lightly toss again.

Serves 6

'The onion. The garlic.
The oil. The beginning.'
(Guy Grossi)

Spaghetti Alio, Olio e Pepperoncino
Spaghetti with Garlic, Oil and Chilli

from Maurizio Esposito

Maurizio says this is a great thing to whip up at the end of a big night out. The secret is in emulsifying the sauce.

400 g spaghetti

salt

olive oil

2 garlic cloves, finely sliced

1 small red chilli, finely sliced

½ cup roughly chopped flat-leaf parsley

pepper

freshly grated parmesan (optional)

Cook the pasta in a large pot of salted boiling water according to the packet instructions.

About 4 minutes before the pasta is ready, heat 100 ml of olive oil in a large frying pan and sauté the garlic and chilli. When the garlic turns nut-brown, add ½ cup of hot pasta water to stop the garlic cooking any further. Remove from the heat while you drain the pasta.

Return the pan to high heat and add the pasta, parsley and a little more olive oil. Keep tossing the pasta – the pasta water and oil will emulsify, thickening and coating the spaghetti. Season to taste with salt and pepper and sprinkle with parmesan if you like.

Serves 4

Panzanella
Bread Salad

from Graziella Alessi

Nothing is wasted in an Italian kitchen. This salad uses stale bread, which soaks up the flavours of the dressing while retaining a slightly crunchy texture – it is incredibly yummy, especially if you use a good loaf of bread. Proper ciabatta should be crusty on the outside and not too doughy or airy inside.

1 day-old ciabatta loaf, crusts cut off, cut into cubes

300 ml extra-virgin olive oil

100 ml balsamic vinegar

1 garlic clove, crushed

5 ripe tomatoes, roughly chopped

1 small red onion, finely sliced

½ bunch basil

salt and pepper

Bake the bread in a warm oven until golden brown and dry. Leave to cool.

Place the oil, vinegar and garlic in a bowl, add the bread and toss together. Add the tomato and onion and tear in the basil leaves. Toss again, season to taste and serve immediately.

Serves 6

'If you don't feel like cooking, stay away from the kitchen. Cooking shouldn't be work but a passionate endeavour.'

Baby Fennel and Blood Orange Salad

from Graziella Alessi

Salads are not just for summer – some of the winter fruits and veggies make magical salads. This winter salad of fennel and blood orange looks as beautiful as it tastes.

2 blood oranges

5 baby fennel bulbs, very finely sliced

6 chervil sprigs, leaves picked

120 ml extra-virgin olive oil

2 tablespoons white-wine vinegar

salt and pepper

Use a small, sharp knife to cut the peel from the oranges, making sure to remove all the white pith. Holding the oranges over a bowl to catch any juice, cut on either side of each segment, removing wedges of flesh but leaving the membranes. Place the wedges in a mixing bowl (use the juice for another purpose).

Add the fennel and chervil leaves to the orange. Drizzle with the oil and vinegar and season to taste with salt and pepper. Toss and serve immediately.

Serves 6

Saltimbocca

from Guy Grossi

Saltimbocca translates as 'jump in the mouth' and it is indeed so delicious that your mouth sings! It is a wonderful veal dish of thin girello steaks that are traditionally pan-fried in butter and served with *gnocchi romano* (semolina gnocchi). Girello is a cut of veal from the back leg. You can buy this as a whole piece then trim off the sinew and cut into 1-cm thick slices. The veal trimmings can be used with vegetables to make a stock (*brodo*), which you can use in this dish instead of a store-bought one.

6 veal girello steaks

6 sage leaves

3 prosciutto slices, cut in half

50 g (¼ cup) plain flour

2 tablespoons olive oil

20 g butter

salt and pepper

1 garlic clove, chopped

1 tablespoon chopped flat-leaf parsley

2 tablespoons stock

splash of dry white wine

Beat the veal steaks with the flat side of a meat mallet to an even thickness. Place a sage leaf on each followed by a piece of prosciutto. Fold the steaks in half to enclose the sage and prosciutto and tap again with the mallet to keep them closed. Lightly dust the steaks with flour.

Heat the olive oil and butter in a heavy-based frying pan and add the veal steaks. Sauté quickly on one side until light golden – the heat should just kiss the meat. Sprinkle with salt, pepper, garlic and parsley before turning over and adding the stock and wine. Cook for another few minutes.

Transfer to serving plates and spoon over the foaming sauce.

Serves 6

'In an Italian home, never even think of saying you're not hungry – they won't understand you!'

Tiramisu

from Vanessa Martin

'*Tiramisu*' means 'pick-me-up' and this dessert is sure to do just that. When Vanessa first made this for me I thought it would be dense and luscious but instead it's wonderfully light after all that beating – dangerously so ... I ate an enormous bowl and could have eaten a second!

6 eggs, separated
220 g (1 cup) caster sugar
500 g mascarpone
1 cup freshly-made hot, strong, espresso coffee
liqueur (Vanessa loves a mixture of Tia Maria, Kahlua and amaretto)
400 g packet *pavesini* biscuits (a slim version of *savoiardi* – if unavailable, use *savoiardi*)
good-quality chocolate, grated

Beat the egg yolks with the sugar until thick and white (this will take at least 15 minutes). Add the mascarpone and beat until just combined but smooth.

Combine the coffee and liqueur (as little or as much as you like) in a bowl. Quickly dip the biscuits into the liquid and set aside on a plate.

Beat the egg whites until thick and stiff then gently fold into the mascarpone mixture.

Layer the soaked biscuits and mascarpone cream in a large glass bowl or individual glass bowls. Refrigerate for at least 2–3 hours. Before serving, top with a generous grating of chocolate.

Serves 6

JAPAN

To explore what makes Japanese cuisine so unique and delicious you must enter a world where food is much more than sustenance. Not only is most Japanese food incredibly refined and elegant, its preparation and presentation have been honed over the centuries and are part of the pleasure of eating – the food is like an edible artwork complete with pure, delicate flavours.

Those clean flavours are the perfect way to start the day according to my friend Tetsuya Wakuda, now a legendary, world-renowned chef. Tetsuya says a bowl of miso soup in the morning is essential. One of the unusual flavours in his world is *dashi* – a gentle stock made from seaweed (in the form of a dried kelp called *kombu*) and shavings of smoked, dried bonito fish. *Dashi* is the basis of miso soup and many other recipes and its flavour is described by Tetsuya as 'tastiness' – in Japanese this is '*umami*', the fifth taste after sweetness, saltiness, bitterness and sourness.

I can attest that you will feel wonderful to your bones after a miso soup made from scratch. You can feel the pure, fresh flavours of this golden broth doing you good. I love the way when you make the *dashi* the *kombu* starts as a bit of shrivelled black stuff, like very dried banana skin, but when soaked in hot water becomes a large piece of flavoursome green seaweed. A bit of a magic trick and one of the many wonders of this special cuisine.

Japanese food is generally not the sort one hoes into – these are dishes to be enjoyed first with the eyes, and the choice of bowl is as important as what is served on it. One of my Japanese friends told me her ten-year-old son was horrified at the thought of eating something she had prepared from an ordinary bowl – his enjoyment would be marred by the less than perfect presentation! No doubt, even at such a young age, he was able to appreciate the importance of attention to detail in a cuisine where the empty parts of a serving platter are seen to emphasise the exquisite beauty of the food.

I must say a Japanese women's cooking group collapsed into giggles as I attempted to eat and drink as carefully and delicately as they did. When I asked for an explanation I was told I held my teacup like a man – around the top like you'd hold a glass of water. Japanese women – well-brought-up ones – hold their tea with two hands, one around the cup and the other lightly underneath. The care these women took with their teacups was also evident in the food they were making – exquisite autumn recipes in autumn colours, including the first persimmons of the season

Essential flavours

BONITO
Steam-processed bonito fillets are dried to wood-like hardness and shaved into flakes, known as *katsuo-bushi*. It is one of the two essential ingredients of the basic soup stock, *dashi*. The bonito, a member of the mackerel family, has been an important part of the Japanese diet from perhaps as early as the eighth century. From about the fifteenth century, the fillets of this fish were dried and used as they are today.

DASHI
Often referred to as the defining ingredient of Japanese cuisine, this is a delicate golden stock made from a combination of *kombu* (dried giant kelp) and *katsuobushi* (flakes of dried bonito fish). It is used to make miso, blanch vegetables or added as an essential ingredient to many dishes. *Dashi* is also available as a ready-made liquid or instant powder.

KONNYAKU
Made from the root of the konjac plant (also known as devil's tongue), *konnyaku* is regarded as a health food especially good for intestinal function. After processing it becomes dense with a slightly chewy texture and it's always parboiled before use. Most commonly used as a vegetable, it is a great absorber of surrounding flavours and is an essential ingredient in *sukiyaki*.

MIRIN
A pale amber-coloured cooking wine used for a hint of sweetness and as a glaze for grilled dishes.

MISO
A fermented paste made predominantly from soybeans, miso has been a fundamental part of Japanese cooking for centuries. It is extremely versatile and is used to make miso soup, to flavour pickles and grilled dishes, or it

can be thinned and made into a dressing. As a general rule, the darker the colour, the stronger the flavour. There are three main types:

Aka (**red**): This has the strongest flavour and is often used in eastern Japan for soup.

Shinshu (**brown**): The most commonly available and widely used miso, it originates from the central Honshu region of Japan.

Shiro (**white**): Also known as *saikyo* miso, this is the palest and sweetest miso and is used in Kyoto for soup. Also excellent in dressings.

SHIITAKE MUSHROOMS

Usually found in dried form and reconstituted in water ready for use in salads, soups, sushi and more. The liquid the mushrooms have soaked in can also be used to flavour dishes.

SHISO

A herb from the mint family, also called perilla, that has a fresh flavour comparable to mint or fennel.

SOY SAUCE (*SHOYU*)

These have a relatively fresh taste and aroma and are generally sweeter and less salty than Chinese sauces. Most commonly available are the light (*usukuchi*) and dark (*koikuchi*) varieties. Light *shoyu* contains a higher salt content and is paler in colour – it is often used with vegetables or clear soups. Dark *shoyu* is more mild and is used as a marinade or in simmered dishes. *Tamari* is another type of *shoyu* that is wheat free and slightly thicker – it is excellent with sashimi.

WASABI

Wasabi root is rarely seen in its fresh state in Australia and is most readily available as a powder or prepared paste. As a green paste it is traditionally served with sushi and sashimi to add a sharp edge to the fresh tastes of the fish.

and red maple leaves to decorate the serving plates. The dishes were all true to the Japanese reverence for celebrating each new season's flavours, textures and colours.

The clean flavours and simplicity of Japanese food also means it's generally extremely healthy. It is low in fat and often uses ingredients that are very beneficial to one's health – fish, seaweed, buckwheat and soy products. So it's no wonder many of us have followed the 'Why Japanese Women Don't Get Fat' model and rejoiced in the results!

On weight loss, Tetsuya is very enthusiastic about a 'zero calorie' substance made from potato starch called *konnyaku* – it looks like a block of grey agar-agar jelly with tiny black dots through it. 'Wow,' I thought, 'What a find!' However its slight chewiness and lack of flavour made me realise this probably wasn't going to be the diet food of the future – at least not for me!

Another of Tetsuya's suggestions has proved wonderful, which is that rice-wine vinegar makes an amazing salad dressing. Instead of mixing a plain vinegar or wine vinegar with oil, the less acidic rice-wine vinegar gives a beautiful, mellow flavour. I'm often intrigued that ingredients suitable for one cuisine can, almost accidentally, be perfect in another.

'Be careful when washing rice – if even one grain goes down the drain, you'll go blind!'

Sea Vegetables

As a group of narrow islands, Japan has great access to the sea and makes good use of its bounty.

Kombu: The second most widely produced seaweed in Japan behind *wakame*. Usually sold in dried form, it is easily reconstituted by soaking in water and is used to make *dashi*.

Nori: Believed to be made from seaweed, nori is actually made from dried algae. It is primarily used to wrap sushi, to garnish and to flavour noodle soups. The darker its colour and greater its aroma, the higher its quality.

Wakame: A variety of seaweed that comes fresh or dried (and like *kombu*, can be easily reconstituted in water). An integral component of miso soup.

Miso Soup

from Yuki Totsuka

If your experience of miso soup has only been of the instant kind, this recipe will be a revelation – it touches your soul. It is made with fresh tofu and *wakame* seaweed, but other classic combinations are daikon and fried tofu, potato and *wakame*, clams and spring onions, and pumpkin and spinach. If using ingredients that need to be cooked (unlike the tofu and *wakame*, which just need to be heated through), you can cook them in the *dashi* (stock) before adding the miso.

DASHI

10 cm piece of *kombu*

750 ml water

15 g *katsuobushi* (bonito flakes)

5 g dried *wakame*

2–3 tablespoons miso (to taste)

150 g tofu, cut into 1.5 cm cubes

finely sliced spring onion

To make the *dashi*, wipe the surface of the *kombu* with a dry or slightly damp cloth (don't wash under water as the surface holds flavour). Using scissors, make a few snips in the *kombu* to help release the flavours when soaking. Place in a saucepan with the water and leave to soak for at least 30 minutes.

Slowly bring the *kombu* and water to the boil. Just before it reaches boiling point, remove the *kombu* and discard. When the water comes to the boil, turn off the heat and stir in an extra ladleful of cold water followed by the *katsuobushi*.

Return the saucepan to the heat until the water comes back to the boil, then remove from the heat again and leave until the *katsuobushi* settles on the bottom of the pan.

Strain the *dashi* through a fine sieve. Don't squeeze out the flakes as this will make the stock too fishy.

To make the miso, soak the *wakame* in cold water for 10 minutes. Drain and squeeze out the excess water. Cut into bite-sized pieces.

Heat the *dashi*. While heating, remove a cup of the *dashi*, dissolve the miso in it and return to the pan. Don't let the soup boil after the miso is added.

Add the tofu and *wakame* and gently heat through. Serve garnished with spring onion.

Serves 6

Norimaki
Nori Rolls
from Masako Fukui

This recipe contains numerous tips for making these beautiful rolls. Take your time and you'll be rewarded with a sensational result. Masako gives four different filling ideas – the *kampyo* filling is deliciously unusual (*kampyo* is strips of dried gourd sold in packets at Japanese grocery stores).

SUSHI RICE

4 cups *koshihikari* rice

120 ml rice vinegar

2½ tablespoons sugar

1 teaspoon salt

KAMPYO FILLING

50 g *kampyo* (dried gourd strips)

salt

200 ml *dashi* stock (see miso soup recipe on page 111, or use instant *dashi* powder or liquid)

3 tablespoons sugar

2½ tablespoons *shoyu* (Japanese soy sauce)

1 tablespoon cooking sake

SHIITAKE FILLING

10 dried shiitake mushrooms, soaked in a bowl of cold water until soft

3 tablespoons sugar

3 tablespoons *shoyu* (Japanese soy sauce)

1 tablespoon cooking sake

CARROT FILLING

1 large carrot, cut into long, thin strips

200 ml *dashi* stock (see above)

2 tablespoons sugar

1 teaspoon salt

1 tablespoon mirin

TAMAGOYAKI (OMELETTE) FILLING

2½ tablespoons *dashi* stock (see page 111)

2 tablespoons sugar

1½ tablespoons *shoyu* (Japanese soy sauce)

1 teaspoon mirin

6 eggs, beaten

TO ASSEMBLE

6 nori sheets

rice vinegar

To make the sushi rice, wash the rice well in cold water and soak in fresh water for 30 minutes. Place the rice and 4 cups of water in a saucepan and cover with a lid. Bring to the boil then reduce to a simmer and cook until all the water is absorbed (alternatively, steam the rice in a rice cooker). Remove the lid, cover with a damp cloth and leave to cool for 15 minutes.

Heat the rice vinegar, sugar and salt over low heat until the sugar and salt dissolve.

Place the rice in a mixing bowl and evenly pour over the vinegar mixture. Mix in well with a cutting action so as not to squash the rice. Fan for a few minutes until the rice has cooled a little (it can still be warm when assembling).

To make the *kampyo* filling, rub the *kampyo* with salt then wash in cold water. Put in a saucepan of water and bring to the boil, then refresh in cold water and squeeze out the excess water. Simmer with the remaining ingredients until tender.

To make the shiitake filling, remove the mushrooms from their soaking water and measure 2½ tablespoons of the water into a saucepan. Thinly slice the mushrooms and remove their stalks if necessary, then add with the remaining ingredients to the pan and cook until all the liquid evaporates.

To make the carrot filling, cook the carrot in boiling water until just beginning to soften. Drain, then simmer in the remaining ingredients until tender.

To make the omelette filling, place ingredients other than the egg in a saucepan and heat until the sugar dissolves. Mix into the egg without over-beating. Cook the omelette in a lightly-oiled frying pan (ideally a Japanese square omelette pan). The omelette should be quite thick. Leave to cool and cut into thick strips.

To assemble the rolls, place a sheet of nori shiny-side down on a work surface (or ideally on a bamboo rolling mat). Wet your hands with rice vinegar and spread 230 g of rice over the nori, leaving a 1 cm border on one long edge. Be careful not to squash the grains of rice as you spread it.

Place the filling ingredients in a line down the centre of the rice. Dip your index finger in rice vinegar and run along the exposed edge of nori to moisten it slightly. Roll the rice and filling up inside the nori to form a squarish cylinder. You should apply firm but gentle pressure (the mat helps if you are using one). Slice the rolls into rounds.

Makes 6 large rolls

Saikyo Yaki
Fish Cooked with *Saikyo* Miso
from Tetsuya Wakuda

Hundreds of years old, this versatile marinade recipe can be used for fish, poultry or beef. I love that one of the world's greatest chefs has shared a recipe that he cooks all the time. *Saikyo* miso is sweet and pale and blends beautifully with the flavour of the fish. He suggests serving this with pickled ginger.

Although garlic isn't popular in Japan, Tetsuya Wakuda says 'Add ginger if you like ginger, a little garlic if you like – after all, you are the one who is going to eat it!' You can buy a special ginger grater from most Asian food stores. Always grate ginger along the grain, not across.

1 cup *saikyo* miso

1 tablespoon cooking sake

2 tablespoons mirin

1 tablespoon grated ginger

½ garlic clove, crushed

2 tablespoons grape-seed oil

4 sea-perch fillets, skin on

Combine the miso, sake and mirin in a bowl, stirring well. Stir in the ginger and garlic and then the grape-seed oil. Spread a little of the marinade in the base of a small rectangular dish. Add a piece of fish, flesh-side down, and cover with more marinade. Top with the remaining fish spread with marinade. Cover and refrigerate overnight.

Scrape off the excess marinade from the pieces of fish. Place on a tray skin-side up and cook under a griller until the skin is golden brown. Serve with pickled ginger.

Serves 4

Aburi Maguro
Seared Tuna Salad
from Kimitaka Azuma

This delicious salad is so fresh, healthy and clean tasting. The recipe makes more dressing than you need but it can be stored in the refrigerator.

2 pieces of sashimi tuna (approximately 4 × 2 × 20 cm each)

salt and white pepper

vegetable oil

1 cup very finely grated daikon

⅓ cup very finely grated white onion

2 tablespoons finely sliced spring onions

1 beetroot, finely julienned

2 tablespoons finely julienned ginger

1 garlic clove, finely sliced and fried to golden

½ tablespoon shredded baby celery leaves

1½ tablespoon shredded shiso (perilla) leaves

PONZU DRESSING

¼ white onion, very finely grated

360 ml Japanese citrus vinegar

200 ml grape-seed oil

½ tablespoon sesame oil

pinch of white pepper

Season the tuna with salt and white pepper. Heat a small amount of oil in a heavy-based frying pan and sear the tuna for about 10 seconds on all sides, so the tuna is coloured on the outside but still raw inside. Leave to cool then cut into 1 cm slices and lay in a wide serving bowl.

To make the dressing, mix the onion with two-thirds of the citrus vinegar. Combine the rest of the vinegar with the grape-seed oil, whisking just briefly. Whisk in the onion and vinegar mixture, sesame oil and pepper.

Pour ½ cup of the dressing over the tuna. Combine the daikon and onion and scatter over the top. Sprinkle with the spring onion, beetroot, ginger, garlic and baby celery and shiso leaves.

Serves 6

JEWISH

What a unique world this is. The orthodox Jewish kitchen is governed by ancient rules that are strictly adhered to. Many devout Jews I've visited have two kitchens and two sets of everything – sinks, plates, cooking pots and cutlery – to separate foods into 'milk' and 'meat', which must not be eaten together. The *kashrut* (kosher) laws are derived from the Torah, the five books written after God spoke directly to Moses, which sets out a blueprint for the Jewish way of life. 'Kosher' basically means 'proper' and these laws relate to what is to be eaten, how it is to be prepared, what it is to be combined with and, finally, how it is to be served.

While the cooking aromas in Jewish kitchens vary according to which part of the diaspora people come from, the basic laws are the same. The way meat is slaughtered and prepared for sale is dictated the *kashrut*. Indeed where food is concerned everything follows these ancient rules that 'go back to the desert', according to the head of one orthodox family.

It seems like a mad rush to have a whole feast ready for the moment on Friday evening when the stars first appear in the sky, marking the start of Shabbat (the Jewish day of rest). However I came to realise that Jewish families would be some of the best time and motion studies in the world! Some foods are prepared in advance, some clever shortcuts are made and everything comes together as it should – and is of course delicious. A lot of the burden seems to fall on the women of the family, who are working around the prohibition of turning any electricity or gas on during Shabbat. Clever Jewish housewives, who turn out vast quantities of food for big families after Temple, traditionally serve either hearty, slow-cooked dishes (like braised brisket or a stew called *cholent*) or dishes that can be served cold (like *gefilte* fish). In recent times a 'Shabbat' mode on ovens has meant that 'keeping it kosher' (and hot and delicious) is possible.

The payoff for the mad flurry at the start of Shabbat is that an entire day is then devoted to family being together and not having to work – something we often forget in this hyper-fast world. And the food! Over Shabbat I have eaten some of the best cakes of my life, including a custard chiffon cake that is like a sweet whisper (made by my friend Merelyn) and a dense orange and almond cake that I now make all the time. I've also tasted *cholent* that reminds me of my Irish heritage and the best chicken soup in the world. I have met women compiling a cookbook of Jewish recipes and learning how to do a six-plait *challah* (sweet egg bread) and I recently ate the first *gefilte* fish I've ever really liked – made by Melbourne food legend Rita Erlich.

EGGS

Popular in all forms in Jewish cooking. They are mostly used for doughs, cakes, *lokshen* (noodles) and the quintessentially Jewish egg and onion salad. In kosher supermarkets only white eggs are available – these have been tested up to the light for blood spotting in strict adherence to kosher law. Otherwise, eggs need to be broken into a cup one by one to check for blood.

MATZO

Unleavened flatbread made from flour and water and baked quickly. It's a substitute for bread during the Jewish holiday of Passover, when eating bread and leavened products is forbidden. According to Jewish tradition, when the Israelite slaves were fleeing from Egypt, they did not have time to wait for their bread to rise – the result was this cracker-like matzo. In commemoration of the Exodus, Jews eat matzo every year during Passover. After baking, matzo may be ground into fine crumbs, known as matzo meal. The coarse version of matzo meal is used to make matzo balls (or *knaidlach*) for chicken soup at Passover. It's added to other foods, such as *gefilte* fish, to hold the ingredients together instead of flour. Passover cakes and biscuits are also made with fine matzo meal – they are more dense than conventional flour versions.

117

Borscht

from Ramona Koval

This is a family recipe from Ramona's book *Jewish Cooking, Jewish Cooks*. It can be served either hot in winter or as a refreshing cold soup in summer. It is made with water, although you can use either water or chicken stock to cook the beetroots (to be kosher, if you're using stock don't serve the soup with sour cream or yoghurt).

1 kg beetroots, topped, tailed and peeled

juice of 1 lemon

2 litres chicken stock or water

3 small potatoes, peeled and diced

1 large onion, roughly chopped

1 large bunch dill, roughly chopped

1 tablespoon sugar

2 teaspoons salt

freshly ground black pepper

extra 750–1000 ml water

6 boiled potatoes if serving the soup hot

sour cream or yoghurt

Place the beetroot in a large saucepan. Add half the lemon juice and the stock or water and bring to the boil over medium heat. Cook for 40 minutes, until the beetroot is soft when pierced with a knife.

Drain the beetroot and cut into small pieces. Return to the empty saucepan and add the potato, onion, dill (reserve a little for garnish), sugar, salt and remaining lemon juice. Season with pepper and add the water. Cover and bring to the boil then simmer for 20–30 minutes.

Puree the soup. Serve either steaming hot with a boiled potato added to each bowl, or chilled and icy cold. Top each serve with a spoonful of sour cream or yoghurt and a sprinkling of dill.

Serves 6

Chicken Soup with Matzo Balls

from Shirley Hirsch

Known as 'Jewish penicillin', chicken soup is regarded as a cure-all and is a mainstay of the Ashkenazi Shabbat table. Begin the soup and matzo balls a day in advance.

1 kg meaty chicken bones

1 onion, cut into chunks

3 carrots, cut into chunks

1 leek, cut into chunks

2 parsnips, cut into chunks

MATZO BALLS

2 eggs

3 pinches of salt

½ teaspoon cinnamon

2 cups coarse matzo meal

125 ml light olive oil

125 ml water

In a large pot, cover the chicken with cold water and bring to the boil. Simmer until the chicken is cooked through. Skim off any foam. Add the vegetables, cover and simmer for 2 hours. Strain the soup, discarding the solids, and refrigerate overnight.

To make the matzo balls, beat the eggs in a bowl. Add the remaining ingredients and mix well. Refrigerate overnight.

To cook the matzo balls, bring a large saucepan of salted water to a simmer. With damp hands, form golf ball-sized portions of the matzo mixture. Drop the balls into the pot. Cover and simmer for 20–25 minutes.

Remove any solidified fat from the soup before reheating. Place several matzo balls in each serving bowl and ladle over the hot soup.

Serves 8–10

Borscht

'My mother always told me to never make chicken soup with anything but kosher chickens.'

Gefilte Fish

from Rita Erlich

A popular mainstay in Ashkenazi Jewish cooking, *gefilte* fish (literally 'stuffed fish') is traditionally made by carefully removing the skin of a fish (leaving it intact), mincing the flesh with ingredients such as egg, spices, onion and carrot, stuffing this back into the skin and baking the fish in the oven. This recipe is much easier as it is made from minced fish fillets formed into patties or balls, which are poached to a delicate shade of pale. Salmon or ocean trout give the *gefilte* fish a lovely rosy hue. It's delicious served with grated horseradish.

STOCK

skin and bones from the fish fillets (see below)

1 carrot, sliced

1 onion, sliced

1 leek, sliced

slice of ginger

1–1.25 litres water

FISH PATTIES

3 large onions, 2 quartered, 1 sliced

6 eggs

1 kg mixed fish fillets such as flathead, snapper, dory, salmon or ocean trout

60 g almond meal

2 teaspoons sugar

salt and white pepper

2 slices of ginger

1 carrot, sliced in thin rounds

To make the stock, place the ingredients in a saucepan and bring to the boil. Simmer for 40 minutes then strain, discarding the solids.

To make the fish patties, boil the quartered onion with 3 of the eggs for about 15 minutes. Allow to cool, then peel the eggs. Mince the boiled onion and egg in a food processor and place in a large mixing bowl.

Mince the fish in the food processor and add to the minced onion and egg, beating well with a wooden spoon to incorporate.

Add the almond meal and sugar and season with salt and pepper. Add the remaining raw eggs one at a time, beating well (the better the mixing, the lighter the patties; allow 10 minutes of beating in total). If you think the mixture needs softening, add some chilled water. Refrigerate the mixture for 10 minutes to set a little. Form into medium-sized patties.

Lay the sliced onion in the base of a wide saucepan and add the ginger. Place the patties over the onions in a tight layer. Top each pattie with a slice of carrot.

Carefully pour in enough stock to come half- to three-quarters of the way up the patties. Gently bring to a simmer and cook for 40 minutes. Leave the patties to cool in the pan, then lift them into a wide dish. Strain the liquid over the patties, discarding the onion. Cover and chill in the refrigerator; the liquid should set into a light jelly.

Serve the carrot-topped patties and a little of their jelly with grated horseradish.

Serves 8

Cholent

from Merelyn Frank

Every Jewish community around the world has its own version of *cholent*. A hearty mix of beef, marrow, beans and barley, this is the perfect slow-cooked meal to prepare before the start of Shabbat on Friday evenings.

This *cholent* is cooked for four hours in a low–moderate oven, but for the ultimate slow-cooking, Merelyn says you can cook it overnight at 100°C. To stick to tradition, brown the meat in *schmaltz* instead of olive oil (*schmaltz* is rendered chicken fat that is sometimes flavoured with onions, apples and seasonings) and buy the ribs from a kosher butcher, where they only use the top half of a carcass (in a regular butcher these would be sold as *asado* cut).

Merelyn serves leftover *cholent* as a base for barbecued lamb chops – heavy but delicious, and you don't need much!

3 tablespoons olive oil

700 g beef top ribs, cut into pieces

700 g beef shin (gravy beef), cut into pieces

2 large onions, chopped

3 garlic cloves, crushed

2 tablespoons sweet paprika

2 litres water

1 tablespoon salt

1 teaspoon freshly ground black pepper

1 cup dried cannellini beans,
washed and soaked overnight

1 cup dried borlotti beans,
washed and soaked overnight

½ cup pearl barley

½ large marrow bone
(ask the butcher to saw it into pieces)

3 desiree potatoes, quartered with the skin on

3 large carrots, cut into chunks

Preheat the oven to 160°C.

Heat the oil in a large ovenproof pot. Brown the meat on all sides then remove from the pot. Add the onion and sauté until dark golden. Stir in the garlic and paprika and add the water, salt and pepper. Return the meat to the pot and add the drained beans and remaining ingredients. Bring to a simmer. Cover the pot with foil then with a tight-fitting lid and bake in the oven for 4 hours.

Check the water levels during cooking to make sure the *cholent* isn't drying out. After 3 hours, the meat should rise to the top of the dish and look brown and crunchy. In 4 hours, the meat will be falling apart, melting into the beans, and the marrow should be falling out of the bones. Taste for seasoning before serving.

Serves 10

'You can never have enough time if you love preparing Jewish food – the sheer quantity and variety of delicious options will take every spare minute you have.'

Orange and Almond Cake

from Batia Slater

This recipe has caused an orange and almond cake revolution! A classic Passover dessert that draws on the Sephardic traditions of Morocco, the Mediterranean and the Middle East, this version has seduced the tastebuds of many – even people who normally never make cakes love its simplicity. The oranges boil for two hours and are then pureed, skin, pips and all.

2 oranges

250 g caster sugar, plus extra for dusting

6 eggs

250 g almond meal

1 teaspoon baking powder

icing sugar

Wash the oranges and cook in boiling water for 2 hours. Drain and allow the oranges to cool before pureeing. This can be done ahead of time.

Preheat the oven to 190°C. Butter a 20 cm springform cake tin and dust it with a little caster sugar. Place the eggs and 250 g of caster sugar in a mixing bowl and beat well. Stir in the orange puree followed by the almond meal and baking powder. Pour into the tin and dust the top with more caster sugar. Bake for 1–1½ hours, until the top is golden brown. Dust with icing sugar to serve.

Serves 10–12

'Never buy anything ready-made if you can make it yourself.'

KOREA

Years ago my friend Yang took me into his world – into emporiums stacked with heavy stone bowls and garlic sold by the sackful, into *kimchi* factories where mounds of wombok (Chinese cabbage) were chopped by cleaver near huge pots of chilli, into butchers where they were busy slicing frozen beef for *bulgogi*, and into restaurants and tiny cafes all packed with Korean people enjoying themselves ... It's such a different world and Korean cuisine and the etiquette that surrounds it are unlike anywhere else on earth.

Korean food is fascinating – not only is it beautifully presented, fresh-tasting and healthy, it's also a very tangible celebration of culture and tradition. Because Korean people view the preparation of food as a link with the past and their ancestors, many dishes have changed very little over the centuries. Whether in Korea or away from it, Korean people are devoted to their food and treat it with great reverence.

Kimchi is a great example. This is the fermented vegetable dish made from salted wombok and sometimes daikon, spring onion or cucumber, which are mixed with chilli powder, garlic and sometimes fish sauce. *Kimchi* originally started as a means of preserving vegetables in salt through the very cold winter but when chilli was brought from the New World in the seventeenth century, the colour and flavour of *kimchi* changed dramatically.

Kimchi can form a simple meal with rice and it is an essential part of breakfast, lunch and dinner. In fact, a meal without *kimchi* is nearly unthinkable. Some Koreans say they actually feel 'weird' without *kimchi*; others speak of the longing and emptiness they feel if they go without it for more than a day. I was intrigued to meet one young man who carried an emergency pack of *kimchi* with him, just in case his mates suggested going out to pizza. 'I just don't feel right unless I eat *kimchi* with whatever I'm having for dinner – whether it's Korean food or pizza, it tastes great and helps digestion.' Now that's devotion!

NASHI PEAR

Grated nashi pear (*bae*) is often used in marinades, especially for beef – as well as tenderising the meat it adds a natural sweetness. Nashi are equally loved as a cleansing, crisp finish to a meal.

SESAME SEEDS AND OIL

With its cultivation dating back thousands of years, sesame has long been harvested for its seeds, which appear after the pods ripen and split. Tiny hulled sesame seeds are used in abundance in Korean cuisine. Often toasted and used whole or ground to a paste, their nutty taste is loved across the country.

Sesame oil can be cold-pressed from raw seeds or, more commonly, hot-pressed from toasted, hulled seeds, which creates a dark colour and nutty flavour. It is often used as a marinade or to drizzle on dishes after cooking.

WOMBOK

A long, barrel-shaped cabbage with tightly packed, crinkled, green–yellow leaves, commonly known as 'Chinese cabbage'. Wombok is used for making Korean *kimchi*.

DOENJANG

A fermented soybean paste made from boiled, ground soybeans which are dried and fermented in blocks then brined. It is a salty condiment used to make rich, thick stocks and stews with vegetables and tofu. It's also used on its own as a condiment with *bulgogi*.

GARLIC

Korean food couldn't exist without garlic. It is used abundantly, either crushed or slivered, and is adored in its raw state as well as used in cooking. Slivers of raw garlic are often served as an accompaniment to *bulgogi*.

GOCHUJANG

A chilli paste made from dried chillies, salt, fermented soybeans and rice powder to produce a dark-red, spicy paste. It is mixed into soups, stews and marinades and dolloped onto dishes like *bibimbap* (seasoned vegetables and rice) and *bulgogi*.

korea

Its digestion-aiding properties are renowned, making Korea one of the most health-conscious nations. Because of its pungency, many Koreans store their *kimchi* in special ceramic jars and some families invest in a *kimchi* refrigerator, which is about the size of a bar fridge and stores a whole winter's supply – only to be found in Korea!

Some families in Korea still gather to make their *kimchi* every year although most buy it ready-made. There is enough work involved in putting meals together already – Korean food is very labour intensive. As well as the main fare of meat or fish, noodles or rice, most meals are served with at least five different side dishes (*panchan*). These could be pickled bean sprouts; sliced potato with a sprinkling of chilli; spinach; stuffed cucumber; whole radish *kimchi*; cabbage *kimchi* ... and that's just the side dishes! While traditions are treasured, all this preparation takes time and as more women enter the workforce in Korea some of the more elaborate meals are being scaled down. Now three side dishes, even bought ready-made, are acceptable!

'Washing your face in the water used to clean rice will make your skin whiter.'

Etiquette

This is a cuisine with many rules and traditions, where Westerners can blunder in and cause offence without knowing it!

Table settings are very important and food is as much about 'eating with the eyes' as the mouth. Korean people like a sense of order and many different colours and textures on the table, as well as many beautifully presented side dishes, or *panchan*. They recognise that the number of side dishes denotes the importance of the meal.

Koreans always use flat, metal chopsticks for side dishes and meat but a spoon for rice and soup. You shouldn't use chopsticks and a spoon at the same time. And once the meal is finished, all utensils should be arranged neatly as they were originally set at the table.

You should never hold a bowl in your hands as you eat.

When eating *bulgogi* (barbecued lean beef wrapped in a lettuce leaf with condiments) the parcel should be eaten in one bite.

When eating *kimchi* one Korean friend recommends you have some chewing gum and brush your teeth afterwards as the garlic will scare people away! Another friend adds: 'We do not talk much directly after eating *kimchi*.' This same man told me most Koreans consume seven heads of garlic a week! It's no wonder kissing is not a big pastime in Korea.

'Never pour drinks using one hand – using both hands is a sign of respect for the person you're serving.'

Japchae

from Youngkyu Kwon

Japchae is a dish of deliciously chewy cellophane noodles made from sweet potato starch. The noodles are tossed with julienned vegetables and sometimes meat (this recipe includes marinated beef), and each component is separately stir-fried. It's a popular Korean dish for parties and can be served hot or cold. Vary the vegetables as you please – others to consider are green beans and spinach, or make a mushroom *japchae* with a selection of Asian mushrooms.

MARINATED BEEF

100 g lean beef, cut into thin strips

1 tablespoon soy sauce

½ tablespoon sesame oil

2 teaspoons sugar

pepper

200 g *japchae* sweet potato noodles

80 ml soy sauce

2 tablespoons sugar

2 tablespoons sesame oil

1 onion, finely sliced

vegetable oil

salt

1 carrot, julienned

1 green capsicum, julienned

6 dried shiitake mushrooms, soaked until soft, finely sliced

1 egg, separated

Combine the beef with the marinade ingredients and set aside.

Soak the noodles in cold water for a few minutes, then cook in plenty of boiling water for 5 minutes. Rinse in cold water and drain well. Cut the noodles into 10–15 cm lengths approximately. Mix with the soy sauce, sugar and sesame oil.

Stir-fry the onion in a little oil with a pinch of salt. Scoop onto a plate and repeat with the carrot, then the capsicum, then the shiitake mushrooms.

Beat the egg yolk and white separately and fry as 2 thin omelettes. Cut into strips and place in a bowl.

Stir-fry the beef and add to the plate of vegetables.

Stir-fry the noodles for a couple of minutes and put into a large mixing bowl. Toss with the meat and vegetables. Add more soy sauce, sugar or sesame oil to taste. Serve garnished with the sliced egg.

Serves 4

'Kimchi tastes best when made by hand.'

Bulgogi
Marinated Beef

from Chung Jae Lee

This is a tasty dish of marinated beef, tenderised and flavoured with a blend of nashi pear and onion then cooked on a hot plate. Koreans love to eat *bulgogi* wrapped in lettuce leaves, sometimes with a small amount of steamed rice in the lettuce too, and with condiments such as *kimchi, gochujang* (chilli paste) or *doenjang* (soybean paste), which are all available from Korean food stores.

600 g beef scotch fillet, sliced as thinly as possible
185 ml soy sauce
3 tablespoons water
1 tablespoon crushed garlic
40 g sugar
pinch of salt and pepper
1 nashi pear, peeled, cored and roughly chopped
1½ onions, 1 roughly chopped and ½ finely sliced
1 tablespoon sesame oil
grape-seed or olive oil
3 spring onions, finely sliced

GARNISHES AND ACCOMPANIMENTS

sesame seeds
pine nuts
red chilli, very finely julienned
lettuce leaves
kimchi, gochujang (chilli paste) or *doenjang* (soybean paste)

Combine the beef with the soy sauce, water, garlic, sugar, salt and pepper. Puree the pear and chopped onion and stir into the beef. Leave to marinate for approximately 30 minutes. Just before cooking, stir through the sesame oil.

Heat a heavy-based frying pan and add a little oil. Grill the beef (in batches if necessary) for around 3 minutes, adding some of the marinade towards the end so the beef doesn't dry out. Add the sliced onion and spring onion and cook for another minute.

Garnish the beef with sesame seeds, pine nuts and chilli. Serve immediately with lettuce leaves and condiments.

Serves 4

Bulgogi

Dolsot Bibimbap
Stone-bowl *Bibimbap*

from Suzanna Kim

This is the most delicious mix of rice, beef and vegetables cooked with garlic and sesame oil, topped with an egg yolk and *gochujang* (chilli paste). The ingredients are cooked individually then beautifully arranged in a stone bowl called a *dolsot*, which is heated until the rice turns golden and crispy on the bottom. You mix everything together when you eat it. You will need four *dolsot* bowls, available from Korean grocery stores.

The amount of garlic used might seem high but remember that this is a culture in which most people eat seven heads of garlic a week! You can use less garlic if you like but once cooked it is delicious and not overpowering.

2 cups short-grain rice

400 g beef scotch fillet,
finely sliced into strips 5 cm long

1½ tablespoons soy sauce

140 ml sesame oil

3 tablespoons crushed garlic

pinch of sugar

salt and pepper

1 cup dried shiitake mushrooms,
soaked until soft, finely sliced

2 small carrots, cut into matchsticks

1 small daikon, cut into matchsticks

2 small zucchini, cut into matchsticks

1 bunch spinach, leaves picked

1 generous cup bean sprouts

4 egg yolks

gochujang (chilli paste)

Rinse the rice in cold water and drain, then repeat twice to make sure the grains are thoroughly washed. Put the rice in a saucepan and place a hand flat over the top. Fill with cold water to the top of your hand. Cover with a lid and simmer until the water is absorbed (approximately 20 minutes).

Combine the beef with 1 tablespoon of the soy sauce, a little sesame oil, 3 teaspoons of the garlic, the sugar and a pinch of pepper. Stir-fry until the beef is golden brown and set aside.

Mix the mushrooms with the remaining soy sauce, a little sesame oil, 2 teaspoons of the garlic and pepper and set aside.

Stir-fry the carrot in a little sesame oil with 2 teaspoons of the garlic and a pinch of salt and pepper. Scoop onto a plate and repeat with the daikon and zucchini.

Bring a saucepan of water to the boil and blanch the spinach leaves for 15 seconds, then scoop out, drain, place in a bowl and toss with some sesame oil, a little garlic, and salt and pepper. Repeat with the bean sprouts.

Put a teaspoon of sesame oil in the base of each stone bowl. Put some rice in the bowls and arrange small mounds of beef and vegetables over the top. Gently place an egg yolk in the middle and a teaspoon (or more to taste) of *gochujang* to the side. Pour another tablespoon of sesame oil around the edge of each bowl.

Place the stone bowls over high heat on the stove for approximately 5 minutes, or until you can hear the rice popping and crackling. Carefully remove the hot bowls from the heat and serve.

Serves 4

LEBANON

Wherever you go in Lebanon, there is a waft of fragrant spices and fresh herbs. The emporiums, bakeries and restaurants all have a beguiling aroma of cinnamon, cumin, coriander, parsley and mint that signals the delicious and exotic dishes awaiting you. If you're in a Lebanese home you'll be treated like royalty. Two steps through the door you'll be greeted by beautiful baking smells or the intense, fresh scent of parsley being carefully cut for tabbouleh – and it will be a miracle if you get any further without being offered food. The first of many delicious offerings is usually roasted nuts or salt-dusted roasted pumpkin seeds. The tradition of hospitality is something that runs deep and when combined with a cuisine that is effortlessly generous and abundant, you have a recipe for pure culinary magic.

'Sahteyn' is a word you'll often hear in Lebanese homes – loosely translated it means 'twice your health' and is a form of welcome to join a family and share delicious food. In a Lebanese household, food is life and sharing it is one of the great joys of being alive. Even for simple dinners at home, there will be a variety of dishes on the table. The meal will start with small dishes known as mezze, which centre around dips and salads. The salads are all presented snap-fresh and dressed with olive oil and lemon juice. It's not unusual to have a number of salads and dips to start a meal – these are all fairly labour intensive but beautiful to look at and taste. Needless to say, dinners can last some hours.

One of the things I've learned from hanging around Lebanese kitchens and cooks is that you must be exacting about ingredients. The parsley for tabbouleh, for example, must be young, soft and just picked – no hard supermarket bunches are allowed here; the same for the mint, and both herbs are bunched and sliced finely (almost shaved). Another hallmark of Lebanese cooking is that many dishes are mixed with the hands and people say it's the touch of the hands that elevates the food to the heavens. Certainly the salads are some of the best I've ever tasted.

I also love the way the food easily translates between cultures – my dear friend Fouad, a legendary chef, remarked that Lebanese kafta (minced lamb and beef that can be shaped as patties or wrapped around skewers) are perfect for a barbecue. And he's right!

Sweets are pure artwork and there are endless variations on a theme – for instance, baklawa comes in many shapes and with differing amounts of nuts and syrup. There are also wickedly creamy sweets filled with a clotted cream called ashta and melting shortbread that is sometimes filled with a date paste or nuts – and much more. Lebanese sweets are generally served in between meals with black coffee or tea and are an essential part of any celebration. Sahteyn!

Essential flavours

ASHTA
A form of clotted cream made by skimming boiling milk. It is used in many Lebanese sweets, especially *nuraset* or ladies' arms and Damascus rose (filo rounds topped with *ashta*, syrup and pistachios).

BAHARAT
Used throughout the Middle East, each region has its own distinctive blend of spices. In Lebanon the blend includes paprika, pepper, cumin, cassia, cloves, coriander seed, cardamom and nutmeg.

BASTURMA
Air-dried beef, similar to pastrami, that is coated with spices and usually sliced finely.

LABNEH
A type of cheese that is made from yoghurt, which is hung in a fine cloth for a day and drained of moisture. It is rich and creamy with a nice tang and is used to spread on bread and as the basis of many dips.

SUMAC

A ground, dried berry with a peppery, lemony flavour and a reddish-purple colour. It is very common in Lebanese dishes such as *fattoush* (a fresh salad of tomato, cucumber, parsley, mint and toasted bread).

TAHINI

A popular paste made from hulled or unhulled sesame seeds. It is thick and creamy with a slightly nutty flavour and is used in many sauces and dips – it is a key ingredient in hoummus.

ZA'ATAR

A blend of thyme, toasted sesame seeds, sumac and salt. It is often mixed with a little olive oil to make a fragrant dip for Lebanese bread or spread with olive oil on *manoush* (a thin pizza that is served as a breakfast dish) and baked, then topped with tomato, mint, onion and black olives.

133

Hoummus

from Greg Malouf

A classic dip that is made almost every day in most Lebanese homes. The secret is to cook the chickpeas until they're really soft. If you can, seek out the prized nine-millimetre chickpeas grown in the Ord River region of Western Australia – they're fabulous.

500 g dried chickpeas
2 tablespoons bicarbonate of soda
1½ tablespoons tahini
1 tablespoon lemon juice
1–2 garlic cloves
2 teaspoons salt
1 tablespoon extra-virgin olive oil
1 teaspoon sweet paprika
finely chopped flat-leaf parsley

The day before you wish to make the hoummus, place the chickpeas in a large saucepan and add enough cold water to cover by 10 cm or more. Add the bicarbonate of soda and leave to soak overnight.

The next day, rinse the chickpeas, return them to the saucepan and cover with more water. Bring to the boil then simmer for approximately 1–2 hours, until the chickpeas are soft and shedding their skins. Drain and allow to cool.

Place the chickpeas in a food processor and blend until soft and creamy. Add the tahini, lemon juice, garlic and salt and blend again until the mixture is smooth. Scoop into a serving bowl and make a well in the centre. Pour the oil into the well and sprinkle paprika and parsley on top.

Makes approximately 4 cups

Baba Ghanouj

from Katya Faraj

It's quite nerve-wracking to just pop a whole eggplant directly on a gas flame, but without the smoky flavour you get as the eggplant sizzles, you wouldn't have a true baba ghanouj. This is a foolproof and creamy recipe for this beautiful dip.

3 medium eggplants
1½ tablespoons tahini
1 tablespoon lemon juice
1–2 garlic cloves
2 teaspoons salt
1 tablespoon extra-virgin olive oil
1 teaspoon sweet paprika
finely chopped flat-leaf parsley
finely diced tomato

Grill the eggplants whole over a gas flame, turning with tongs until the skin is evenly blistered and the flesh is soft. Soak in cold water for 10 minutes to cool.

Peel the eggplants and leave to drain for 15–20 minutes.

Place the eggplants in a food processor with the tahini, lemon juice, garlic and salt and process until well combined and creamy. You may wish to add extra tahini, lemon juice or salt to taste.

Scoop into a serving bowl and make a well in the centre. Pour the oil into the well and sprinkle paprika, parsley and tomato on top.

Makes approximately 3 cups

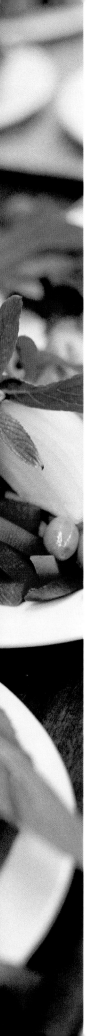

'Respect the ingredients that you cook with – they are a gift and precious.'

Tabbouleh
from Samira Saab

This recipe is a revelation – make it and see how crisp and lovely this salad should really be. Tightly bunching the parsley in your hand ready for cutting is crucial, as is using a very sharp knife – both help you to shave the parsley as finely as possible. Tabbouleh can be prepared a couple of hours ahead, but add the salt, pepper and oil just before serving. Serve it alongside almost any Lebanese dish (try the *kafta* on this page), or simply spoon onto baby cos lettuce leaves, roll up and enjoy.

1 bunch fresh, soft flat-leaf parsley

handful of mint leaves

1–2 lemons

2 tablespoons fine burghul

3–4 medium tomatoes, diced

4 spring onions, finely chopped

salt and pepper

olive oil

Gather the parsley in a tight wad in your hand and finely shred the leaves with a very sharp knife, almost in a shaving action. Tip into a colander. Do the same with the mint. Wash the chopped herbs and drain well.

Squeeze the lemon juice over the burghul and leave to soften for 10 minutes.

Combine the parsley and mint, softened burghul, tomato and spring onion in a bowl. Season with salt and pepper, add olive oil and mix with your hands.

Serves 4

Kafta
from Fouad Sayed

These minced-meat skewers are like the ultimate handmade sausages and they're incredibly simple. Make sure you buy the best-quality minced lamb and beef – or even better, mince the meat yourself. If you don't have metal skewers you can simply shape the mixture into patties. Great on the barbie, great in a pan, great in the oven – just great!

1 cup finely chopped flat-leaf parsley

500 g minced lamb

500 g minced beef

1 large onion, very finely chopped

1 teaspoon salt

½ teaspoon freshly ground white pepper

flatbread, to serve

tabbouleh, to serve

Place all the ingredients in a large bowl and use your hands to combine and knead the mixture until smooth.

Dampen your hands with water and shape the mixture around metal skewers. Barbecue until golden brown and cooked through.

To serve, split open some flatbread and fill with tabbouleh. Top with a *kafta*, close the bread around it and hold firmly as you slide out the skewer. Use torn-off pieces of bread to pick up some of the *kafta* and tabbouleh.

Serves 10–12

'Before you use any Lebanese food, you make the sign of the cross over it and say *"Bis mis Salib"* (In the name of the Cross).'

Kousa Mahshi
Stuffed Zucchini

from Judy Saba

I was thrilled when my friend Judy shared this family recipe with me, and found it fun to hollow out the zucchini using a *manakra* (a tool like a long apple corer designed for this purpose; you can find them in Middle Eastern food stores). The best zucchini to use is the small, slightly bulbous, pale green variety often sold as Lebanese zucchini. To adapt this recipe for vegetarians, use chickpeas instead of minced beef.

STUFFING

1 cup long-grain rice, washed
250 g lean minced beef
1 medium tomato, finely diced
½ onion, finely diced
⅓ cup chopped flat-leaf parsley
⅓ cup chopped mint
⅓ cup chopped coriander
¼ teaspoon chilli powder
1 teaspoon *baharat* or allspice
1 teaspoon ground cumin
½ teaspoon freshly ground black pepper
2 teaspoons salt
20 g butter, softened
2 tablespoons olive oil

10 small Lebanese zucchini, approximately 10 cm long
salt
2 heaped tablespoons tomato paste
natural yoghurt

Thoroughly mix the stuffing ingredients together.

Cut off the zucchini stalks, then slice off the dried tips at the opposite ends without removing too much flesh. Carefully hollow out the zucchini from the stalk end by pushing and turning a *manakra* into the flesh. The tool will remove thin fingers of flesh at a time; keep hollowing until you have a generous cavity (reserve the zucchini flesh for another purpose such as an omelette). Fill a bowl with water and add a teaspoon of salt. Wash the zucchini in the salted water (this helps to keep them firm when cooking), then drain.

Fill each zucchini with the stuffing, leaving 1 cm free at the top to allow the filling to expand. It's easiest to fill the zucchini by hand, tapping them on the bench every now and then to settle the stuffing down. If you have any leftover stuffing, form it into meatballs.

Fill a large saucepan with water and add 2 tablespoons of salt and the tomato paste. Add the stuffed zucchini and any meatballs and bring to the boil. Simmer over low heat for about 1 hour, allowing the sauce to reduce. Serve the stuffed zucchini with a little of the sauce and a dollop of yoghurt.

Serves 4–6

'Tarator-Style' Baked Salmon

from Greg Malouf

This is one of the best dishes I've eaten in my life and is now our show-off dinner party and Christmas lunch dish. The combination of perfectly cooked fish, a tahini and yoghurt dressing, freshly chopped herbs and walnuts, and a hint of chilli is fresh and delicious. The dish is served at room temperature, so you can cook the salmon up to four hours in advance.

DRESSING

1 garlic clove

1 teaspoon sea salt

400 g natural yoghurt

100 ml tahini

lemon juice

1 Tasmanian salmon (4–4.5 kg)

sea salt and freshly ground white pepper

170 ml extra-virgin olive oil

150 g walnuts

juice of 1–2 lemons

1 medium red onion, finely diced

3 long red chillies, seeded and finely diced

2 cups coriander leaves, chopped

½ cup mint leaves, shredded

20 g sumac

To make the dressing, place the garlic and salt in a mortar and crush well. Stir the garlic, yoghurt and tahini together until it becomes a thick paste. Thin slightly with lemon juice (it should be the consistency of pure cream). Taste for salt and refrigerate.

Preheat the oven to 150°C. Place the salmon on a large sheet of baking paper. Season all over with salt and pepper and drizzle with 2½ tablespoons of the oil. Wrap the salmon in the paper, place on a tray and bake in the centre of the oven for 25 minutes. Gently turn the salmon over and cook for a further 25 minutes, by which time it should be medium–rare. Remove from the oven and open the paper to stop the salmon cooking further. Leave to cool to room temperature.

Turn the oven up to 200°C and roast the walnuts for 5 minutes. Remove from the oven and rub briskly in a clean tea towel to remove as much of their skin as possible. Chop finely and set aside.

Close to serving time, use a sharp knife to cut through the skin along the back of the salmon from head to tail. Peel away the skin from one side. Scrape away the thin layer of grey flesh (the blood line) to expose the pink flesh underneath. Carefully transfer the salmon to a large serving plate. Brush ½ cup of the yoghurt dressing over the top of the salmon.

In a bowl, whisk the remaining oil with the lemon juice, salt and pepper. Add the onion and chilli and whisk lightly. Add the chopped walnuts, herbs and sumac. Spoon the salad over the salmon, covering it as neatly as possible.

Use a metal spoon to 'cut' portions of the salmon and salad. Serve with the remaining dressing.

Serves 10–12

'If you lick the saucepan, it will rain on your wedding day!'

MALAYSIA

If I could have my childhood over again, I'd grow up in Malaysia. Every expatriate I've spoken to sighs wistfully as they recall sumptuous banquets and simply prepared yet exquisite dishes. Like the story of the *kway teow man*, a mobile foodstall dedicated to a single great Malaysian offering – *char kway teow* noodles. This dish uses glossy, fat rice noodles mixed with plump, fresh prawns, thin discs of sweet–savoury Chinese *lup cheong* sausage, sometimes a little diced chicken, bean sprouts, garlic chives and a dash of soy sauce and chilli. It's all tossed together in a smoking-hot wok and the finishing touch is a beaten egg, which is whisked through to make a creamy sauce. The whole dish is made even more enticing by that special X-factor, the 'breath of the wok' – that's the '*char*' in the dish's name. And to think that this wonder actually comes to your front doorstep – does it get better than that?

Char kway teow encapsulates the magic of Malaysian food – a layering of tastes and textures that is well thought-out, elegantly spiced, simply beautiful and a perfect blend of Indian, Malaysian, Chinese and Nyonya (Straits Chinese) flavours. Malaysia has a rich cultural mix and in a wider sense this dish allows a glimpse of the way the world could be, with many races existing harmoniously together.

Malaysian food is also the result of a whole nation of dedicated – no, obsessive – food lovers who focus on taste and texture to achieve culinary nirvana. This nirvana has been described to me by my chef friend Jess as 'making your tastebuds jump up and down!'.

I had a glimpse of this nirvana when I discovered a flavour secret in the cheat's laksa recipe that follows – not only does the base flavour of nutty sweetness come from the dried shrimp used, it's also from the prawn heads and shells, which are cooked briefly in hot oil. What a revelation to see the oil change colour and catch the delicious aroma of the scraps that most of us would throw in the bin! In all these recipes I also found that you can get fairly close to authentic restaurant or hawker stall flavours at home when you know how.

The sweets that finish Malaysian meals are marvellous concoctions of rice flour, coconut and palm sugar. These take various forms, from the multicoloured steamed rice confections called *kueh*, to *sago gula melaka* in all its wonderfully sweet, dark stickiness. This is a great cuisine!

LUP CHEONG

Dried sausages that are red in colour and usually made from pork meat and spices. They are sweet and slightly spicy. Slice very thinly and stir-fry, or steam whole then slice.

PALM SUGAR

A golden sugar with a rich caramel flavour and a hint of coconut. It can be grated or sliced. If not available, brown sugar may be substituted.

PANDAN LEAF

The Asian equivalent of vanilla bean. Its subtle aroma is released when bruised by tying one or two long leaves into a knot. The leaves can also be used to wrap chicken or fish before cooking. Pandan leaf is also available as an essence and a powder to flavour and colour cakes. It is often used when cooking curries, rice and desserts.

THICK CARAMEL SOY SAUCE

Even more viscous than dark soy sauce, this is used to add a depth of colour and flavour to many dishes. Surprisingly, despite its name, it is not sweet.

Char Kway Teow

from Jess Ong

This is known fondly as Sunday night noodles in our house. It's everything a good dish should be – full of great flavour and texture with the silky noodles contrasting with the crunchy fresh sprouts and the creamy egg. Heat the wok well and have all the ingredients standing by in bowls ready to cook. The wok must be very hot as the secret to this dish is cooking quickly over high heat. A good tip is to heat the noodles first (if they are cold from the fridge), which is easily done in the microwave. And only cook enough for one person at a time to avoid the wok being too full and the ingredients 'stewing'.

80 ml oil

2 *lup cheong* sausages, sliced

12 fish balls, sliced

8 spring onions, sliced

8 garlic cloves, chopped

5 handfuls fresh rice noodles, warmed

1 tablespoon dark soy sauce

1 tablespoon light soy sauce

24 shelled green prawns

4 eggs, beaten

4 handfuls bean sprouts

⅓ cup chopped garlic chives

Use a quarter of the ingredients to cook for each person individually. Heat the wok over high heat. When thoroughly heated, add oil, sausage, fish balls, spring onion and garlic and stir-fry for a few minutes. Add noodles and toss briefly, then add soy sauces and toss through the noodles. Scrape everything to the side of the wok and add prawns, cooking until they change colour. Move the prawns to the side and add egg. Cook until the egg is nearly set, then gently fold it into the noodles. Add bean sprouts and chives, toss, and serve immediately.

Serves 4

Beef Rendang

from Alvin Tan

This is a recipe to treasure and make again and again – thanks to my friend Alvin for sharing it. Try to source all the ingredients (from Asian food stores) for the best authentic flavour, and remember that once you've found turmeric leaves they'll freeze well for next time. Like all great slow-cooked dishes, rendang calls for meat with a bit of fat through it – it will become succulent, soft and absolutely delicious.

6 dried long chillies, torn in half (seeded if you want less heat), soaked in hot water until soft

150 g red onions, chopped

5 garlic cloves, chopped

3 cm piece of galangal, chopped

3 cm piece of young ginger, chopped

1 lemongrass stalk, finely chopped

1 cup desiccated coconut

3 tablespoons vegetable oil

¾ turmeric leaf, rolled and finely chopped (optional)

6 kaffir lime leaves, rolled and sliced

1 kg topside or chuck steak, cut into 3 cm cubes

250 ml coconut milk

4 tablespoons Malaysian 'meat' curry powder

125 ml water

1–2 tablespoons thick caramel soy sauce

salt

Place the chilli, onion, garlic, galangal, ginger and lemongrass in a blender or food processor and blend to a paste, adding some soaking water from the chillies as needed.

Heat a frying pan over low heat and toast the coconut to golden. Grind in a mortar, blender or food processor and set aside.

Heat the oil in a heavy-based saucepan and add the paste and the turmeric and lime leaves. Fry for 3–4 minutes, until fragrant. Add the meat, then stir in the coconut milk and curry powder. Add the water and toasted coconut (which will thicken the rendang) and bring to a simmer. Cook for 1–1½ hours, until the meat is tender. Add extra water during cooking if the rendang is drying out. To finish, add the soy sauce and season to taste with salt.

Serves 4–6

'In Malaysia, tastebuds are triggered by various sounds. A cow's bell ringing is the mobile hawker selling *pulut hitam* (sweet coconut black rice), a beep is for laksa, a bicycle bell for satay, a lady's bellowing for Nyonya *kueh* (rice-flour sweets) ...'

Cheat's Laksa

from Aryan Mansour

This was first described to me as a ten-minute laksa but it takes a little bit longer to prepare – but not much! What I love is that you're adding delicious fresh ingredients to a commercial laksa paste (look for this in Asian food stores), so a lot of the work is already done for you. This is a great dish to serve for a group of friends if you've set the table already and have all the garnishing to hand. Make it up to the adding of the noodles and you'll be blessed as a culinary genius!

4–5 shallots, chopped

6–7 garlic cloves, chopped

thumb-sized piece of ginger, chopped

1 red chilli (more if you want extra kick)

1 heaped tablespoon dried shrimp

125 ml water

12 green prawns

80 ml vegetable oil

4 tablespoons laksa paste

1 litre chicken stock or water

400 ml coconut cream

fish balls

fried tofu puffs, cut in half

1 teaspoon sugar

fish sauce

salt

juice of 1 lime, plus extra wedges to serve

dried rice vermicelli

fresh egg noodles

shredded cooked chicken

bean sprouts

finely sliced spring onion

finely sliced red chilli

coriander leaves

fried shallots

Place the shallots, garlic, ginger, chilli, dried shrimp and water in a blender or food processor and blend to a smooth paste.

Shell the prawns. Heat the oil in a large saucepan and fry the shells for about 1 minute, until they turn red. Scoop out the shells leaving the coloured oil. Add the blended paste to the oil and fry for a minute before adding the laksa paste. Fry until fragrant, then add the stock and bring to the boil. Add the coconut cream and turn the heat back to a simmer. Add the fish balls, tofu and sugar, along with fish sauce and salt to taste. Add the lime juice.

Cook the rice noodles in a separate saucepan of boiling water, then scoop into a colander. Add the egg noodles to the water to heat through and remove to a separate colander. Poach the shelled prawns in the same water.

Put some noodles and prawns in each serving bowl. Ladle over the broth and top with chicken and bean sprouts. Scatter with spring onion, chilli, coriander and fried shallots. Add a wedge of lime to squeeze in before eating.

Serves 4

Nasi Lemak
Coconut Rice

from Alvin Tan

Nasi Lemak is known as the national dish of
Malaysia and is served with *ikan bilis*, roasted
peanuts, hard-boiled eggs and spicy sambals.
Delicious and fragrant, *Nasi Lemak* is a perfect
accompaniment to beef rendang. I never cook
plain old rice any more after learning this
recipe! You can cook this in a rice cooker if
you have one.

3 cups long-grain rice
200 ml coconut milk
200 ml water
2 cm piece of ginger, bruised
1 pandan leaf, split and tied in a knot
¾ teaspoon salt

Rinse the rice twice and drain. Put in a saucepan
with the remaining ingredients, cover with a lid
and bring to the boil. Simmer gently until the
liquid is absorbed (about 15 minutes). Remove
from the heat and leave covered for another
5 minutes before serving.

Serves 6

Sago Gula Melaka
Sago with Palm Sugar Syrup

from Suzanne Goh

Like little pale pearls is how the sago looks once
cooked. Add the mellow caramel made from
palm sugar and it's a match made in heaven.
This pudding looks really impressive when
it's set in a fluted ring mould.

300 g sago
1 egg white
200 g palm sugar, chopped
125 ml water
75 g (⅓ cup) white sugar
400 ml coconut milk

Bring a large saucepan of water to the boil and
add the sago. Stir as the water returns to the boil
to stop the pearls sticking to each other. Cook
until the sago floats to the surface and is trans-
parent (approximately 15 minutes). Drain and
rinse in cold water a couple of times to remove
the starch.

Beat the egg white until soft peaks form. Stir
in the sago. Pour into a jelly mould and chill for
at least 1 hour to set.

Heat the palm sugar and water over medium
heat, stirring to dissolve the sugar. Stir in the
white sugar. When completely dissolved, strain
through a fine sieve and leave to cool.

Turn the sago pudding onto a serving plate.
Cut into wedges and serve topped with a little
coconut milk and syrup.

Serves 6

MALTA

When you hear the story of how Maltese people have survived and thrived for centuries on their rocky island in the centre of the Mediterranean (between Sicily and North Africa), you have to hand it to these tenacious people. Most of the land isn't suitable for grazing or cultivation and yet has given birth to some beautiful rustic recipes that sing of Mediterranean flavour and freshness.

That same spirit of getting on with it persists in the homes of Maltese immigrants. One inspiring woman called Polly missed the cheese she had grown up with so much that she decided to buy a couple of cows and learn to milk them so she could make the cheese herself. Impressive!

After a morning spent cheese making, when I visited Polly she whipped into her kitchen to make some wonderful *bragioli* (beef olives). A real Maltese favourite, this consists of a rolled escalope of beef filled with minced veal, herbs and cheese then cooked in a lovely fresh tomato sauce. She served the cooking sauce with some pasta then the meat was the main course – ingenious and delicious. The famous Maltese stews of rabbit (*stuffat tal-fenek*) and octopus (*stuffat tal-qarnit*) are served the same way.

Other simple but yummy things I tasted were a dip called *bigilla* made from dried fava beans (broad beans) that are cooked then mashed with some garlic, chilli and anchovies and eaten with crusty bread; and a Maltese open sandwich made from crusty bread called *hobz biz-zejt* (which translates as 'bread with oil'). To make *hobz biz-zejt*, thick slices of bread are spread with the beloved sweetish tomato paste called *kunserva* and topped with ingredients such as tuna, anchovies, capers, olives and garlic plus black pepper and a drizzle of olive oil. It is very Mediterranean and very tasty.

And how could I forget the most famous snack of Malta – the flaky, golden pastries traditionally filled with ricotta and mushy peas called *pastizzi*, which are sold on street corners and village bars and eaten hot with black tea or coffee.

Because of its close proximity to Italy, there are a lot of Italian influences in Maltese dishes like *timpana* (a deep pasta pie) and *ravjul* (ravioli stuffed with ricotta cheese) but the ravioli are generally larger than the Italian variety and Maltese pasta is usually cooked to a softer texture than al dente.

Maltese sweets also reveal the influence of other countries – Arabic culinary traditions are seen in *qaq tal-ghasel*, a pastry stuffed with a date and honey mixture; and the English bread and butter pudding has been transformed into *puddina*, a more solid chocolate version with dried fruit, which is eaten hot or cold and is also great with a cup of tea. Chilled fruit is always served as part of a dessert spread – stone fruits, figs, melons, pears, grapes, citrus fruits and pomegranates.

CAPERS

These small, salty buds grow wild in bushes along the roadside and are used in many dishes. They are essential to the ultimate Maltese open sandwich, *hobz biz-zejt*.

EXTRA-VIRGIN OLIVE OIL

Olive trees grow in abundance on the rocky island. Olive oil is used liberally in the Maltese cuisine in salad dressings and as cooking oil.

GBEJNIET

Gbejniet is the name for a type of cheese adored by the Maltese. This is generally made with cow's milk. There is a soft fresh version like a silky cross between mozzarella and ricotta; a sun-dried version of the same, which hardens after a month into a little sweet, nutty round of cheese; and another version of hard cheese, which is rolled in a pepper powder and served with grapes or figs or as part of an antipasto selection.

KUNSERVA

This rather sweet tomato paste is used in pasta sauces and to boost any dish that contains tomatoes. It is a key ingredient in the favourite national snack, the *hobz biz-zejt* sandwich.

PULSES

Pulses in various guises are widely used in Maltese cooking. Green split peas are popular for soups and in the famous mushy pea and ricotta filling for *pastizzi* pastries. Broad beans are used fresh and dried in soups and in the beloved *bigilla* dip eaten with crusty bread.

Soppa tal-Armla
Widow's Soup

from Alex Vella

A simple, delicious soup made from fresh
vegetables including kohlrabi, peas and broad
beans. It's healthy and low fat. If you can find
soft *gbejniet* cheese (available from selected
delis and cheese makers), pop it into the hot
soup for a few minutes before serving and you'll
enjoy the beautiful taste of molten cheese too.

1 tablespoon butter

1 tablespoon olive oil

1 onion, diced

3–4 garlic cloves, crushed

⅔ cup chopped flat-leaf parsley

2 potatoes, peeled and chopped

2 carrots, peeled and chopped

1 kohlrabi, peeled and chopped

2 celery stalks, sliced

1 cup podded broad beans (fresh or frozen)

1 cup podded peas (fresh or frozen)

½ large or 1 small cauliflower, cut into bite-sized pieces

1½ tablespoons tomato paste

chicken or vegetable stock

salt and pepper

6 soft *gbejniet* (small Maltese cheeses)

Heat the butter and oil in a large saucepan and
add the onion, garlic and most of the parsley.
Sauté until soft. Add the vegetables, tomato
paste and enough stock to cover. Stir well and
season to taste with salt and pepper. Bring to
the boil, cover and simmer for 15–20 minutes,
until the vegetables are just cooked.

Add the *gbejniet* and press down lightly to
submerge. Cover and cook for a couple of minutes to heat the cheese. Add the remaining
parsley to the soup and stir through.

Ladle the soup into bowls, topping each
with a round of *gbejniet*.

Serves 6

Hobz biz-Zejt
Open Sandwich

from Shane Delia

Malta's number one snack food is an open
sandwich slathered with *kunserva* (sweetish
tomato paste) and topped with the best the
Mediterranean has to offer. Shane especially
likes to use white anchovies, which are pickled
in vinegar rather than preserved in salt or oil
and have a mild, sweet flavour.

slices of dense, crusty bread

kunserva (Maltese tomato paste)

capers

white anchovies or tinned tuna in oil, drained

sea salt and freshly ground black pepper

flat-leaf parsley leaves

extra-virgin olive oil

Spread the bread with *kunserva*. Sprinkle capers
over the top, then add anchovies or tuna. Season
with salt and pepper, scatter with parsley and
drizzle generously with oil. Enjoy!

'Give bread only to people
who know how to eat it
(Get an expert if you want
a job done properly).'

Hobz biz-Zejt

'Only the cook knows
exactly what went in
the pot.'

Timpana

from Louis Bigeni

Timpana is the ultimate pasta pie. Macaroni or penne is cooked and added to a rich bolognaise-style sauce, often enhanced by chicken livers. With the addition of cheese and eggs, the pasta and sauce is spooned into a pastry case and cooked until golden.

75 g butter
250 g onions, finely diced
2 garlic cloves, crushed
150 g bacon, finely diced
150 g minced pork
150 g minced beef
150 g chicken livers, diced (optional)
250 ml chicken or beef stock
100 g tomato paste
125 ml tomato puree
250 g macaroni or penne
75 g parmesan, grated
75 g tasty cheese, grated
4 eggs, beaten
salt and pepper
250 g puff pastry sheets

GLAZE

1 egg
2½ tablespoons milk

Heat the butter in a saucepan and add the onion and garlic. Sauté for 5 minutes. Add the bacon and pork, stirring well to separate, then add the beef and continue cooking for 10 minutes, stirring every so often. Add the chicken livers if using and cook for 5 minutes. Add the stock, stir well and bring to the boil. Simmer for 20 minutes. Add the tomato paste and puree, simmer briefly and remove from the heat.

Meanwhile, cook the pasta in a large pot of salted boiling water until just undercooked. Drain, then mix through the sauce. Stir in the cheeses and egg and season with salt and pepper.

Preheat the oven to 180°C. Line a buttered baking dish with the pastry, extending it up the sides. Spoon in the pasta and cover with another layer of pastry. Prick the *timpana* all over with a knife to let steam escape. Beat the egg and milk for the glaze and paint it over the *timpana*. Bake for 1–1¼ hours.

Serves 6–8

Timpana

Bragioli
Beef Olives

from Polly Vella

The joy of this recipe is that you don't need the best cuts of meat to make a delicious meal. Thin slices of tenderised beef are stuffed with minced veal, herbs and flavourings and gently cooked in a tomato-based sauce. This can also be served as two meals in the traditional Maltese way with the cooking sauce paired with pasta as a first course.

SAUCE

3 tablespoons olive oil

2 large onions, diced

5 garlic cloves, crushed

400 g tin tomatoes

1 cup flat-leaf parsley leaves

½ cup basil leaves

2 bay leaves

250 ml red wine

500 ml water

salt and pepper

6 thin slices of topside or round steak

400 g minced veal

2 bacon rashers, diced

2 garlic cloves, crushed

½ cup finely chopped flat-leaf parsley

1 tablespoon finely chopped oregano

1 spring onion, finely sliced

½ cup grated *gbejniet* (Maltese cheese)

2 eggs, beaten

salt and pepper

To make the sauce, heat the oil in a large saucepan and add the onion and garlic. Fry until softened. Add the remaining ingredients and leave to simmer while you prepare the *bragioli*.

Flatten the beef slices with a mallet and set aside. Mix the remaining ingredients together well, seasoning with salt and pepper. Place a generous tablespoon of mixture on each slice of beef, spreading out well. Roll up and secure with toothpicks or tie with butcher's string. Place the rolls in the sauce and simmer for 1½ hours over low heat.

Serves 6

'A donkey does not appreciate cake (sometimes people don't realise when they are onto a good thing).'

Stuffat tal-Fenek
Rabbit Stew
from Paul Camilleri

This is a marvellous slow-cooked dish that's full of flavour, with meat so tender it falls off the bone.

1 rabbit (1.5–2 kg)
350 ml red wine
6 bay leaves
6 garlic cloves, 4 peeled and left whole, 2 finely chopped
80 ml extra-virgin olive oil
salt and pepper
1 onion, finely diced
3 tablespoons tomato paste
1.5 litres tomato puree
250 ml water
3–4 potatoes, peeled and cut into chunks

Remove the rabbit kidneys and liver and set aside. Chop the rabbit into pieces: remove the front and back legs and cut each in half, and chop the body or saddle into 5 pieces. Place the rabbit pieces, kidneys and liver in a large bowl and add the wine, half the bay leaves and the whole garlic. Marinate in the refrigerator overnight, turning the meat a few times.

Strain off the marinade liquid and reserve. Discard the garlic and bay leaves.

Preheat the oven to 150°C. Heat the oil in a heavy-based ovenproof pot and gently brown the rabbit on all sides until well sealed and golden. Season with salt and pepper. Remove from the pot.

Add the onion and chopped garlic to the pot and fry until beginning to soften. Add the tomato paste and marinade liquid and cook for a minute. Add the tomato puree and water and mix well. Return the rabbit to the pot and add the potatoes and remaining bay leaves. Bring to a simmer then remove from the heat, cover with a lid and bake for 2½–3 hours.

Serves 6

Puddina
Bread and Butter Pudding
from Rita O'Dwyer

With ingenuity the Maltese have adapted this dish from the English (Malta was once a British colony) and added an Arabic twist. Day-old bread is soaked in water then mixed with generous quantities of dried fruit, almonds and cocoa. *Puddina* is served in slices with black tea as an afternoon pick-me-up.

1 day-old loaf of bread
370 g (1⅔ cup) sugar
2 tablespoons custard powder
2 tablespoons cornflour
35 g (⅓ cup) cocoa
2 eggs, beaten
500 g mixed dried fruit such as sultanas, raisins, currants and chopped peel
250 g almonds
250 g glacé cherries, halved
vanilla extract
80 ml whisky, brandy or sherry

Tear the bread into small pieces and soak in cold water for 15 minutes until soft.

Preheat the oven to 200°C. Tip the bread into a colander and squeeze out the excess water using a potato masher. Place the bread in a mixing bowl and stir in the sugar, custard powder, cornflour and cocoa. Add the eggs and mix well. Add the dried fruit, half the almonds and half the glacé cherries. Add vanilla to taste and the whisky, brandy or sherry. Pour into a baking dish and decorate the top with the remaining almonds and cherries. Bake for 45–60 minutes, or until a skewer comes out clean. Serve in slices, warm or at room temperature.

Serves 10

MAURITIUS

If you had to invent a cuisine and could choose your favourite influences from around the world, you'd probably come up with something like the food of Mauritius. This combines techniques and ingredients from some of the most diverse nations on earth and blends them harmoniously and deliciously into a unique national cuisine. Indian and Sri Lankan curries, breads and pickles are cooked alongside slow-braised European daubes and Chinese stir-fried noodles – all given an African twist with local ingredients.

Take the sauce used every day by most Mauritians called *rougaille*. It's a clever mix of common ingredients such as tomatoes, onions, garlic and chillies, which are cooked with a couple of spices into a delicious fresh-tasting sauce. Vegetables, meats and seafood can then be cooked in the *rougaille* and eaten with *achards* (pickled vegetables) and dhal or rice. One of the things I was struck by is that most Mauritian dishes are cooked quickly – if you live in the tropics, you've got better things to do than stand over a hot stove!

Another quick dish to assemble is *vindaye* (pickled fish) – beautiful fresh fish (or octopus) is fried quickly then coated in a mixture of turmeric, mustard seeds, chilli, garlic, ginger, oil and vinegar. *Vindaye* was created to preserve fish before the days of refrigeration but it is still made in the traditional way and is one of the dishes that Mauritians hold close to their hearts.

Spices are also adored and used abundantly – turmeric, cinnamon, cardamom and cloves are found in many dishes, including the distinctive curries of the island. These curries rarely contain coconut milk and, interestingly, often feature more typically European herbs like thyme.

It's worth crossing the ocean for *gateaux piments* – these are incredibly more-ish, spiced split-pea cakes, a bit like falafel, which are available on every street corner – and *dholl puri*, a flatbread filled with a thin layer of mashed yellow split peas topped with all sorts of crunchy, yummy pickled vegetables and chutneys. It is always served as 'a pair of *dholl puri*', which doesn't mean two wraps but a double-layered one.

Mauritians love their sweets and have invented some beautiful tarts and biscuits that combine French techniques with local ingredients. The classic *tarte banane* is one indulgent example and I adore the impossibly cute pink-iced shortbreads sandwiched with raspberry jam called *napolitaines*. And as you would expect of a tropical island, fruit is abundant and enjoyed in cooking or as refreshing snacks. Green mango is finely shredded in salads or pickled in the sun with chilli and salt, and sliced pineapple with chilli salt is one of the most commonly sold snacks. The perfect food for lazing on the beach!

BANANA

Used green in curries, or ripe and cooked with sugar to fill lattice-topped tarts fried to perfection to make *beignets* (fritters).

CHILLI

Chillies are always used to complement a meal and most Mauritian families will have chilli paste in jars in their fridge. The most popular chillies are *petit piment* (little chilli), also known as *piment petard* (firecracker chilli) because it is so hot. *Piment rodrigues* is another type of small, hot chilli. Chillies are also eaten in snacks from a young age – one common way is crushed with salt and sprinkled over slivered, crunchy green mango or pineapple.

COCONUT

Finely grated fresh coconut is traditionally combined with mint, chilli and garlic for a refreshing chutney.

MURUNGA LEAVES

Rarely seen in Australia but well known in Sri Lanka as drumstick leaves, these are commonly grown in Mauritian backyards. Their slippery texture and tangy flavour is loved across the island and they are stir-fried with onion and garlic or made into protein-rich soups.

MUSTARD SEEDS

Dark brown or black seeds are most commonly used in Mauritian cooking, cooked in oil at the start of a curry or pickle to add a mildly nutty flavour.

SHALLOTS

Small, golden, papery-skinned bulbs with a more delicate and sweet flavour than their onion relation.

THYME

Thyme is often used in Mauritian curries and in the many French-derived braised meat dishes.

TURMERIC

A popular spice, used both fresh and powdered. Fresh turmeric is used in *achards*, pickles and curry pastes and dried turmeric is used in curry powders.

YELLOW SPLIT PEAS

A common staple in Mauritian cooking. They are made into curries and soups, provide the filling for *dholl puri* and are the key ingredient in *gateaux piment*.

Dholl Puri

from Kavi Hurrydoss

These flatbreads have a filling of cooked yellow split peas. They're served warm wrapped around curries, *achards* (pickled vegetables) and chutneys to make a yummy snack. Try with the two *achards* on page 160 and the coriander chutney on this page.

½ tablespoon cumin seeds
250 g yellow split peas, soaked overnight
salt
1 kg plain flour
½ teaspoon turmeric
400 ml warm water
vegetable oil

Toast the cumin seeds in a dry frying pan. Grind in a mortar.

Drain and rinse the peas and boil in fresh water until just tender. Drain well and blend with the cumin in a food processor (the mixture should be like a powder). Add salt to taste.

Place the flour, turmeric and 2 pinches of salt in a large bowl and mix well. Add the water, mix to a smooth dough and knead for about 5 minutes. Cover the dough with a damp cloth and leave for 20–30 minutes.

Form the dough into balls weighing about 60 g. Make an indent in the centre of each ball and stuff with the pea mixture. Seal the dough around the filling. Roll the balls out on a floured surface to very thin rounds.

Brush a frying pan (non-stick is ideal) with oil and cook each *dholl puri* over high heat for 2 minutes on each side. Before flipping, brush the top with a little oil.

Makes 20–30 flatbreads

Coriander Chutney

from Kavi Hurrydoss

A fresh-tasting chutney that works its magic in *dholl puris* and alongside any grills or barbecues. Best eaten on the day it's made.

2 garlic cloves
4 small red chillies
2 bunches coriander, chopped
salt

Blend the garlic, chilli, coriander and salt to taste until the ingredients form a paste. You can do this using a mortar and pestle or food processor. Check the seasoning, adding more salt if desired.

Makes 1 generous cup

'Dholl puri must be eaten hot (both in terms of temperature and chillies).'

'The best curries are
cooked in old pots.'

Duck Curry

from Jocelyn Riviere

A delicious, simple, falling-from-the-bone duck curry in a rich, thick sauce. It is full of flavour but less tricky to make than other curries as it relies on curry powder rather than a complex spice blend (you will find the best curry powder at an Indian grocery store). It is lovely served with shallot *achard* (see page 160).

8 cm piece of ginger, chopped

6–8 large garlic cloves, chopped

1–2 small red chillies

salt

1 duck (1.5–1.8 kg)

freshly ground white pepper

vegetable oil

2 medium onions, finely chopped

small handful of curry leaves

4 tablespoons good-quality Indian curry powder, mixed with water to make a wet paste

4 medium-sized ripe tomatoes, seeds removed, roughly chopped

½ bunch coriander, roughly chopped

Place the ginger, garlic, chilli and a pinch of salt in a mortar and pound to a paste.

Trim the duck of excess skin and fat. Chop the duck into medium-sized pieces, leaving the drumsticks whole. Place the pieces in a bowl and season well with salt and white pepper, tossing to coat.

Heat a large, heavy-based saucepan over medium–high heat. When hot, add a little oil and brown the duck pieces in batches. When all the pieces are browned, remove them from the pan and turn the heat down to medium. There should be a little melted duck fat left in the pan.

Add the onion and sauté until light brown. Add the ginger, garlic and chilli paste. Fry for about 2 minutes, then turn the heat down to medium–low and add the curry leaves and curry powder. Cook, stirring, for another 2 minutes. Add a little water, the duck pieces and any juices. Mix well and add extra water to come halfway up the contents of the pan. Season to taste. Bring to the boil then cover with a lid and simmer for 45–60 minutes, stirring occasionally until the meat is tender and almost falling off the bone.

Remove the lid and add the tomato. Turn the heat up a little to allow the tomato to break down and the sauce to reduce. Check the seasoning and add the coriander just before serving.

Serves 6

'Never cook a curry
without salt.'

'Poor people never go hungry – there's always tasty and cheap *bouillon mooroome* (soup made from a backyard plant with a small green leaf).'

Achards
Pickled Vegetables

from Kavi Hurrydoss

Two different recipes for these deliciously crunchy pickled vegetables.

SHALLOT *ACHARD*

500 g shallots, quartered (leave enough base to hold the quarters together)

salt

10 garlic cloves

50 g ginger, chopped

25 g fresh turmeric, chopped

1 tablespoon black mustard seeds

1 tablespoon yellow mustard seeds

250 ml vegetable oil

2 long green chillies, sliced into strips

3 tablespoons white vinegar

VEGETABLE *ACHARD*

180 ml vegetable oil

2 large onions, finely sliced

10 garlic cloves, finely sliced

4 long red or green chillies, sliced into strips

2 tablespoons black mustard seeds

250 g cabbage, finely sliced

250 g carrots, julienned

250 g green beans, sliced into strips

250 g cauliflower, finely sliced

2 tablespoons white vinegar

salt

To make the shallot *achard*, toss the shallots in some salt and leave for 5 minutes. Rinse in cold water and pat dry with a clean tea towel.

Place the garlic, ginger, turmeric and mustard seeds in a mortar and pound to a paste.

Heat the oil in a frying pan over low heat. Once hot but not bubbling, add the garlic mixture and stir briefly (don't let it fry). Add the shallots and chilli and cook gently for about 10 minutes – the shallots should still be a little crunchy. Add the vinegar and season to taste. Fill sterilised jars and store in the refrigerator. Leave for at least 2 days before serving.

To make the vegetable *achard*, heat the oil in a large frying pan and sweat the onion, garlic, chilli and mustard seeds. Add the remaining vegetables and mix well. Remove from the heat. Add the vinegar and season to taste. Fill sterilised jars and store in the refrigerator. Leave for at least 2 days before serving.

Both *achards* will keep for 1 week.

Vegetable Achard

Fish *Vindaye*
from Robyn Touchard

Pickled fish in a jar sounds unappetising until you try this beautiful, easy recipe for white fish fillets infused with ginger, garlic and spices – it's filled with flavour, low in fat (which always helps!) and high in protein and omega 3. I add *vindaye* to steamed rice for lunch or an easy dinner ... and I imagine that if I lived in tropical Mauritius, I'd want to eat this all the time to maximise the time spent under a palm tree rather than in the kitchen!

vegetable oil

1 kg firm, thick, white fish fillets or cutlets

2 medium onions, thickly sliced

1 tablespoon grated ginger

5 garlic cloves

2 teaspoons turmeric

200 ml white vinegar

1 teaspoon black mustard seeds, lightly ground

2 small red chillies, finely sliced

Heat oil for shallow-frying in a pan over medium heat. Fry the fish fillets until pale gold on both sides. Remove from the pan.

In the same oil, briefly stir-fry the onion, ginger and garlic cloves. Stir the turmeric into the vinegar and add to the pan, mixing well. Return the fish to the pan and sprinkle over the mustard seeds and chilli. Mix gently to coat the fish in onion and spices. Put the fish into a large sterilised jar and top with the onions (which should still be crunchy) and liquid. Store in the refrigerator for a few days before using (it will keep for up to 2 weeks).
Serves 4–6

Prawn *Rougaille*
from Vijay Baboo

A simple recipe of prawns cooked in Mauritius' favourite spicy tomato sauce.

olive oil

1 red onion, chopped

1 tablespoon finely chopped garlic

125 ml white wine

500 g tomatoes, peeled and chopped

1 tablespoon ground cumin

1 teaspoon sweet paprika

1 teaspoon salt

1 teaspoon white pepper

2 small red or green chillies, finely chopped

½ bunch flat-leaf parsley, finely chopped

2 thyme sprigs, leaves picked

1 kg green king prawns, shelled, heads and tails intact

½ bunch coriander, chopped

Heat 2 tablespoons of olive oil in a saucepan over medium heat. Add the onion and half the garlic and fry until golden. Pour in half the wine to soften the onion, then add the tomatoes and cook for a few minutes over high heat to reduce. Stir in the cumin, paprika, salt and pepper and an extra drizzle of olive oil. Add the chilli, parsley and thyme and remove from the heat.

Heat a little more oil in a frying pan and fry the remaining garlic until fragrant. Add the prawns, season with pepper and cook for 2 minutes. Pour in the remaining wine to deglaze the pan.

Tip the prawns into the *rougaille* (tomato sauce) and stir through the coriander.
Serves 4

Fish *Vindaye*

MEXICO

Those who know and love true Mexican food rate it as one of the great cuisines on the planet – ancient yet highly developed.

Expatriate home kitchens are a little slice of Mexico, full of cooking aromas that make you hungry – the tang of freshly squeezed lime, the warm smell of just-pressed corn tortillas cooking on the griddle and the toasty, rich waft of tomatoes and chillies roasting over a flame. It's tantalising and there's also an atmosphere of fun – shaping tamales then wrapping them in corn husks is done so quickly when done with friends.

Mexican foods such as tortillas, cactus, corn, chilli and tomatoes go back to pre-Hispanic times when the great Mayan and Aztec cultures held sway. The arrival of the Spanish in the sixteenth century saw new ingredients and produce introduced: sheep, pigs and cows as well as dairy products, garlic, wheat and many different herbs and spices. Spanish culinary traditions were also fostered by the missionaries that scattered across the country.

In Mexico each region has its specialities. Some are incredibly complex dishes, others are simple and quick. All of them have a fabulous depth of flavour and combine savoury and earthy ingredients with fresh herbs and at least two types of chilli at any one time (fresh or dried).

Many Mexican ingredients are readily available anywhere, while others can be grown at home – *tomatillos* or *epazote* (a native herb) – or ordered through specialist food importers. Useful implements I saw in Mexican kitchens are the lime squeezer; the Mexican mortar and pestle; the *comal* (a griddle for cooking tortillas, toasting chillies and garlic); and the earthenware *cazuelas*, although a heavy pot or Dutch oven will work as well.

There is much to learn about Mexican cuisine – for example, true guacamole doesn't include sour cream, mayonnaise or cream; and a taco is made with a soft corn tortilla not a crunchy one. There are many wonderful variations on the tortilla theme, all delicious – tacos are filled with cooked beans, salsa and grilled meat; burritos are made with a flour tortilla and filled with cheese, rice, beans, meat, onions and salsa; quesadillas are also made with a flour tortilla and filled with cheese and any number of additions and then returned to the hotplate to melt together. Tortillas are fundamental to each meal and work as cutlery, plate and napkin.

Moles, or sauces, are an essential part of Mexican cuisine and the basis of many of their delicious dishes. Some ancient *moles* combine up to 200 ingredients that are pounded or blended together, then meat or vegetables are added and cooked in the sauces. I tasted one of the top ten dishes of my life (so far!) in Mexico – a turkey *mole poblano* served wrapped in a leaf. It was a rich, black sauce full of incredible flavour including mellow, raisin-like chilli and a hint of chocolate. What a beautiful cuisine!

Chilli

This is the main flavouring ingredient in Mexican food with both fresh and dried forms used. To use most dried chillies, discard the stem and seeds, gently fry the chilli in oil until the chilli changes colour, then simmer in hot water for ten minutes. Common chilli varieties include:

Ancho: A mild, sweet dried chilli. When fresh it is known as *poblano* and looks similar to a large, pointed green capsicum. Its beautiful flavour is a traditional base for *moles*.

Guajillo (pronounced 'gwah-hee-yoh'): A large mild chilli. When dried it has a very tough leathery skin so may require long soaking. Its sweet heat is used in salsas, chilli sauces, soups and stews.

Habanero: A super hot variety of chilli that is available fresh and dried. It has a tropical fruitiness as well as a fiery heat that is useful in sauces.

Jalapeño ('hah-luh-pane-yo'): The most common chilli in Mexican cooking. It is usually sold green and adds a warm spiciness to many dishes. When smoked and dried it is known as *chipotle* ('chee-poht-leh').

Pasilla ('pah-see-ya'): A mild to medium–hot dried chilli. Literally 'little raisin', it is also traditionally used as a base for *moles*.

Essential flavours

ACHIOTE

Known as 'annatto' in English, this is a red seed with a mild, earthy flavour. It is used in cooking for both its bright colour and subtle flavour and can also be used to dye fabric – in fact it is one of several ancient ingredients that were used as body paint. It is sold as a pressed block or in a common spice blend including salt, pepper and garlic.

AVOCADO

The avocado, which is native to South America, is thought to have originated in southern Mexico. It was cultivated well before the arrival of Europeans. Avocado is used in salsas and to make guacamole.

CHOCOLATE

The first people known to make chocolate were the ancient cultures of Mexico and central America. Mexican chocolate is dark and bitter and flavoured with cinnamon, almond and cloves. In Mexico chocolate is used as a flavouring in many *moles* (sauces) and commonly used to make hot chocolate drinks.

CORN

In its various guises corn is an indispensable part of Mexican cuisine. *Masa*, or corn flour, is ground from white, yellow or blue corn and is used to make tortilla. These soft, pancake-like flatbreads are steamed then eaten with most meals. Hominy is a dried white corn that is used to make a much-loved stew called *pozole*. It is so popular that some small restaurants in Mexico serve only this dish.

LIME

A key flavouring in many Mexican dishes, as in much of Latin America. Lime is widely used in salsas, marinades and margaritas.

MEXICAN CORIANDER

Native to Mexico and South America, this herb is from the same family as coriander, but has long leaves and a stronger taste. It is the most commonly used fresh herb in Mexican cooking. Coriander can be used in its place.

TOMATILLOS

Tomatillos look like a small green tomato but are actually a member of the gooseberry family. They have a very tart flavour and are used in many dishes, including salsas and stews. Canned *tomatillos* can be bought at Spanish and South American grocery stores.

Guacamole

from Luipta Feint

This perfect, simple guacamole uses the best avocados mixed with fresh chilli, coriander, onion, tomato and lime. To help keep the vibrant green colour of the avocados, sit the avocado stones in the prepared guacamole and remove just before serving.

3 ripe avocados

½ fresh jalapeño chilli (optional), finely chopped

½ tablespoon chopped coriander

a little chopped red onion

1 tomato, diced

juice of ½ lime

1 teaspoon salt

Halve the avocados, remove the seeds and use a spoon to scoop the flesh into a bowl. Add the chilli, coriander and onion. Mash together with a fork. Gently fold in the tomato, lime juice and salt. Taste for seasoning.

Makes 4 cups

Pico di Gallo
Tomato Salsa

from Lupita Feint

Its simplicity makes this a great all-purpose tomato salsa. It should be made on the day using the freshest ingredients – fresh is always best. You can add diced avocado for extra colour and flavour.

3 tomatoes, diced

½–1 fresh jalapeño chilli, finely chopped

3 tablespoons chopped coriander

½ red onion, diced

1 teaspoon salt

Combine the ingredients, tasting for seasoning.

Makes 2½ cups

'When chopping chillies if you happen to rub your hand in your eyes, quickly rub your eyes on somebody else's hair and that will get rid of the pain.'

Pollo Pibil
Yucatán Barbecued Chicken

from Mary Carmen Dias

The lovely orange colour and mellow flavour of this barbecued chicken comes from *achiote*, a spice paste made with annatto popular in the Yucatán region. Serve this chicken and salsa inside corn tortillas. The marinade can also be used for prawns – simply marinate green prawns in the same way as the chicken, thread them onto bamboo skewers and cook on a barbecue with a little olive oil for just a few minutes.

4 chicken thigh fillets

½ x 100 g packet 'El Yucateco' *achiote* paste

juice of ½ orange

½ teaspoon salt

80 ml vegetable oil

1 red onion, finely sliced

2 tomatoes, sliced

RED ONION SALSA

1 red onion, finely sliced

1 tablespoon olive oil

½ tablespoon vinegar

splash of fresh orange juice

1 tablespoon dried oregano

salt

Prick the chicken thighs all over with a fork to allow the marinade to be absorbed. Using your hands, crumble the *achiote* paste into a wide bowl and add the orange juice and salt to make a smooth sauce. Thoroughly rub the mixture into the chicken.

Tear off 4 large squares of foil. Wrap each chicken thigh in foil. Refrigerate the parcels for at least 2 hours or ideally overnight.

Combine the salsa ingredients in a bowl and refrigerate for at least 1 hour so the onion softens a little.

Preheat the barbecue.

Heat the vegetable oil in a frying pan and sauté the onion until translucent. Add the tomato slices and fry them gently on both sides until just soft. Unwrap the chicken parcels and add some onion and tomato to each one, then rewrap.

Cook the parcels on the barbecue for about 20 minutes, being careful not to overcook the chicken. Turn the parcels over halfway through cooking. Unwrap the cooked parcels and serve the chicken in corn tortillas topped with the salsa.

Serves 4

'Never arrive early or on time if you are invited to a Mexican home – thirty minutes after the stipulated time is perfect.'

Sopa de Tortilla
Tortilla Soup

from Gina Castaneda

There's a nice depth of flavour in this soup, which comes from the roasted tomatoes and onion and from the raisin-like dried chillies called *pasilla*. Strips of crunchy, fried tortillas are added to the soup just before serving. Fetta is not traditional but it makes a good substitute for Mexican cheese.

3 ripe tomatoes, halved
½ onion
2 garlic cloves
3 dried *pasilla* chillies
1.5 litres chicken stock
oil
salt and pepper
8–10 corn tortillas, cut in half, then in strips
½ red onion, diced
150 g fetta, diced
2 avocados, diced
3 limes, halved
125 ml thick cream

Roast the tomatoes, onion and garlic in a cast-iron pan until charred. Toast the chillies by holding them with tongs over a gas flame (they may catch fire). This heightens their flavour. Soak the chillies in hot water until soft, then remove the seeds.

Puree the tomatoes, onion, garlic and 2 of the chillies in a blender with a bit of the stock until smooth. Heat a little oil in a frying pan and sauté the tomato puree for a few minutes, then remove from the heat.

Bring the remaining stock to the boil in a saucepan and stir in the tomato puree. Season with salt and pepper and cook, covered, over medium heat for 15 minutes.

Wipe out the frying pan and add a little more oil. Fry the tortilla strips in batches until golden brown. Remove and drain on paper towel.

Arrange the red onion, fetta, avocado and lime on a plate. Slice the remaining chilli and add to the plate. Put the cream in a bowl or jug.

Add some of the fried tortilla to the soup. Ladle the soup into bowls and garnish with more tortilla. Each person can add red onion, fetta, avocado, lime, chilli and cream to taste.

Serves 6

'No pregnant women can help make tamales or they won't cook evenly and will be *pintos* (spotted).'

Mole Verde (Green Sauce) with Pork

from Kimberley Chiswell

Tender pork cooked in a beautiful, fresh green *mole*, ingeniously coloured by the pumpkin seeds, vegetables, green chillies and herbs. Serve with Mexican rice and corn tortillas.

1 kg pork leg meat, cut into 2 cm cubes

1 bay leaf

½ small onion

salt

3 tablespoons sesame seeds

50 g almonds

100 g pumpkin seeds

15 spring onions, roughly chopped

1 garlic clove

400 g tin tomatillos

1 large green capsicum, seeded and roughly chopped

2 hot green chillies

1 bunch coriander, roughly chopped

ground cumin

pepper

olive oil

Place the pork in a saucepan with the bay leaf, onion and salt. Cover with water and bring to the boil, then simmer until tender (approximately 1 hour).

Toast the sesame seeds in a dry frying pan until golden. Remove from the pan and repeat with the almonds and then the pumpkin seeds. Puree the seeds and nuts in a blender with a little water from the pork. Set aside.

Put the spring onions, garlic, tomatillos, capsicum, chilli and coriander in the blender with cumin, salt and pepper to taste. Add 2 cups of water from the pork and puree to a bright green sauce.

Heat a little oil in a saucepan and fry the seed and nut mixture for a few minutes. Add the green sauce and simmer for 5 minutes. Add the cooked pork and simmer for a few more minutes.

Serves 6

Mexican Hot Chocolate

from Yvonne de Keizer

We all love this thick, frothy chocolate with its hint of cinnamon. A *molinillo* (chocolate whisk) and a block of Mexican drinking chocolate are the perfect present for the cook with everything!

Place about a litre of milk and 90 g Mexican chocolate in a saucepan. Slowly bring to the boil, then reduce the heat to a slow simmer. Whisk the mixture using a *molinillo*: hold the *molinillo* between both hands and rub your hands together until the chocolate is dissolved and the milk is velvety and frothy. Pour into cups.

MOROCCO

One of the most seductive cuisines, Moroccan food casts its spell as soon as you inhale – your nose fills with wonderful wafts of cinnamon, cumin, paprika and saffron and the fresh, green scent of coriander and parsley. Moroccan expatriate kitchens hint at the smells that would hit you walking through the souks in Morocco, where brilliantly coloured spices are piled in pyramid shapes – a far cry from our neat little spice racks in gleaming Western supermarkets!

My discovery of the food of this part of Africa took place many years ago when, after a visit to Tunisia (one of the three countries of the Maghreb – the others are Algeria and Morocco), I found my longing for exotic places, food and customs very well sated. I later visited Morocco and found the same delicious food and the same generous opening up of one's home, which comes from the Islamic teaching that all guests should be welcomed and fed (how generous they are!). I was lucky enough to spend time with a family in a small village and to prepare meals with the women of the family. It's fair to say that my life's course was set from that moment.

On this trip ensued some of the most memorable meals of my life. Beside a campfire in the northern Sahara I shared a communal dish of fragrant, spicy couscous cooked with vegetables and a lamb sacrificed in our honour; on a Mediterranean beach I shared freshly caught fish cooked with spices over charcoal with local fishermen; and in a village in the High Atlas Mountains I enjoyed a luscious carrot salad made with cinnamon and orange juice. The simple wonder of the street food is also enough to make you swoon. *Brik al oeuf* has stayed in my memory as one of the best food combinations of all time – this flaky golden delight is made by cracking an egg onto a square of pastry, adding generous spoonfuls of harissa, tuna and capers, then folding it all up and frying in oil. It is eaten hot with the yolk still runny. Marvellous!

The same warmth and generosity I experienced in Morocco is shown in expatriate homes. Your hands are cleaned and perfumed with orange-blossom water at the front door, then fresh dates stuffed with almonds are offered as the first of numerous traditional dishes prepared for you with love and care. Shut your eyes and you can almost imagine the desert at the back door.

Etiquette

With overwhelming hospitality and an abundance of beautifully prepared food come a few rules of etiquette:

At a Moroccan feast never serve couscous before other courses. It fills up the guests so they won't be able to eat more of the other lovely dishes to come.

Never say no to food offered at a dinner party even if you don't like the dish on offer. You must try at least one or two mouthfuls, otherwise you will be regarded as snobbish and rude.

Most sensible Moroccans never eat meals consisting of chickpeas or fava beans before an important date for the sake of the other participants!

In Morocco it is traditional to eat with your hands. This requires some rules and great skill. The idea is to form a couscous ball with the three fingers and thumb of the right hand, then to pop the couscous ball into your mouth without your fingers coming into contact with your lips. Never use the left hand.

Refrain from eating garlic during the month of Ramadan – this will prevent 'garlic breath' throughout the fasting days when you do not drink water or eat between sun-up and sun-down.

Always say 'B'smilah' ('In the name of Allah') before the start of a meal.

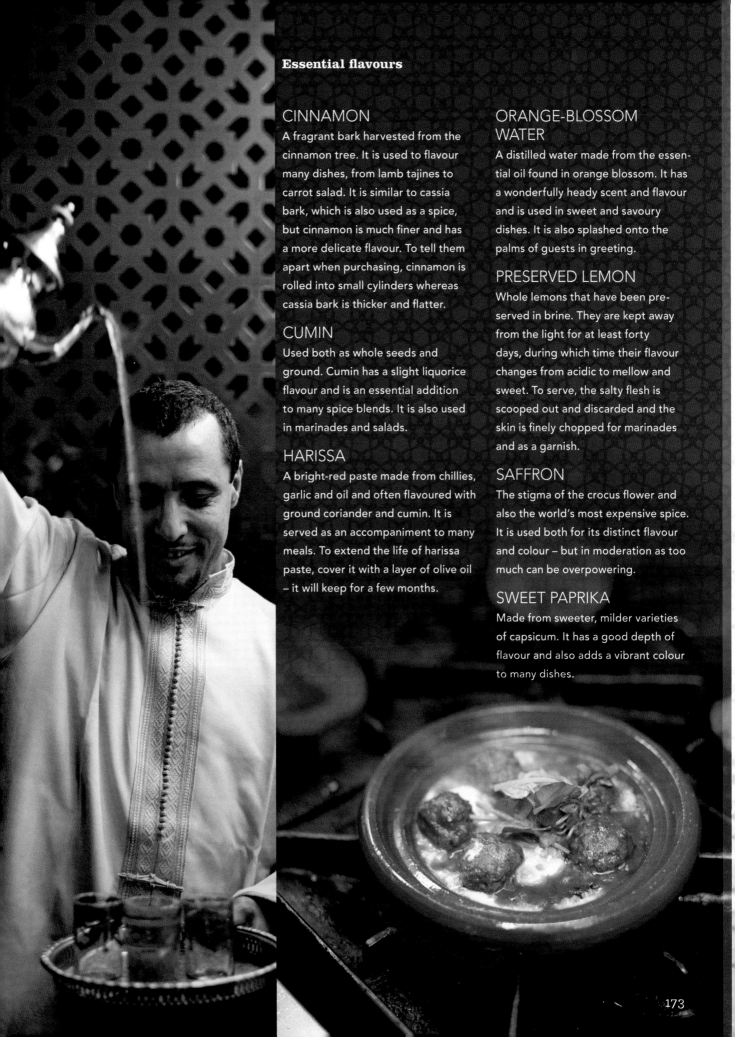

Essential flavours

173

CINNAMON

A fragrant bark harvested from the cinnamon tree. It is used to flavour many dishes, from lamb tajines to carrot salad. It is similar to cassia bark, which is also used as a spice, but cinnamon is much finer and has a more delicate flavour. To tell them apart when purchasing, cinnamon is rolled into small cylinders whereas cassia bark is thicker and flatter.

CUMIN

Used both as whole seeds and ground. Cumin has a slight liquorice flavour and is an essential addition to many spice blends. It is also used in marinades and salads.

HARISSA

A bright-red paste made from chillies, garlic and oil and often flavoured with ground coriander and cumin. It is served as an accompaniment to many meals. To extend the life of harissa paste, cover it with a layer of olive oil – it will keep for a few months.

ORANGE-BLOSSOM WATER

A distilled water made from the essential oil found in orange blossom. It has a wonderfully heady scent and flavour and is used in sweet and savoury dishes. It is also splashed onto the palms of guests in greeting.

PRESERVED LEMON

Whole lemons that have been preserved in brine. They are kept away from the light for at least forty days, during which time their flavour changes from acidic to mellow and sweet. To serve, the salty flesh is scooped out and discarded and the skin is finely chopped for marinades and as a garnish.

SAFFRON

The stigma of the crocus flower and also the world's most expensive spice. It is used both for its distinct flavour and colour – but in moderation as too much can be overpowering.

SWEET PAPRIKA

Made from sweeter, milder varieties of capsicum. It has a good depth of flavour and also adds a vibrant colour to many dishes.

Mechoui (Barbecued Lamb) with Minted Yoghurt

from Aziz Bakalla

Here is a dead-easy marinade for lamb that is full of incredible flavour. The cool taste of mint and the tang of yoghurt team beautifully with the barbecued meat. As well as backstraps or fillets, you can try this with chops.

1 kg lamb backstraps or fillets,
cut into long strips about 2 cm wide

1 tablespoon ground cumin

1 tablespoon sweet paprika

2 tablespoons chopped garlic

1 tablespoon chopped coriander

1 tablespoon chopped flat-leaf parsley

1 tablespoon lemon juice

generous drizzle of olive oil

salt

MINTED YOGHURT

1 cup natural yoghurt

¼ teaspoon sugar

3 teaspoons chopped mint

Put the lamb in a bowl and add the remaining ingredients. Use your hands to thoroughly coat the lamb. Cover and refrigerate for 1 hour.

Combine the ingredients for the minted yoghurt in a blender and keep cold in the refrigerator until ready to serve.

Barbecue the lamb to medium–rare and serve with the yoghurt.

Serves 4

Cheat's Couscous with Seven Vegetables

from Saana Zaki

The secret to making the best instant couscous is in the steaming method. The couscous absorbs the fragrant steam from the ingredients being cooked below to become light and fluffy. (Moroccans say that couscous that has been made only by absorbing boiling water is 'uncooked' and they marvel that many people have yet to discover the magic of true couscous.) As well as improving the flavour of the couscous, the vegetables in this dish look colourful and delicious together and the whole dish can be on the table in well under an hour. The other secret of great couscous is in the finishing touch – in Morocco this is *smen* (preserved butter), but Saana uses light blue-vein cheese to add the same little kick.

1 swede, cut into large chunks

1–2 parsnips, cut into large chunks

1–2 carrots, cut into large chunks

1–2 zucchini, cut into large chunks

small piece of pumpkin, skin left on, cut into large chunks

4 roma tomatoes

1 cup podded broad beans (fresh or frozen)

1 tablespoon ground coriander

1 tablespoon ground ginger

1 tablespoon ground cumin

1 tablespoon sweet paprika

handful of coriander sprigs

handful of flat-leaf parsley sprigs

1 litre stock (ideally homemade)

500 g instant couscous

2–3 tablespoons vegetable oil

1 teaspoon salt

150 g light blue-vein cheese (such as Blue Castello)

Put the vegetables (including the whole tomatoes and broad beans) in the bottom of a large pot that has a steam basket attachment. Add the spices, herbs and stock. Bring to the boil, cover with a lid and reduce the heat to a simmer.

Meanwhile, put the couscous in a bowl and add the vegetable oil. Stir with your hands to coat the grains. Add the salt and just enough water to moisten the grains but not drown them. Stir well so the grains absorb the water evenly. Transfer to the steam basket and place over the vegetables. Cover with a lid.

Once the couscous begins to steam, remove the basket and tip the couscous into a bowl. Crumble the cheese over the couscous and stir so it melts through. Sprinkle on a little more water and stir again. Return the couscous to the basket.

Place back over the pot of vegetables, cover with a lid and wait until the couscous begins to steam again. Tip the couscous onto a large platter and spoon over the vegetables and a little stock.

Serves 6

'Among walnuts only empty ones speak.'

'What you have put into
your pot comes out on
your apron.'

Chicken Tajine with Preserved Lemon and Olives

from Hassan M'souli

This dish is wonderful. Although it takes a little while to prepare, all that fades when you bring the tajine to the table, lift off the conical lid and watch as your family and friends take a deep, satisfied breath. Serve with couscous and harissa. Like curries, it is even better on the second day.

CHERMOULA MARINADE

2 garlic cloves, chopped

½ preserved lemon, rind only, rinsed and finely sliced

2 onions, chopped

½ small red chilli

1 tablespoon sweet paprika

1 tablespoon ground cumin

2 tablespoons chopped coriander

2 tablespoons chopped flat-leaf parsley

2 bay leaves, torn in half

½ teaspoon saffron threads, soaked in a little water

125 ml olive oil

salt

1 small chicken (1–1.2 kg)

2 tomatoes, 1 chopped, 1 sliced

2 onions, 1 chopped, 1 sliced

2 large potatoes, cut into wedges

150 g pitted green olives

1 bunch coriander, chopped

250 ml water

1 preserved lemon, rind only,
rinsed and cut into 6 or 8 wedges

Combine the marinade ingredients in a food processor and blend until finely chopped and thoroughly combined. Leave for 30 minutes before using (or you can make this up to 7 days in advance and store it in the refrigerator).

Wash and dry the chicken. Cut out the backbone and trim off the wing tips and any excess fat. Chop into pieces. Place in a bowl and rub with half of the marinade. Refrigerate for at least 2 hours or ideally overnight.

Combine the chopped tomato and onion with a little more marinade and spread over the base of a tajine (this will prevent the chicken from burning on the bottom). Arrange the chicken pieces in the centre of the tajine. Coat the potato wedges in a little more marinade and arrange around the chicken. Top with the sliced onion, then the sliced tomato, and push the olives into the gaps. Combine the remaining marinade with the coriander and water and pour over the top. Decorate with preserved lemon wedges.

Cover the tajine with the lid and cook over a very low heat on the stove for 45 minutes. Don't stir or lift the lid during cooking.

Take the tajine to the table and serve with couscous and harissa.

Serves 6

'A peacock has too little in its head and too much in its tail.'

Bissara
Fava-bean Dip

from Aziz Bakalla

Served warm as part of a mezze selection, *bissara* is a delicious and mellow dip. With its simple but effective spicing it is a low-cost, high-protein comfort food – and it's easy to make too. The recipe uses dried, split fava beans (broad beans), which are yellow; dried whole fava beans still have their skins on and are browny-green.

2 cups dried split fava beans
(broad beans), soaked overnight

olive oil

1 tablespoon chopped garlic

ground cumin

1.5 litres water

salt and pepper

sweet paprika

1 black olive

Drain the beans and pick out any discoloured ones.

Heat 2 tablespoons of oil in a saucepan and fry the garlic until fragrant. Stir in 3 teaspoons of cumin then add the beans and water. Cover and bring to the boil then reduce the heat to a simmer. Cook until the beans have absorbed all the water and have broken down to a smooth, velvety puree, like thick soup. Season with salt and pepper and pour into a serving bowl. Garnish with paprika and extra cumin. Place an olive in the centre and drizzle with more olive oil. Serve with flatbread.

Makes 3–4 cups

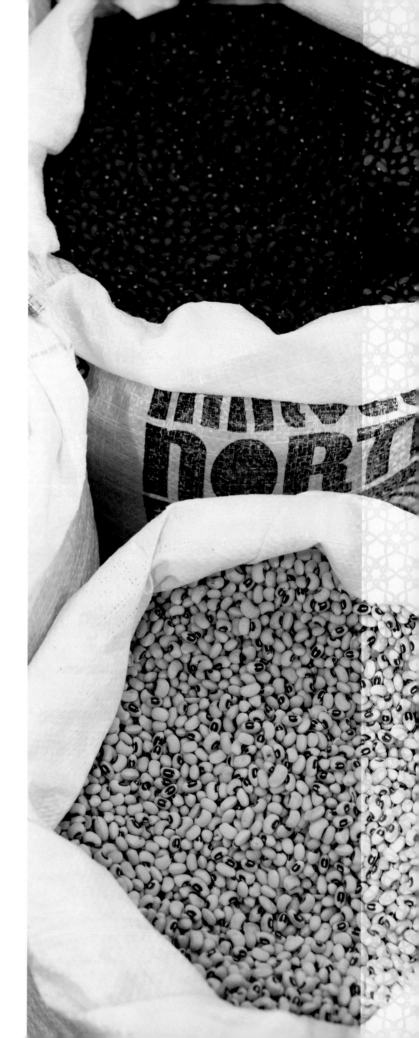

'Without fingers the
hand would be a spoon.'

Carrot and Orange Salad

from Sara Ennaim

Put any ideas out of your head of a delicate salad lightly tossed in a little dressing – this version is a lot more liquid! In fact it is so full of juice that it's served in tea glasses or bowls with small spoons. The combination of fresh flavours wakes up the tastebuds and it is great as an appetiser or between courses in a Moroccan banquet. Make sure you get carrots that are snap-fresh.

500 g carrots, peeled
4 oranges
75 g (⅓ cup) sugar
1 tablespoon orange-blossom water
1 teaspoon cinnamon

Grate or finely chop the carrots in a food processor. Place the carrot in a bowl and squeeze the oranges over the top. Add the sugar, orange-blossom water and cinnamon and mix together.

Serves 6

Fruit Salad with Moroccan Dressing

from Omar Majdi

This is the perfect end to a banquet – sweet, refreshing and warm with the spice of cassia. Use colourful seasonal fruit such as grapes, rockmelon, apple, pear, mandarin and banana and make the dressing in advance if you like as it keeps for at least a week in the refrigerator.

DRESSING

250 ml water
3 tablespoons sugar
small piece of cassia bark
2 tablespoons lemon juice
½ tablespoon orange-blossom water

mixed seasonal fruit, cut into chunks
10 mint leaves, torn

Place the dressing ingredients in a saucepan and bring to the boil, then reduce the heat and simmer for 5 minutes. Leave to cool then refrigerate for 1 hour. Mix the fruit and mint with the dressing.

PAKISTAN

One of the things I enjoy most about finding out about different cuisines is the opportunity to spend time in other people's kitchens. In Pakistani homes I've learned many new and intriguing things, one of which is that women mix up chapattis (thin, round disks of unleavened whole-wheat bread) every morning then cook them on a heavy griddle to have hot for breakfast. To them it is as easy as pouring cereal into a bowl – and much more delicious.

In Pakistani food, spices are treasured, used cleverly and replenished every couple of weeks. Spicing is a measure of the esteem in which one holds a guest – I've learned that when presenting dishes such as the classic biryani (a spectacular combination of spiced rice cooked with meat), Pakistani people love to see the whole threads of saffron strewn among the toasted nuts and fresh herbs that characteristically garnish this masterpiece. When it comes to sweets, especially the beautiful reduced-milk sweets and *burfis*, edible gold and silver leaf are used to signify importance and these precious materials are widely used for wedding feasts.

Although the country of Pakistan is relatively new (it was partitioned from India in 1947), the cuisine of the region has developed over centuries and incorporates elements from neighbouring India, Afghanistan and Iran. It is also heavily influenced by the predominantly Muslim population. Its blend of Indian, Far Eastern and Middle Eastern cooking techniques creates a simply beautiful cuisine.

Some of the key dishes are slow cooked – the famous *haleem* (a mix of grains, pulses, lamb and spices) is cooked for up to seven hours. I love the way Pakistanis use the phrase '*Haleem* – king of curries' as a mark of the respect they have for this rich comfort food. It is lovely and viscous, garnished with the fresh tastes of lemon, coriander and ginger and scooped up with Pakistan's favourite accompaniment – bread. This is either leavened naan that has been cooked in a tandoor oven, or unleavened chapattis or roti that have been cooked on the stove top.

As well as great bread, Pakistanis also produce some of the best rice in the world – their long-grain basmati rice is especially prized and is used to make biryani.

Sweets are as generous as the chefs in Pakistan and are rich with ghee, sugar and nuts such as pistachios and almonds. *Halwa* (meaning 'sweet') is one of the most popular sweets and can be made with flour or semolina, or even carrot or pumpkin. Many sweets are infused with fragrant essences like rosewater or crushed cardamom pods – delicate, exotic and a beautiful finish to a Pakistani feast.

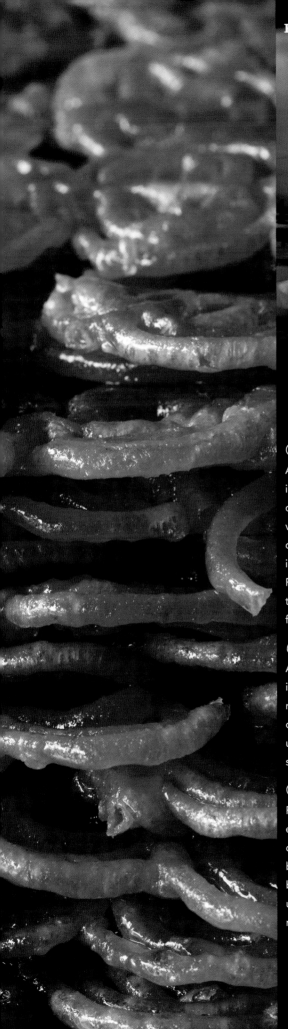

CARDAMOM

A dried seed pod from a herb belonging to the ginger family, cardamom comes in both green and brown varieties. Green cardamom pods are crushed to release the black seeds inside and are used extensively in Pakistani cuisine. Stronger in flavour, the larger brown variety is reserved for meat and vegetable dishes.

CHAAT MASALA

A sour blend of spices typically including *amchur* (dried green-mango powder), dried ginger, cumin, coriander and black pepper. This is used for the favourite fried dough snacks called *chaat*.

CUMIN

Regular brown cumin or the more exotic black cumin are used in many dishes including curries, rice dishes, breads and chutney. The seeds can be ground or used whole. They are usually toasted before use to release their flavour.

DAL

Dried beans, peas and lentils (whether whole or split) are known as 'dal'. They are a staple in Pakistani cuisine and are high in both protein and fibre. There are many varieties including *urid*, *chana*, *mung*, *toor* and *masoor* dal. Once cooked as a dish they are referred to as 'dhal'.

DRIED PLUMS

These impart a rich, tart flavour and are often used in dishes like biryani.

DRIED POMEGRANATE SEEDS

These seeds have a lovely sweet and sour flavour and are used both whole and ground.

GARAM MASALA

A toasted and ground mixture of spices that includes cumin, coriander seed, chilli and cardamom. Try to buy the freshest spices and make just the amount you need – the fragrance and flavour of the masala will deteriorate over time.

GHEE

Clarified butter with a higher burning point than unclarified butter and most oils. It is adored in curries, slathered on hot naan and used in sweets.

SAFFRON

The hand-picked red stigma of the crocus flower. Saffron is the most expensive spice in the world and is believed to have been first cultivated in Kashmir in the third century. Loved for its unique flavour and colouring ability, it is used extensively in curries, biryani and Pakistani sweets.

Mantu
from Basil Daniell

Beautiful little dumplings that are perfect starters or great party food – they're easy to make and fun for children too. Basil grew up with these in Pakistan and devised his recipe using the readily available wonton wrappers. They are served with yoghurt and parsley, although you can also add a dollop of dhal.

3 tablespoons vegetable oil or clarified butter (ghee)

500 g lean minced lamb

4 onions, finely chopped

2 teaspoons finely chopped garlic

½ teaspoon ground coriander

1 teaspoon ground cumin

¼ teaspoon chilli powder

½ teaspoon salt

40 Shanghai (square white) wonton wrappers

natural yoghurt

chopped flat-leaf parsley

Heat the oil or ghee in a wok or frying pan and add the lamb. Fry over low heat until lightly browned, stirring to separate the meat. Add the onion and stir-fry until it is translucent. Add the garlic, spices and salt and stir-fry for another 3 minutes or until fragrant. Transfer to a bowl to cool.

Place a heaped teaspoon of lamb filling in the middle of a wonton wrapper. Brush the edges with a little water and draw two opposite corners together to meet in the middle. Draw in the other two corners and seal the edges. You should have a square pouch. Repeat with the remaining wrappers and filling.

Place the *mantu* in a steamer, making sure they don't touch, and steam for 10 minutes. Top each *mantu* with a spoonful of yoghurt and a sprinkling of parsley.

Makes 40 *Mantu*

Dhal
from Basil Daniell

An easy dhal that can be served as a side dish to any curry or as an accompaniment to *mantu*.

200 g red lentils

1 litre water

¼–1 teaspoon chilli powder

1 teaspoon ground coriander

1 teaspoon salt

2 tablespoons clarified butter (ghee) or vegetable oil

2 garlic cloves, bruised

1–2 dried chillies

Place the lentils and water in a large saucepan and bring to the boil. Reduce the heat to a simmer and skim off any scum that rises to the surface. Cover and simmer for 40–50 minutes, or until the lentils are soft and the water has been absorbed. Stir in the chilli powder, ground coriander and salt.

Heat the ghee or oil in a small frying pan until very hot. Add the garlic and dried chillies and fry until the garlic is golden, stirring constantly so it doesn't burn. Stir the garlic, chilli and oil into the lentils. Cover the dhal to retain the aromas until serving.

Serves 4

Tandoori Chicken

from Nighat Hussan

This recipe is from a beautiful Pakistani woman called Nighat who makes her own bread every morning and thinks nothing of catering for fifty people! The chicken with its incredible fresh mint sauce is simple and very, very delicious. Serve with roti, tomato and lettuce.

200 g natural yoghurt

1 tablespoon finely grated ginger

1 tablespoon crushed garlic

1 tablespoon tandoori paste

½ teaspoon tandoori food colouring (optional)

2 teaspoons ground cumin

2 teaspoons ground coriander

1 teaspoon garam masala

½ teaspoon chilli powder

½ teaspoon turmeric

salt

1 kg chicken breast or thigh fillets

MINT SAUCE

200 g natural yoghurt

1 bunch mint, roughly chopped

1 bunch coriander, roughly chopped

½ small onion, roughly chopped

1 tomato, roughly chopped

2 tablespoons dried pomegranate seeds, ground

1 teaspoon turmeric

chilli powder

salt

To prepare the chicken, combine the ingredients except for the chicken in a bowl, stirring until well combined. Add the chicken and coat well (the best way is to rub the mixture in with your hands). Marinate in the refrigerator for at least 2 hours.

To make the mint sauce, combine the ingredients in a blender, adding chilli powder and salt to taste. Blend until smooth.

Preheat the oven to its highest temperature. Bake the chicken for 20 minutes, then reduce the temperature to 120°C and cook until tender. Serve with the mint sauce.

Serves 4–6

Sindhi Biryani

from Sonya Kayani

A marvellous creation of layers of perfectly cooked goat curry, beautiful rice and a fresh mix of tomato, herbs and chilli, all decorated with nuts and onion rings. This is a feast in its own right, but Sonya likes to serve it with a chopped salad called a *cachumbar* containing tomato, red onion, lettuce and vinegar, and with a yoghurt raita containing mint and cumin.

vegetable oil

3 medium onions, finely sliced

1 kg boneless goat meat, cut into large cubes

3 tablespoons grated ginger

1 tablespoon crushed garlic

100 g natural yoghurt

1 tablespoon chilli powder

2 teaspoons turmeric

2 teaspoons sweet paprika

1 tablespoon ground coriander

2 heaped teaspoons ground cumin

2 teaspoons cumin seeds

10 cloves

4 cinnamon sticks

14 green cardamom pods

3 brown cardamom pods

5 bay leaves

10 dried plums

1 tablespoon salt

8 peppercorns, ground

4 long green chillies, 3 left whole, 1 finely sliced

3 medium potatoes

500 g basmati rice, soaked for 30 minutes

1 tablespoon saffron threads, soaked briefly in milk

3 medium tomatoes, cut into thin wedges

1 bunch coriander, chopped

1 bunch mint, chopped

onion rings, fried until dark brown and caramelised

25 g sultanas

25 g slivered almonds

25 g walnuts

25 g cashews

Heat a little vegetable oil in a large saucepan and fry the onion until golden brown. Add the goat and fry for a few minutes. Stir in the ginger and garlic, then add the yoghurt, ground spices, whole spices (reserve 8 green cardamom pods for the rice), bay leaves, dried plums, salt and pepper. Add the whole chillies and 250 ml of water. Cover and simmer for 45 minutes.

Meanwhile, boil the potatoes whole until tender, then drain and cut in half. Keep warm. Drain the rice and boil with the reserved cardamom. When cooked, drain and put half into a bowl. Add the saffron milk and stir until the rice is evenly yellow. Keep the plain and saffron rice warm.

Combine the tomato, coriander, mint and sliced green chilli. Add one-third of the tomato mixture to the goat curry. Cover and cook for a further 5–10 minutes.

Spoon half of the plain rice onto a large serving platter. Top with the goat curry. Spoon over half of the saffron rice and scatter with half of the remaining tomato mixture. Scatter with the boiled potatoes, then add final layers of plain rice and saffron rice. Scatter with the fried onion. Top with the remaining tomato mixture then sprinkle over the sultanas and nuts. Serve immediately.

Serves 6

Haleem –
'King of Curries'

from Javed Chaudry

This is the ultimate slow-cooked wonder, full of gentle spices and warm comfort, and a Pakistani favourite. *Haleem* gets its lovely sticky consistency from constant stirring, so give yourself up to the hypnotic cooking and enjoy the aromas as you do.

½ cup each of *chana* dal, *urid* dal, *mung* dal and barley

½ cup wheat berries

1 kg beef or lamb on the bone, meat cut into chunks

2 tablespoons crushed garlic

2 tablespoons grated ginger

2.5 litres water

2 tablespoons clarified butter (ghee)

pinch of saffron colour (optional)

¼ teaspoon ground fenugreek

1 tablespoon ground coriander

1 tablespoon ground cumin

1 tablespoon *chaat masala* spice mix

1 tablespoon chilli powder

1 teaspoon turmeric

salt

125 ml vegetable oil

2 onions, sliced

1 tablespoon garam masala

TO SERVE

chaat masala spice mix

finely sliced green chilli

julienned ginger

coriander leaves

sliced lemon

Soak the dal and barley together overnight. Partly crush the wheat berries in a mortar and pestle and soak for 1½ hours.

Put the lentils and grains, meat and bones, garlic, ginger and water in a large, heavy-based pot and bring to the boil. Simmer for around 2 hours, stirring occasionally.

Remove the bones and continue to cook until the meat starts to fall apart (about another hour).

Add the ghee, saffron colour, fenugreek, coriander, cumin, *chaat masala*, chilli powder, turmeric and salt and cook for another hour, stirring regularly to help the ingredients break down and blend into each other. The stew will start to look very thick and sticky.

Heat the vegetable oil in a frying pan and fry the onion until brown and caramelised. Add the onion (reserving ¼ cup) and garam masala to the stew. Cook for a further 15 minutes.

Scoop onto plates and garnish with the remaining fried onions, *chaat masala*, chilli, ginger, coriander and lemon. Serve with roti, naan or chapattis.

Serves 8

Carrot *Halwa*

from Sumaira Cheema

This is an incredibly easy version of this tasty sweet, best eaten warm when the cardamom is most fragrant.

1 kg carrots, grated
100 g clarified butter (ghee), plus 1 tablespoon extra
7 cardamom pods, cracked, husks discarded
15 almonds, cut into thin slivers
15 pistachios, cut into thin slivers
200 g sugar
⅓ cup milk powder
2 tablespoons cream

Steam the grated carrot for 10 minutes until fairly soft. (Alternatively, you can cook the carrot in a microwave.)

Melt 100 g of ghee in a non-stick frying pan over high heat. Add the cardamom seeds and fry for 2 minutes until fragrant. Add the carrot and fry over high heat for another 2 minutes. Add most of the almonds and pistachios and keep frying, stirring occasionally, until the ghee starts to separate from the carrot. Add the sugar and mix well. Turn the heat back to medium and cook for another 5 minutes.

Soften the extra ghee in a small saucepan and add the milk powder and cream, stirring until well combined. Add to the carrots and stir over high heat for another 2 minutes. Serve hot or warm garnished with the remaining nuts and a scoop of vanilla ice cream.

Serves 4

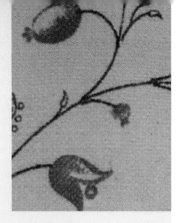

'Always brown the onions in whatever dish you are making – this is fundamental to getting the right taste.'

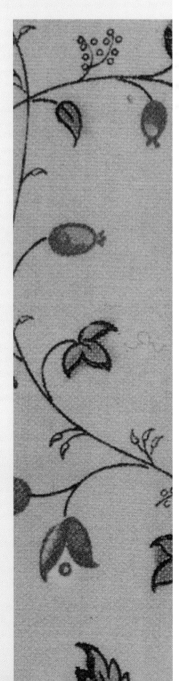

PERSIAN

Of all the cuisines I've explored, Persian would have to be the one I found most surprising – its wide range of ingredients are used to create some very unusual dishes. Persia was one of the ancient empires of the earth and its people have produced beautiful food for thousands of years. High-lights include exquisite rice dishes flavoured with saffron and studded with green pistachios, stews prepared with dried limes and handfuls of fragrant herbs, kebabs fit for a sultan, sweets that melt in your mouth … and some really 'out there' dishes as well.

One treasured Persian tradition is *dizi*. Named after the small metal pot it's cooked in, this is a slow-cooked dish of meat, dried beans, a few spices, a little fat and water. Once cooked the liquid is poured out and eaten like a soup with bread. Then a metal masher that looks like a tall mushroom is used to squash the soft meat and beans that remain in the *dizi* and the result, which some devotees have called 'Persian pâté', is served with bread, fresh mint and slivers of red onion. This was customarily a meal adored by labourers as it sustained them through a long working day – I loved seeing some of the glossy young members of the Persian community tucking into hearty *dizi* too.

Also typical of Persia – and unusual – is a sweet called *falooda*, said to be the only thing capable of cooling you down on a 40-degree Tehran day. It's like an exotic slushie made with crushed ice and vermicelli noo-dles, which freeze in the icy mix. When you start eating the noodles they soften in your mouth.

At the pinnacle of all these great food experiences are the excellent kebabs, which are adored, and top kebab makers are in great demand – to skewer the fine lean meat for *barg* or lamb fillet kebab, to mould the minced meat on a sword-like skewer for *koobideh kebab*, to marinate the meat and to cook up to forty kebabs at a time, making sure they cook evenly and perfectly over charcoal or gas.

There is so much in Persian cuisine that is delightful – even the rice. Called 'pearls of Persian cuisine', rice is the centre of the meal rather than a side dish and it is exceptional – fragrant and fluffy, with each grain long and perfect. This is the result of using aged rice, which is at least two to three years old. Saffron is also prized and is used cleverly – I love seeing my friend Nadia grind a few precious strands with a little sugar and then soak it in some water; the saffron-flavoured liquid is then used for cooking rice, or it's added to chicken dishes or mixed through butter. In fact, Persian people seem to be surrounded by the scent of saffron, as well as rosewater … Divine.

Essential flavours

DRIED BARBERRIES
A dried fruit that looks like a cranberry grown mainly in the South Khorasan province of Iran. Its sour taste may be mellowed by adding sugar when cooking.

DRIED LIME
These limes are a low-acid variety that are salted then dried, before being sold whole or powdered. Buy whole limes, which are light as a feather, and crack them open before adding to stews to release maximum flavour. They soften and add a deep, musky and slightly sweet note after slow cooking.

PISTACHIOS
Due to its perfect hot, dry climate, these nuts have been grown and highly prized in Iran since ancient times. The principal producing area is Kerman, which is located in the arid southeast. Iranian pistachios are greener and more flavoursome than those grown else-where and they're widely used to garnish food or in many biscuit and dessert recipes. In any Iranian house-hold, pistachios are always offered to guests.

ROSEWATER
Prized for many centuries, rosewater and rose petals are used to scent, flavour and decorate many foods, particularly sweet desserts and biscuits. Rosewater syrup is the basis of many refreshing drinks.

SAFFRON
With its exotic aroma and flavour, Persian food, from starters and entrees through to desserts, relies on this beautiful spice. Iran is the largest producer of saffron in the world and Persian saffron is said to be the strongest in flavour and colour.

Zereshk Polow
Barberry Rice

from Nadia Sajadi

Known as 'celebration rice' or 'jewelled rice', this is often cooked for weddings. It is made with wild, red barberries (*zereshk*), which give the dish its jewel-like appearance and an exotic, slightly tart taste.

4 cups long-grain rice, rinsed

4 tablespoons salt

3 pinches saffron threads

sugar

½ teaspoon turmeric

¼ teaspoon sweet paprika

½ teaspoon *baharat*

¼ teaspoon black pepper

1 teaspoon salt

2 garlic cloves, crushed

1 tablespoon lemon juice

1 chicken, quartered

1 onion, finely sliced

olive oil

1 large potato, sliced

4 tablespoons butter

1 cup dried barberries, rinsed

2 tablespoons almonds, cut into slivers

2 tablespoons pistachios, cut into slivers

Rinse the rice and put in a bowl with the salt. Cover with water. Soak for 1–2 hours.

Meanwhile, place the saffron and a small pinch of sugar in a mortar and grind to a fine powder. Place in a cup and fill one-third full with hot water. Set aside.

Combine the spices, pepper and salt in a small bowl. Add the garlic, lemon juice, 250 ml of hot water and a tablespoon of the saffron water. Stir well.

Preheat the oven to 160°C. Wash the chicken, pat dry and place in a deep baking tray. Scatter with the onion and pour over the spice and garlic mixture. Cover with foil and bake for 1 hour.

Three-quarters fill a large saucepan with water and bring to the boil. Drain the rice and add to the water with 2–3 tablespoons of olive oil if desired to stop the grains sticking to each other. Boil the rice for 10–15 minutes stirring gently a few times, until al dente. Drain in a colander.

Put the pot back on the stove and add 3–4 tablespoons of oil. Lay the sliced potato in the base (to protect the rice, but also to create a delicious edible crust of rice and potato). Top with the drained rice and cover with a lid. Cook until the rice begins to steam (about 3–5 minutes), then turn the heat to low and wrap the lid in a tea towel (covering the underside) and place back on the pot. The tea towel catches the condensation, stopping it from dripping back onto the rice. Leave to steam for 45–60 minutes. By the end you should have perfect, fluffy, separated rice.

Meanwhile heat half the butter in a frying pan and add the barberries. Sauté for a few minutes then add 2 tablespoons of sugar and 2 tablespoons of the saffron water. Stir briefly then remove from the heat.

Place a layer of rice on a serving platter, followed by a sprinkling of barberries, nuts and a little saffron water. Keep layering, mounding up into the shape of a cone. Leave some barberries and nuts for the top. Melt the remaining butter and mix together in a bowl with the remaining saffron water. Mix in a large dollop rice.

Arrange the chicken quarters around the platter then spoon the saffron rice on top of the mound. Add a final sprinkling of barberries and nuts.

Serves 4 - 6

Zereshk Polow

Kashk-e Bademjan
Grilled Eggplant and Cheese Dip
from Afsaneh Charani

In Persian households this is made every morning ready for lunch – the sound of the chopping of walnuts and parsley for the topping echoes throughout Persian neighbourhoods. The salty *kashk* cheese is a fermented by-product from cheese making and is available from Middle Eastern grocery stores. With its strong flavour it resembles a liquid fetta cheese and is lovely mixed with the golden eggplant and dried mint.

olive oil

4 eggplants, peeled and finely sliced

1 onion, finely chopped

1 heaped teaspoon turmeric

3 garlic cloves, finely chopped

2 tablespoons dried mint

2 tablespoons *kashk*

salt and pepper

chopped walnuts

chopped flat-leaf parsley

Heat 2 tablespoons of oil in a non-stick frying pan until really hot, then fry the eggplant until soft and golden. Drain on paper towel. Add the onion with a little more oil to the pan and fry until translucent, then stir in the turmeric. Push the onion to one side and add the garlic. Fry until fragrant then push to another side of the pan. Remove the pan from the heat, add the mint and fry briefly in the remaining heat.

Put the eggplant in a bowl and mash.

Heat a little more oil in a saucepan and add the eggplant, *kashk*, most of the onion, garlic and mint (reserve some of each for garnish), and salt and pepper. Warm the ingredients through and combine. Spoon into a serving bowl and top with the remaining onion, garlic and mint. Sprinkle with walnuts and parsley and serve warm.

Makes 3–4 cups

Qormeh Sabzi
from Jason Aghamri

Qormeh sabzi is a delicious Persian *khoresh*, or stew. *Sabzi* is the herb mix integral to the dish and includes parsley, coriander, garlic chives and fresh or dried fenugreek leaves. The herbs are added in mountains and it's no wonder the dish turns a marvellously dark green – and the aroma of fenugreek fills the house (be warned!). This recipe is cooked with duck, but it can also be cooked with chicken or lamb – or you could even do a vegetarian version.

2½ tablespoons clarified butter (ghee) or vegetable oil

1 large onion, chopped

1 duck, chopped into large pieces

pinch of turmeric

100 g flat-leaf parsley, chopped

100 g garlic chives, chopped

50 g coriander, chopped

50 g dried fenugreek leaves

chicken stock or water

6 dried limes, cracked

200 g cooked kidney beans

salt and pepper

Heat the ghee or oil in a large, heavy-based saucepan over medium heat. Add the onion and stir for a few minutes until it softens. Add the duck pieces and turmeric and fry until the duck is golden brown. Remove the duck from the pan.

Add the fresh herbs and dried fenugreek to the pan and fry, stirring, until the herbs darken. Return the duck to the pot and add stock or water to just cover the meat. Add the dried lime and kidney beans and bring to the boil. Season with salt and pepper. Simmer for 1½ hours. Serve with rice.

Serves 6

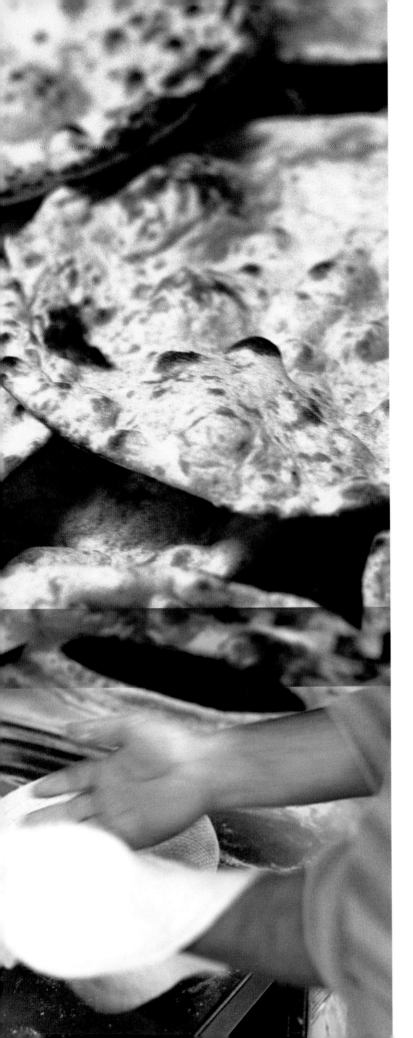

Falooda

from *Jalal Dastyari*

Falooda is Iran's take on the slushie and it is perfect on hot days. Ice made from frozen sugar syrup is crushed and mixed with rice noodles and rosewater, and topped with lime juice or with strawberry, sour cherry or pomegranate syrup (available from Middle Eastern stores). It is deliciously refreshing!

1 litre water

250 g sugar (or more to taste)

180 g rice vermicelli, cooked and drained

2 teaspoons rosewater

fresh lime juice or strawberry, sour cherry or pomegranate syrup

Heat the water and sugar, stirring until the sugar dissolves. Leave to cool, then freeze in a block for 24 hours.

Once frozen solid, place the ice in a large metal bowl and crush it with a hard implement such as a large pestle (you might need to let the ice thaw a little). Then put gloves on and use your hands to crush further, until the ice is smooth. Add the rice vermicelli and mix through – the noodles will become hard. Add the rosewater. Scoop into glasses and drizzle each with a tablespoon of lime juice or a little fruit syrup and serve immediately.

Serves 6–8

'There is a loving thing people say at the end of the meal which is loosely translated as "May your hand be relieved of the pain of preparing all this," to which the cook replies "Salute to your soul and body."'

PORTUGAL

One of the things I find endlessly fascinating about food is that each cuisine is an edible snapshot of history. In Portugal the country's fortunes changed with two simple ingredients – cod, caught in the cold waters off Scandinavia, and salt. When combined these allowed cod to be preserved, which in turn fuelled a great nation of explorers who set off for new lands, opening trade routes and discovering new foods as they went. The Portuguese diaspora soon stretched into colonies in Angola and Mozambique in Africa, the Canary Islands off the African coast, the trading port of Goa in India, and Brazil in South America. And it all started with the beloved salted cod or *bacalhau,* which resembles a thick, smelly, salt-crusted parchment.

My friend Fatima has been entranced by this fish all her life – after it's been chopped into large chunks and soaked for twenty-four hours, you can start to see its magic too. Here is a perfectly white fish that flakes beautifully and can be used in a vast range of recipes. Fatima also adores the large, plump Portuguese sardines with their thick skins and decent layer of fat. She buries her sardines (bought frozen from Portuguese grocery stores) under rock salt in a baking dish and bakes them in the oven; once cooked she slides their skins off like a wetsuit and dresses the fillets with slivers of roasted capsicum, parsley and the lovely thick, green olive oil of Portugal. What a great Portuguese combination.

Actually the smell of sardines cooking over charcoal is my lasting memory of the country. In every small town terracotta braziers were smoking as this favourite fish was being simply grilled to accompany pale green Portuguese wine (*vinho verde*).

While the coastline bordering the Atlantic and Mediterranean is famous for great seafood dishes, inland the pig rules. People raise chickens and sheep as well but the pig is fundamental to much of the food and to village life. Villages spend time during winter slaughtering pigs and making numerous smallgoods, including the garlic- and paprika-laced *chouriço* sausage and the blood sausage *morcilla*.

Another edible slice of history is the now-familiar Portuguese chicken. It is hard not to love this flattened, marinated chicken, which is served with the chilli-spiked *piri piri* sauce – a recipe developed in Angola when it was a Portuguese colony. The dish became a big hit in Portugal and South Africa and is now making its way around the world like those early explorers.

Another familiar food from Portugal is the *pasteis de nata*, or custard tart. Like many popular desserts it is made largely from eggs and sugar, which create a creamy and luscious filling for crisp golden pastry. What a great gift to the world!

BACALHAU

Cod that has been dried then preserved in salt. It is said that in Portuguese cooking there is a different dish using *bacalhau* for every day of the year. It needs to be soaked for 24 hours in several changes of water before using – this reconstitutes the fish and removes excess salt.

BAY LEAVES

They can be bought as whole dried leaves or ground. Bay leaves are one of the few herbs that don't lose their flavour when dried, rather the flavour becomes more intense.

CHOURIÇO

A smoked pork sausage that is flavoured with garlic and paprika, which gives it a rich, red colour. *Chouriço* can be bought fresh or dried. One traditional way of heating and serving it is in an *asador* (a terracotta cooking dish). The *chouriço* sits in the *asador* on a rack and a type of Portuguese grappa is poured beneath it and set alight. This gives a wonderful smoky flavour to the sausage.

PAPRIKA

Known as *colorau* in Portuguese, this is without doubt the most widely used spice in Portuguese cooking. A sweet, smoked paprika is commonly used rather than a hot version.

QUINCE PASTE

A staple in every home and often served with a mild cheese. Children eat it on sandwiches and it is regarded by some as the Portuguese equivalent to Vegemite.

ROCK SALT

This salt is a larger crystal than regular salt and is widely used – chicken and beef are coated with rock salt before hitting the barbie and sardines are covered in it and baked.

195

Chanfana

from Cidalia Rendeiro

A gorgeous peasant recipe for lamb, which becomes incredibly tender after its bath in wine and paprika followed by slow cooking. Find the right pot and the work is done – it marinates, it cooks and you eat. What could be simpler. Serve with new potatoes boiled in their skins.

1 large onion, finely chopped

1 large head of garlic,
cloves separated, peeled and bruised

3 kg lamb shoulder, trimmed of excess fat,
cut into large chunks

rock salt

white pepper

dried bay leaves

sweet paprika

2 bottles red wine (or enough to cover the meat)

80 ml olive oil

1 bunch flat-leaf parsley

Scatter some of the onion in the base of a large casserole pot, followed by some garlic and a layer of lamb chunks. Sprinkle with rock salt, white pepper, a torn bay leaf and 1 teaspoon of paprika. Repeat the layers until all the lamb is used. Pour in red wine to cover the lamb. Cover the pot and leave to marinate for at least 4 hours, unrefrigerated.

Preheat the oven to 200°C. Check the wine level – you may need to top it up as the meat soaks some up while marinating. Pour over the olive oil and place the stems of parsley on top. Cover with a tight-fitting lid or foil, making sure the pot is well sealed around the edges. Cook for about 45 minutes (or until you can smell the wonderful aroma), then reduce the heat to 180°C and cook for another 2¼ hours.

Serves 6–8

'Cook what you feel like eating – it will turn out to be delicious.'

Charcoal Chicken with *Piri Piri* Sauce

from Luis Fernandez

This recipe is a derivation of the famous one from Angola, where Luis' grandmother devised a marinade and sauce that would later travel the world. Angola was of course a colony of Portugal and many Portuguese families were encouraged to settle there. The Fernandez family was one.

1 large chicken

8 garlic cloves, crushed

juice of 2 lemons

1 teaspoon bay leaf powder

2 teaspoons sweet paprika

80 ml scotch whisky

2 tablespoons butter, softened

rock salt

PIRI PIRI SAUCE

10–12 small red chillies, finely chopped (or less to taste)

pinch of salt

juice of ½ lemon

100 ml olive oil

2 tablespoons garlic powder
(fresh garlic makes the sauce too runny)

Trim the chicken of excess fat. Use a sharp knife or kitchen scissors to cut the chicken through the breastbone. Open the chicken out, turn over and flatten it by pressing down on the backbone. Make a small cut under each wing to help the chicken flatten further. Make several slashes in the flesh with a sharp knife to allow the flavours of the marinade to get in and the fat to drain out. Prick the chicken all over with a fork.

Combine the garlic, lemon juice, bay leaf powder, paprika, whisky and butter, mixing well. Brush the chicken on both sides with the mixture and sprinkle with rock salt. Cover and marinate in the refrigerator for 30–45 minutes.

Mix the *piri piri* ingredients into a thickish sauce.

Cook the chicken on a hot charcoal barbecue, turning frequently and basting continuously with the leftover marinade, for 30 minutes or until golden brown. Cut the chicken into pieces and brush with the *piri piri* sauce.

Serves 6

'Olive oil, bread and wine
are essential on any table.'

Bacalhau com Broa

from Fatima Barroso

A beautiful combination of thick white fish, little potatoes and a crunchy topping of cornbread (*broa*) crumbs. (This dense bread is available from Portuguese bakeries.) Perfect with a glass of mellow Portuguese red wine! Begin soaking the *bacalhau* the day before.

600 g thick *bacalhau* fillet

milk

½ red onion, cut into chunks

3 dried bay leaves

3 garlic cloves, 2 left whole, 1 chopped

1 teaspoon peppercorns

1 kg small new potatoes

olive oil

salt

1 red capsicum, cut into thin strips

4 brown onions, finely sliced

4 thick slices of cornbread

4 flat-leaf parsley stalks, leaves picked and chopped

3 egg yolks

¾ cup pitted black olives (Portuguese if possible)

Cover the *bacalhau* with water and soak for 24 hours, changing the water 3 times.

Drain the fish, place it in a saucepan and cover with milk. Add the red onion, bay leaves, whole garlic and peppercorns. Simmer gently for 20 minutes.

Meanwhile, roast the potatoes with olive oil and salt in a hot oven until golden brown. At the same time roast the strips of capsicum.

Heat more olive oil in a heavy-based saucepan and fry the sliced onion over high heat until browned. Reduce the heat and cook gently until soft and nearly caramelised.

Finely crumble the cornbread into a bowl and mix with the chopped garlic, parsley and egg yolks.

Remove the fish from the milk (the milk can be used on another occasion to make a bechamel sauce). Remove the skin and bones and break the fish into chunks.

Preheat the oven to 180°C. Place the roasted potatoes on a board and smash each one with your fist to flatten them. Lay them in a baking dish and cover with the fish chunks, followed by the soft onions and the breadcrumb mixture. Drizzle with olive oil and season with black pepper. Stud with olives and scatter with strips of roasted capsicum. Bake for 20–30 minutes. Drizzle with more olive oil before serving.

Serves 6

Bacalhau com Broa

Migas

from Andrea de Souza

This is a wonderful salad with its finely sliced dark green leaves, crunchy breadcrumbs, pine nuts, and beans for colour and texture. Great on its own or with grilled meat and Andrea says it's terrific with a classic Aussie barbecue!

1 bunch kale (Chinese broccoli is a good substitute), leaves only

3 tablespoons olive oil

1 garlic clove, cut in half

½ cup fresh breadcrumbs (preferably from Portuguese cornbread or a good sourdough)

½ cup pine nuts

¾ cup cooked black-eyed beans

salt and pepper

Wash the kale and pat dry. Place the leaves on top of each other and roll up into a tight cylinder. Use a sharp knife to shred the leaves very, very finely.

Heat the oil in a frying pan. Throw in the garlic and fry briefly to flavour the oil, then remove. Add the breadcrumbs and fry until golden brown. Add the kale, pine nuts and black-eyed beans and toss until heated through. Season with salt and pepper.

Serves 6

'As you read a recipe, learn to visualise how it will look and taste. Don't be afraid to change the ingredients according to your taste.'

Caramel Flan

from John De Almeida

A classic Portuguese dessert and easy to make! It is very similar to the French crème caramel.

CARAMEL

50–75 ml water

200 g sugar

CUSTARD

200 g sugar

12 eggs

1 litre milk

1 cinnamon stick

1 strip of lemon rind

1 teaspoon vanilla extract

To make the caramel, pour the water into a heavy-based saucepan and add the sugar, pouring it into the centre of the water so it doesn't touch the sides of the pan. Cook over medium heat for 10 minutes without stirring. The caramel will slowly colour from blonde to a rich, dark brunette. Pour into ramekins to set.

To make the custard, put the sugar in a bowl and whisk in the eggs one at a time until the mixture is slightly frothy.

Put the milk, cinnamon, lemon and vanilla in a saucepan and bring to boil, then remove from the heat and stir into the egg mixture, being careful not to over-stir.

Preheat the oven to 150°C. Strain the mixture into a jug, then pour into each ramekin, swirling as you do so the toffee doesn't crack in one spot. Place the ramekins in an ovenproof dish and fill the dish with water to halfway up the ramekins. Bake for 30 minutes, turning the dish around after 15 minutes so the flans cook evenly. Rest for 30 minutes before running a knife around the edges of the ramekins and turning the flans onto serving plates.

Makes 6–8 flans

Caramel Flan

SINGAPORE

When I think of Singapore, I think of spicy food being cooked and eaten in warm tropical air – wafts of *rempah* (spice paste) cooking; fish grilling; noodles being stir-fried; satay sticks being fanned over charcoal … This to me is heaven. Even now that air conditioning has moved a lot of the hawker centres (groups of small food stalls) inside, food and the quest for delicious specialities remain a national obsession.

Every taxi driver is a culinary expert – you can't say that about most countries but Singapore is unique. It started as a fishing village and morphed into one of Asia's most dynamic cities, a centre for some of the best food in Southeast Asia. Settlers and traders from China, India and Malaysia all brought their own cuisines to Singapore, which have flourished. A distinctly new cuisine has developed as well called Peranakan or Nyonya. This was the result of local Malay women marrying Chinese merchants and labourers – the fusion of Chinese Hokkien ingredients and Malay flavourings has resulted in hot and spicy dishes that often start with a *rempah* made from chilli, shallots, lemongrass, candlenuts, turmeric and *belachan* (shrimp paste).

My friend Helina remembers the days when the laksa man would either cycle or walk the streets, ready to assemble noodles, stock, coconut milk and more into a tasty dish served right at her door. She also recalls evenings watching Chinese operas while munching on the classic Singaporean salad called *rojak* (crunchy fruit and vegetables in a salty–sweet dressing sprinkled with peanuts); family celebrations with chicken rice (delicate poached chicken served with rice cooked in stock) as the centrepiece; and, in the days before blenders, mounds of aromatic herbs and spices being pounded before each meal.

As well as *rojak*, Singapore has many other distinctive dishes, including *otak-otak*, which is fish cooked with coconut milk, chilli paste, galangal and herbs then wrapped in a banana leaf; *poh pia*, which are soft spring rolls; fish-head curry, which is often eaten from a banana leaf; and the renowned Singapore chilli crab, which is stir-fried with tomato sauce, soy sauce, sugar and, of course, plenty of chilli.

Tropical fruit is a great way to finish a Singaporean banquet but this food obsessed country has many of its own dessert recipes as well, including *bubur cha-cha*, a colourful mix of sago, sweet potato, sometimes black-eyed beans, tropical fruit and coconut milk.

CHILLI

Large or small but usually red, chillies are an integral ingredient of most dishes including Singapore chilli crab.

PANDAN LEAF

Pandan leaves are used in both savoury and sweet dishes. They are often put into the pot when rice is cooked, to perfume it.

SHRIMP PASTE

Known as *belachan*, this has an awful smell but once roasted the odour fades and the paste adds a beautiful depth of flavour to many dishes. It is sold as a pressed block. To use, cut a small amount from the block, wrap it in foil and place in a hot oven or hold over a flame for a minute or two using tongs. Then remove from the heat and once it is cool, crumble and add to your dish.

TOMATO SAUCE

Somewhat surprisingly, this is used for richness and sweetness in sauces when no further chilli is desired. It's an integral part of the sauce used to make Singapore chilli crab.

Hainanese Chicken Rice

from Tiffany Wong

This is a classic Singaporean dish of delicately poached chicken infused with ginger, which is accompanied by rice cooked in chicken stock, a bowl of the hot stock itself, and various sauces. Tiffany makes quick chilli and ginger sauces and also serves this with kecap manis and cucumber.

CHICKEN

1 very fresh chicken (preferably free-range), fat trimmed and reserved for the rice

1 tablespoon Chinese rice wine

2 tablespoons light soy sauce

1 garlic clove, roughly chopped

6 slices of ginger

2 spring onions, roughly chopped

1 teaspoon sesame oil

½ teaspoon salt

STOCK

1 kg chicken carcasses (or legs or wings)

3 slices of ginger

2 spring onions

CHILLI SAUCE

10 long red chillies, seeded and roughly chopped

1–2 garlic cloves, roughly chopped

5 cm piece of ginger, roughly chopped

lime juice

salt

GINGER SAUCE

75 g ginger, roughly chopped

6 garlic cloves, roughly chopped

½ tablespoon lime juice

½ teaspoon salt

'Singaporeans greet each other with: "Have you eaten rice today?"'

RICE

fat from the chicken (or peanut oil as a healthier alternative)

2–3 cm piece of ginger, grated

3–4 garlic cloves, finely chopped

3 cups long-grain rice, rinsed and well drained

1–2 teaspoons salt

2 pandan leaves, each tied in a knot (optional)

TO SERVE

sliced spring onion or blanched shredded cabbage

kecap manis

sliced cucumber

Rub the inside of the chicken with the rice wine and half the soy sauce. Pound the garlic, half the ginger and half the spring onion to a paste in a mortar (or blend in a food processor). Rub the paste inside the chicken.

Bring a large pot of water to the boil, then turn off the heat and add the chicken, remaining ginger and spring onion. Cover with a lid and leave to stand in the water for 1 hour. After the first 5 minutes, lift the chicken out and drain the water from its cavity, then return to the water. Repeat 2 or 3 times during the hour (this ensures that there's enough hot water inside the chicken to cook it through). After 30 minutes, bring the water back to almost boiling then turn the heat off again. Cooking the chicken without boiling it ensures it is tender and juicy.

Remove the chicken from the water. Combine the remaining soy sauce with the sesame oil and salt and rub into the chicken. Leave to cool.

To make the stock, add the chicken carcasses, ginger and spring onions to the pot of water and boil for 1–2 hours, until the stock has a strong chicken flavour. Strain the stock through muslin cloth.

'Street food in Singapore –
It's cheap! It's hot! It's *shiok*
(delicious)!'

Meanwhile, make the chilli sauce. Pound the chilli, garlic and ginger to a paste in a mortar (or blend in a food processor). Add ½ tablespoon of chicken stock and lime juice and salt to taste.

To make the ginger sauce, pound the ginger and garlic to a paste in a mortar (or blend in a food processor) and add the lime juice, salt and 2 tablespoons of chicken stock.

To make the chicken rice, heat the chicken fat in a wok until it releases oil, then add the ginger and garlic and fry until golden. Discard any solid pieces of fat. Add the rice and salt and stir-fry briskly for 1–2 minutes. Transfer the rice to a saucepan or rice cooker and add 3½ cups (875 ml) of chicken stock and the pandan leaves if using. Cover with a lid and cook until the stock is absorbed (you may need to add a little more stock towards the end if the rice seems dry).

To serve, slice the chicken into bite-sized pieces. Reheat the remaining chicken stock and ladle into small serving bowls, garnishing with sliced spring onion or blanched shredded cabbage. Serve the stock alongside the chicken, rice, chilli sauce, ginger sauce, kecap manis and cucumber.

Serves 6

'Shop till you drop.
Eat till you pop!'

Assam Fish
Tamarind Fish

from Chui Lee Luk

Sweetened with many shallots, this tangy tamarind-based sauce is a perfect match for thick cutlets of oily fish such as mackerel. The fish is dusted in turmeric-laced flour then fried and added to the sauce. A wonderful dish that is perfect as a main dish or shared as part of a banquet.

REMPAH (SPICE PASTE)

10 shallots

2 long red chillies

½ head of garlic, peeled

1.5 cm piece of young ginger

½ teaspoon shrimp paste, roasted

1½ tablespoons tamarind pulp

500 ml water

400–500 g thick Spanish mackerel cutlets
(or other strong-flavoured oily fish)

plain flour

turmeric

oil

1 lemongrass stalk, bruised

2 tomatoes, peeled, seeded and quartered

2 long red chillies, halved lengthwise, seeded

2 long green chillies, halved lengthwise, seeded

sugar

salt

Pound the *rempah* ingredients to a fine paste in a mortar, or blend in a food processor.

Combine the tamarind pulp and water and leave to soften, then strain.

Coat the fish pieces in flour mixed with a little turmeric. Heat some oil in a frying pan and fry the fish pieces until lightly coloured. Set aside.

Heat a little more oil in a heavy-based saucepan and fry the *rempah* paste over high heat until fragrant. Add the lemongrass, tomato, chillies and tamarind water and bring to the boil. Season to taste with sugar and salt – the flavour should be a mix of hot, sweet, sour and salty. Add the fried fish and simmer over low heat for 5 minutes.

Serves 2

'To eat well means
to have lots of wealth.'

Rojak

from Helina Lee

This is the freshest tasting salad – crunchy
fruit and vegetables with fried tofu in a sweetly
sticky, slightly sour dressing, sprinkled with
roasted peanuts. It includes some unusual
ingredients, but they can be found at Asian
grocers. Yam bean (also called *jicama*) is a pale
brown tuber with crisp white, slightly sweet
flesh. Water spinach (called *kang kong* in Malay
but common throughout Asia) is a crunchy,
hollow-stemmed green with long pointed
leaves. Fried dough sticks are deep-fried strips
of unsweetened dough and are also known as
Chinese doughnuts or crispy crullers. Serve
this salad with bamboo skewers, as done in
Singapore.

DRESSING

2 tablespoons tamarind pulp

1–2 teaspoons crushed red chilli (small or
long chillies depending on desired heat)

1 tablespoon shrimp paste from a block
(*belachan*), roasted

2 tablespoons shrimp paste from a jar

2–3 tablespoons grated palm sugar

juice of ½ lemon

handful of bean sprouts

handful of water spinach, ends trimmed

2 large fried tofu puffs

1 fried dough stick

handful of peeled, sliced green mango

handful of peeled, sliced pineapple

handful of peeled, sliced yam bean (*jicama*)

handful of sliced cucumber

½ cup roughly crushed roasted peanuts

To make the dressing, soak the tamarind pulp in
a little water until soft. Strain it into a large bowl
– it should be a thick puree. Add the remaining
dressing ingredients and mix well to a thick
sauce consistency. Taste to see if you have added
enough chilli and palm sugar.

Blanch the bean sprouts for 10 seconds in
boiling water. Remove with a slotted spoon and
leave to drain. Repeat with the water spinach.
Drain and roughly cut.

Place the tofu puffs and dough stick under a
griller or in a hot oven for a few minutes to crisp
up. Leave to cool, then cut into bite-sized pieces.

Add the sliced fruit and vegetables to the
dressing along with the bean sprouts, water
spinach, tofu and dough stick. Mix well, coating
everything in the dressing. Spoon into serving
bowls and scatter with the peanuts.

Serves 4

'Food = everything: they learn this from when they're very young.'

Singapore Chilli Crab
from Alex Lee

A whole crab, preferably a mud crab, is served in a thick, sweetish tomato sauce warmed by chilli. Traditionally it's served with triangles of dry white toast but, whatever the accompaniment, eating it with your hands is a must!

1 large mud crab
2 onions, roughly chopped
8 small red chillies
125 ml oil
thumb-sized piece of shrimp paste
½ tablespoon white vinegar
1 tablespoon tomato paste
400 ml tomato puree
2 tablespoons tomato sauce
80 ml light soy sauce
75 g (⅓ cup) sugar
½ teaspoon salt
¼ teaspoon cornflour or potato starch, mixed with 125 ml water
1 egg
coriander leaves

Remove the crab's top shell (retain for garnish if you like) then chop the crab into quarters. Crack the claws to allow the flavours to get in. Wash the pieces well.

Blend the onion and chilli to a puree in a food processor.

Heat the oil in a wok and add the onion and chilli puree and the shrimp paste and fry until most of the liquid evaporates. Add the vinegar, tomato paste, puree and sauce, soy sauce, sugar and salt and mix through. Add the crab and cook over high heat until the shells turn red. Add the cornflour or potato starch followed by the egg and gently stir through to thicken the sauce. Garnish with coriander.

Serves 2

Fried *Ikan Bilis* and Peanuts

from Helina Lee

Ikan bilis, or dried anchovies, are a popular snack. This dish of *ikan bilis* with peanuts and chilli paste is just the thing to have with a cold Tiger beer (Singapore's local brew) and the salty flavours make a great prelude to a meal. It can also be served with the famous *nasi lemak* (see page 147).

300 g *ikan bilis*, plus 2 tablespoons extra

200 g raw peanuts with skins on

1 onion, chopped

2–3 garlic cloves

small red chillies to taste

8 candlenuts

1 tablespoon chilli powder

oil

Dry-fry 300 g of *ikan bilis* and the peanuts in a large, heavy-based frying pan over low heat for 30 minutes. Remove from the pan and leave to cool.

Pound the extra *ikan bilis* to a powder in a mortar. Add the remaining ingredients other than the oil and pound to a paste (or you can use a food processor).

Heat a little oil in the frying pan and fry the paste until fragrant, then mix in the *ikan bilis* and peanuts, stirring well to coat. Cool and store in an airtight container.

Makes 2 cups

Bubur Cha-Cha

from Chee Ong

This dessert is the most colourful mix of tastes and textures – a perfect finish to a flavoursome meal. There are many versions and this recipe includes sago, sweet potato and taro. Taro are brown-skinned tubers covered in rough ridges – their flesh comes in various colours but is often white flecked with purple. You can find them at Asian grocery stores.

½ cup grated light palm sugar

750 ml water

1 pandan leaf, tied in a knot

200 g taro, peeled and cubed

200 g sweet potato, peeled and cubed

75 g large coloured sago

COCONUT SOUP

½ cup grated light palm sugar

125 ml water from the coconut (below)

1 pandan leaf, tied in a knot

750 ml coconut cream

pinch of salt

COCONUT CRISPS

1 coconut, cracked and peeled

Put the palm sugar, water and pandan leaf in a saucepan and bring to the boil, stirring until the sugar dissolves. Add the taro and sweet potato and simmer until just soft. Leave to cool then chill in the refrigerator.

Boil the sago in plenty of water until soft, then drain and rinse in cold water. Tip into a bowl, fill with cold water and set aside.

To make the coconut soup, place the palm sugar, half of the coconut water and the pandan leaf in a saucepan and boil until lightly caramelised. Remove from the heat while you pour in the remaining coconut water. Return to the heat and simmer for 1 minute. Turn off the heat and stir in the coconut cream and salt. Leave to cool, then chill.

To make the coconut crisps, preheat the oven to 150°C. Shave thin slices of coconut with a knife. Place the coconut on an oven tray and bake for around 1 hour, until light golden and dry. Leave to cool.

To serve, put pieces of taro and sweet potato into bowls. Scatter with sago and spoon over a little coconut soup. Garnish with coconut chips.

Serves 4–6

SOUTH
AMERICA

It's amazing to think that much of the world's favourite food originally came from this vast and beautiful continent – chocolate from Honduras, potatoes from the Andes, chillies from Ecuador, and from all over the region tomatoes, peanuts and corn of many varieties. Imagine *kimchi* without chilli, spaghetti bolognaise without tomato, fish without the chips, and all of us without chocolate! The world as we know it would be a much less vibrant place.

The dishes created across the continent are also exceptional. My Peruvian friend Jorge divides the continent by the Andes. On the west side the land is suited to grazing and countries there love their meat and barbecues (and what feasts of meat they are!) and on the east side they grow a huge variety of potatoes, corn, chillies and tomatoes.

I find it hard to imagine that there are 2000 types of potatoes – some tiny, some huge, all of many different colours and featuring in countless recipes. *Papa amarilla* is the yellow potato of Peru; *papa seca* is the dried potato of the Andes; and *chuño* is a freeze-dried potato from Bolivia, which (when dried) looks like little stones. Potatoes are also used to make flour. And then there's the corn – some yellow, some white, some giant, some dried ... Jorge says you could live on corn for a year and never get tired of it. It's used by the Colombians and Venezuelans to make *arepas* (corn cakes like thick tortillas that are filled or topped with meat or cheese for snacks); Peruvians use the dried, toasted kernels to accompany the marinated seafood ceviche and the Argentinians use soaked white corn to make *mazamorra* (a sweet, milky pudding).

Among all the dishes I've tried over the years, I have to say one of the most challenging was the *chinchulines* served as part of an Argentinian *asado*. I had been really looking forward to learning the secrets of this legendary meat feast – the cuts of grilled meat, the *chimichurri* sauce and *chinchulines*, which sounded at first like a great name for a cocktail. In fact it's the intestines of a cow. These are a local delicacy and often served with *mollejas* (sweetbreads), chorizos and *morcillas* (blood sausages). After a tentative mouthful of *chinchulines* – a bit rubbery and a bit fatty – I spat it out. I'm glad I tried it but don't really want to again! However the *asado* beef, perfectly cooked, is tender and delicious with the vibrant *chimichurri* sauce – now that's a great barbecue!

ADOBO SPICE MIX

This mix of oregano, paprika, chilli and thyme is the base of the famous *chimichurri* sauce for barbecued meat. It is also used as a marinade.

AJI CHILLI

Also known as the 'Peruvian chilli', these long yellow/orange chillies have a fruity rather than spicy flavour, being more like a capsicum than a chilli. They are sold as dried whole chillies or ground into powder.

BEEF

South America, particularly Argentina, is a meat lover's paradise. Meat, mostly beef, is usually barbecued. The most popular cuts are the *vacio* (flank steak) and *asado de tira* (spare ribs). Other favourites include *chinchulines* (chitterlings or intestines) and *mollejas* (sweetbreads).

CASSAVA

A root vegetable closely related to potato, the cassava makes flour and great chips.

CHORIZO

The chorizo sausage is an essential part of South American cuisine. Made from pork, flavoured with paprika and garlic, it is used in stews, grilled on the barbie or enjoyed on its own as a snack.

CORIANDER

Known in Spanish as *cilantro*, coriander features prominently in South American cuisine and is an essential ingredient in the versatile *pebre* salsa.

QUINOA

A seed that has been cultivated in the Andean highlands since 3000 BC. It has a light, fluffy texture when cooked. Its mild and slightly nutty flavour makes it a perfect alternative to rice or couscous and it also makes great salads.

'My grandma told me to always get involved in the kitchen work because "The one in charge of serving up in the kitchen always gets the best portions!"'

Empanadas

from Yvonne Cutro

Debate rages over which country invented the empanada and many varieties using different sorts of pastry abound. Empanadas are the ultimate snack food. They can be filled with any combination of cheese, chilli, meat, tuna, prawns, vegetables, egg and olives. Some are baked whereas others are deep-fried.

3 tablespoons vegetable oil

130 g butter

200 g onions, chopped

200 g spring onions, chopped

½ teaspoon *aji* chilli powder

1 kg minced beef (not too lean)

250 ml hot beef stock

3 tablespoons sugar

salt

1 teaspoon sweet paprika

½ teaspoon cinnamon

½ teaspoon ground cloves (optional)

1 kg shortcrust pastry

plain flour

handful of green olives, chopped

130 g sultanas

3 hard-boiled eggs, peeled and roughly chopped

ground cumin

extra butter, melted

Heat the oil and butter in a large, heavy-based saucepan over medium heat and add the onion and spring onion. Fry until the onion is translucent. Add the *aji* powder, then the beef. Cook until the meat is brown, then add the hot stock and simmer until the beef is cooked through. Add the sugar and season with salt, then add the paprika, cinnamon, ground cloves and a little water. Cook over low heat until the liquid has evaporated. Leave to cool.

Preheat the oven to 200°C. Take pieces of pastry about the size of golf balls and roll out to circles 10–15 cm in diameter. Dust lightly with flour. Put a generous spoonful of meat filling in the centre of each round and add a few pieces of olive, some sultanas and egg. Sprinkle with cumin. Fold the pastry into a half-moon, then fold in the edges, crimping them with your fingers as you go. Place the empanadas on a greased tray and brush the tops with melted butter. Bake for 25 minutes or until golden.

Makes 12–15 empanadas

Ceviche

from Alejandro Saravia

Most South American countries now have their own version of ceviche but it's thought to be Peruvian in origin. Essentially it is marinated raw fish or crustacean that is 'cooked' by the acidity of citrus juice (you can try prawns in this recipe instead of fish if you like). Passionfruit and tamarillo have been added to the marinade for extra flavour. It is a delightful, refreshing, hot-weather meal and reported by some South Americans to be a cure for a hangover! Alejandro serves it with cinnamon-scented sweet potato, but it is often served with *cancha serrana* (dried corn kernels that are roasted and salted).

1 small sweet potato, peeled

1 tablespoon raw sugar

1 cinnamon stick

1 long red chilli

juice of 2 limes

sea salt and freshly ground black pepper

2 skinless, boneless white fish fillets such as snapper, as fresh as possible, cut into 2 cm cubes

ice cubes

½ red onion, finely sliced

1 tablespoon finely chopped coriander

Boil the sweet potato with the sugar and cinnamon until just soft. Leave to cool, then cut into 2 cm cubes.

Blanch the chilli then peel off the skin and remove the seeds. Place in a mortar with a little lime juice, salt and pepper and grind to a paste.

Combine the fish, remaining lime juice and a few ice cubes in a bowl. Add the onion, a pinch of salt, a little pepper and a little chilli paste to taste and mix together. Stir in the coriander. Place in a serving bowl with the sweet potato on the side. Eat immediately: the fresher, the better.

Serves 2

Pebre

from Gema Badiola

In Chile this all-purpose salsa is a big favourite, often served with pumpkin fritters and some good local wine. It's also an excellent accompaniment to barbecued meat and fish. *Pebre* includes a large quantity of onion, but soaking the onion in sugar, then salt, softens the raw flavour. (Instead of onion you could use a bunch of finely chopped chives.)

4 medium onions, diced

2 tablespoons raw sugar

salt

3 tomatoes, diced

½ green capsicum (or red or yellow for a more colourful salsa), diced

3–4 garlic cloves, finely chopped

2 green Chilean chillies, seeded and finely chopped (or use Chilean chilli paste)

2–3 bunches coriander, finely chopped (including stems)

juice of ½ lemon

2 tablespoons white vinegar

3 tablespoons grape-seed oil

dried oregano

pepper

Put the onion in a colander and sprinkle with the sugar and some hot water (not boiling). Mix with your hands and leave to stand for 10 minutes. Rinse the onion and mix in a handful of salt. Transfer to a bowl, fill with cold water and leave to stand for a further 10 minutes, then tip the onion back into the colander, rinse again and drain well.

Combine the tomato, capsicum, garlic, chilli and coriander in a bowl. Add the onion, lemon juice, vinegar and oil and mix well. Sprinkle with a little oregano and add salt and pepper to taste.

Makes 4 cups

Arepas

from Juan Gomez

This Colombian snack food consists of a cornmeal patty cooked in a frying pan and served simply with butter and salt or with any number of fillings. Split the *arepas* open and fill with avocado, cheese, tomato, meat, fried chicken, beans or salsa. Or try the '*arepa* pizza' where chorizo, cheese and spicy chicken or beef strips are used as a topping rather than a filling. In northern Colombia, fried egg *arepas* are a favourite – the egg is fried into the patty. *Arepas* are also a good accompaniment to main meals.

1 kg dried snow corn (white corn), soaked overnight

1 tablespoon butter

1 tablespoon salt

Drain the corn and cook in boiling water for 1 hour or until al dente. Drain and place in a food processor with the butter and salt. Grind as finely as possible. Transfer to a work surface and knead for a few minutes until the dough is smooth without any lumps.

Take balls of dough weighing around 120 g each and flatten with a rolling pin to patties 5 mm–1 cm thick.

Heat a non-stick frying pan or barbecue (without any oil or butter) and cook the *arepas* for 5 minutes on one side, then 3 minutes on the other (the *arepas* are ready to be turned when you can slide them around).

Makes 10–12 *arepas*

'To praise a good cook say "*De tus manos veneno!*" (From your hands, even poison!), meaning that no matter what she cooks, she has the gift of turning it into a magical meal.'

INGREDIENTS: GUAVA PULP, REFINED SUGAR AND CITRIC ACID DISTRIBUTED BY/DISTRIBUIDO POR: PROVEEDORA DE ALIMENTOS DEL PACIFICO ANGELES, CA.90021 · PRODUCT OF ECUADOR

Asado and *Chimichurri*

from Fabian Concha

Asado is a technique for cooking cuts of meat (usually beef) as well as sausages and offal on a barbecue. It is a traditional dish of Argentina, Chile, Uruguay and Paraguay and generally goes hand in hand with *chimichurri*, a spicy, garlicky parsley sauce. The meat is cooked without any embellishments, just very slowly over coals, until it melts in your mouth and cuts like butter. Fabian uses two barbecues – a covered Weber to cook sausages like fresh chorizos, *morcillas* (blood sausages), beef intestines and sweetbreads, and an open grill for large pieces of flank steak and long lengths of beef spare ribs which he covers with newspaper and cooks for about an hour, turning every 15 minutes.

CHIMICHURRI

1 cup finely chopped flat-leaf parsley

3 garlic cloves, finely chopped

125 ml olive oil

3 tablespoons balsamic vinegar

3 tablespoons brown vinegar

½ teaspoon chilli powder

1 teaspoon *adobo* spice mix

salt

Mix the ingredients together and pour over the cooked meat to serve.

Makes 1 cup

Manjar Blanco

from Carmen Almenara

Manjar blanco is a custard of milk, vanilla and sugar that is simmered until thick, rich and caramelised. It is a traditional sweet enjoyed daily throughout South America – as a filling for pastries, the sweet centre of *alfajor* biscuits and *tejas* (filled chocolates) or simply enjoyed on its own – one devotee described it as 'pan-scrapingly good!'

1 tablespoon butter

1 litre full-cream milk

230 g white sugar

¼ teaspoon bicarbonate of soda

1 vanilla bean, split

50 g brown sugar

30 g liquid glucose

Heat the butter, a quarter of the milk, the white sugar, bicarbonate of soda and vanilla in a saucepan. Bring to the boil and cook, stirring constantly with a wooden spoon, until the mixture starts turning a caramel colour. Add another quarter of milk and the brown sugar. Continue stirring. When the mixture starts thickening, add another quarter of milk. As it thickens again, add the remaining milk and the glucose, turn down the heat and continue stirring until the custard is thick enough for you to see the bottom of the saucepan when you move the spoon through it, or until a little custard put on a plate doesn't run. The custard cooks for approximately 40 minutes in total. Remove from the heat and keep stirring for a few minutes before pouring into a bowl.

Makes approximately 4 cups

SPAIN

In Australia we have fallen head over heels for the Spanish tapas tradition, fully embracing this array of delicious snacks that is traditionally served with a drink as a prelude to a meal. We love the sizzle of garlic prawns, will cross town for good Iberian *jamón*, have dived into sangria like it's water and have learned just how good Spanish olive oil, paprika and saffron can be. We're also learning that Spanish food is incredibly varied due to the influence and enrichment of the Moors, Arabs, Sephardic Jews, French and Italians who have all settled at various times in the country. The result is food with soul.

Each region in Spain has its own specialities, dictated by geography. Spain's long coastline, its rugged mountains, its baking plains and its rich farming land are all background to a vast range of dishes, which all have one thing in common – they're simple, unpretentious and use beautifully fresh, seasonal ingredients.

To the Spanish, eating is more than simply looking after hunger pangs – food is savoured and enjoyed communally and many culinary traditions have evolved over the years. I especially love the Spanish version of the fellas manning the barbecue – on a Sunday the women go to church and the men stay home to make paella for the army of family and friends that arrive sometime after midday. There's a lot of male pride bound up in getting the special *calasparra* or *bomba* rice cooked just right in olive oil and stock, and the added seafood, meat and vegetables also cooked to perfection. When they're finished the aroma of saffron hangs in the air and the whole paella pan looks like the best edible artwork on earth.

Most people are familiar with some of the main Spanish exports like paella and sangria and are still coming up to speed with the lesser-known ones, such as the fabulous *zarzuela* seafood stew and *fino*, a dry sherry that makes a great aperitif and goes well with the strong flavours of many tapas dishes. It's always worth seeking out the best and most authentic ingredients – good Spanish paprika, saffron and olive oil – and being generous with garlic and wine also help!

CHEESE

Spain produces some beautiful cheeses such as the hard sheep's milk *manchego* (look for '*queso puro de oveja*' on the label) and the piquant cow's milk *mahón*. From Andalucia to the Basque country – each region of Spain has its own specialty cheeses just as France has.

GARLIC

What would Spanish food be without garlic? Known as *ajo* in Spanish, garlic is used extensively in Spanish cooking.

JAMÓN

The most common variety, which is found all over Spain, is *jamón serrano* (mountain ham). This is a young salt-cured ham that is deep red in colour and served in thin raw slices. It dries out a little with age but when fresh it will melt in your mouth. *Jamón de pata negra* is made from free-range black Iberian pigs, which have grazed on acorns. This *jamón* is aged for 18 months and because of the care taken to produce it, it's very expensive. It has a nutty, slightly sweet flavour and a melting texture.

OLIVE OIL

Known as *aceite de oliva*, Spanish olive oil is 'fruitier' than Italian versions and is used for cooking, salad dressings and also drizzled over dishes to finish.

PAPRIKA

A spice made of dried, ground capsicums. There are many different varieties – smoked (*ahumado*), sweet (*dulce*), spicy (*picante*) or the intense, sun-dried *pimentón de Murcia*. For an authentic Spanish flavour it is important you use the right type specified in a recipe.

SAFFRON

The stigma from the crocus flower and the most expensive spice in the world. Fortunately a small amount is enough to impart its distinctive flavour, enticing aroma and rich colour. It is essential for making paella.

SHERRY VINEGAR

Both sherry and vinegar have been produced in southern Spain for centuries. Like balsamic vinegar, sherry vinegars are aged for up to 75 years and are used to enhance the flavours of soups, stews, sauces and dressings.

Gazpacho *Andaluz*

from Penelope Lopez

A classic chilled vegetable soup. The mixture can be refrigerated overnight and then pureed just before serving.

2 litres water
250 ml white vinegar
125 ml extra-virgin olive oil
1 day-old vienna or *pane di casa* loaf, crusts removed, roughly cut
2 garlic cloves, sliced
1 onion, chopped
5–6 medium-sized soft red tomatoes, peeled, roughly chopped
1 red capsicum, seeded, roughly chopped
1 green capsicum, seeded, roughly chopped
1 large cucumber, half peeled (a little skin left on adds flavour), roughly chopped
3 tablespoons salt

Combine the water, vinegar and olive oil in a large bowl. Add the bread, garlic and vegetables. Mix well with your hands and add the salt. Cover and chill in the refrigerator.

Puree the mixture in a blender and strain before serving.

Serves 8

Gambas al Pil-Pil

from Penelope Lopez

Buy a terracotta *cazuela* dish to cook this in and master the recipe – you'll look great and friends will never come down with colds!

Cooking anything in a *cazuela* will give it that special Spanish 'something' – the smaller clay dishes can be used on the stove to make dishes such as this, the larger ones to bake meat on the bone until it is really tender or to gently cook vegetable dishes.

olive oil
4 garlic cloves, sliced
small red chilli, chopped
12 green prawns, shelled, tails intact
pinch of salt
2 tablespoons white wine
½ tablespoon chopped flat-leaf parsley

Pour oil into a small frying pan or *cazuela* dish to about 1.5 cm deep. Heat over medium–high heat. Add the garlic, chilli and prawns – they should start sizzling immediately. Cook for 15 seconds then turn the prawns over. Add the salt, white wine and parsley, then serve straight away.

Serves 2–3

Gambas al Pil-Pil

San Jacob

from Frank Camorra

This lovely pork dish is meltingly wonderful, with molten cheese inside and a crisp breadcrumb coating. Serve it on top of *asadillo de pimientos* (see the recipe following) – a great combination!

4 pork loin medallions (150 g each)

salt

thyme leaves

4 slices of *jamón*

4 slices of *mahón* cheese

plain flour

2 eggs, lightly beaten

fresh breadcrumbs

olive oil

Lay each medallion out flat and slice through the middle horizontally without cutting all the way to the end. Open the medallions out like little books and flatten them slightly with a meat mallet. Season with a little salt and add some thyme leaves. Top each medallion with a slice of *jamón* and cheese. Close over and seal by lightly tapping with the mallet. Dust lightly in flour, dip into the beaten egg and coat with breadcrumbs.

Preheat the oven to 180°C. Heat a frying pan with olive oil and gently pan-fry the pork on both sides. Transfer to the oven for about 10 minutes, until cooked through. Drain on paper towel and serve on top of *asadillo de pimientos*.

Serves 4

Asadillo de Pimientos

from Frank Camorra

A simple summer salad of roasted capsicum, onion and garlic with tomato and cumin. Use the best extra-virgin olive oil you can find.

6 red capsicums

2 onions

2 heads of garlic

250 ml extra-virgin olive oil
(arbequina if possible)

sea salt

500 g tomatoes, peeled,
seeded and roughly chopped

½ bunch flat-leaf parsley, roughly chopped

125 ml sherry vinegar

1 tablespoon cumin seeds, toasted and crushed

Preheat the oven to 180°C. Place the whole capsicums, onions and heads of garlic in a baking dish. Drizzle with some of the olive oil and sprinkle with sea salt. Roast for 30 minutes or until the onion is soft. Transfer to a bowl, cover with plastic wrap (the steam will help loosen the skins) and set aside until cool enough to handle.

Put the tomato and parsley in a separate bowl. Squeeze the onions from their skins, roughly chop them and add to the tomato. Cut the tops off the heads of garlic and squeeze the cloves into the bowl. Peel the capsicums and discard the seeds. Tear the flesh into strips and add to the bowl. Pour over the remaining oil and the sherry vinegar. Sprinkle with the cumin and add salt to taste. Toss well with your hands.

Serves 4

"Vamos con el arroz" (We are going with the rice) means dinner will be ready when the rice is cooked so everyone better be ready too!'

Paella

from Carlos Lopez

Traditionally paella is made on a Sunday and because women need a day off from cooking it is usually made by the men. I have bought a paella pan and gas ring so my family are always enjoying this lovely dish.

Calasparra is a low-starch, short-grain rice and when cooked it is fluffy with separate grains. It is the best rice to use for paella – it can absorb heaps of liquid so it bursts with flavour. To increase the quantities and serve more people (although you will need a giant paella dish), allow about 80 g of rice per person.

2 red capsicums, 1 left whole, 1 finely chopped

10 saffron threads

salt

3 tablespoons olive oil

1 onion, finely chopped

2 garlic cloves, crushed

1 large tomato, peeled and finely chopped

300 g chicken breast or thigh fillets, diced

200 g squid, diced

300 g *calasparra* rice

750 ml fish stock

3 teaspoons Spanish smoked paprika

4 large green prawns

1 blue swimmer crab, halved

8 mussels

12 pippies

200 g peas

⅓ cup chopped flat-leaf parsley

Roast the whole capsicum in a moderate oven until blistered, then peel it, discard the seeds and tear the flesh into thin strips. Set aside.

Grind the saffron with some salt in a mortar.

Heat the oil in a large paella pan (or frying pan) over medium heat. Add the onion, garlic, tomato, fresh capsicum, chicken, squid and rice and stir for 1 minute. Add the stock, paprika and crushed saffron, stir for the last time and bring to the boil. When the stock boils and the grains begin to swell, lay the prawns and crab on top. Cook over medium heat for about 10 minutes until the stock has reduced enough that you can see the rice underneath. Push the mussels and pippies into the rice and cook until their shells open. Scatter with the peas, strips of roasted capsicum and parsley and cook for another 5 minutes over low heat.

Serves 4

Tortilla de Patatas
Potato Omelette

from Paola Horta

This is simplicity itself – as well as being creamy and delicious. It is great to add to your tapas repertoire, to take to a picnic or to add to a Mediterranean spread.

250 ml olive oil
4 medium potatoes, peeled, quartered and thinly sliced
6 eggs
salt

Heat the oil in a large frying pan and gently cook the potatoes, stirring from time to time so they don't burn on the bottom. Once the potatoes are almost soft, drain them in a colander set over a bowl to remove the excess oil (keep it for another use). Leave 2 tablespoons of oil in the pan.

Beat the eggs in a bowl and season with salt. Add the potatoes, mix well and check the seasoning.

Reheat the frying pan over medium heat and pour in the potato and egg mixture. As the omelette begins to cook, shake the pan from time to time so the omelette doesn't stick to the bottom. Once the bottom of the omelette has set, turn it by placing a plate on the pan and quickly turning the pan and plate over. Gently slide the omelette back into the pan and continue cooking, shaking the pan from time to time, until the omelette is set through.

Serves 6–8

Arroz con Leche
Rice Pudding

from Rosalia Ugarte

I'm sure my family have clocked their one-hundredth round on this recipe – we love it and make it all the time. Although using the condensed milk might be cheating a little bit, it makes a creamy, luscious and very indulgent dessert – thank you Rosalia! (In case you're wondering, Rosalia says this definitely can't be made with skim milk – 'You use full-cream then go for a run!')

250 g medium-grain rice
1.25 litres full-cream milk
1–2 cinnamon sticks
1 strip of lemon rind
395 g tin sweetened condensed milk
ground cinnamon

Place the rice in a saucepan and cover with water. Bring to the boil and cook for 5 minutes. Drain.

Heat the milk in the saucepan with the cinnamon sticks and lemon rind. When it comes to the boil, add the rice and turn the heat down to low. Cook, stirring constantly, until the rice is half cooked. Add the condensed milk and continue cooking and stirring until the rice is cooked through (test by squashing a rice grain in your fingers). Spoon into bowls and dust with ground cinnamon.

Serves 8

SRI LANKA

If Sri Lankan cuisine has a signature smell and sound it would have to be the intense fresh aroma and firecracker sound of fresh curry leaves and mustard seeds popping in hot oil. This is the prelude to many incredible dishes and with a start like this even a simple plate of greens is transformed into something with sexiness and soul.

It's hard not to fall in love with this food, which is a combination of Muslim, Tamil and Sinhalese recipes. It also seems that every nationality that has visited and traded over the centuries has left a mark on the cuisine – the Dutch, Portuguese, English, Arabs, Malays, Moors and Indians have all added some of their magic to the fresh fruit, vegetables and spices that are grown locally in abundance.

Some ingredients are virtually unknown outside Sri Lanka such as drumsticks, which are a long, bitter pod used in curries and accompaniments – their leaves are a popular addition to the favourite crab curry. It's rare to find a Sri Lankan family that hasn't planted their own curry leaf tree in the backyard, although the drumstick tree needs the intense heat of the tropics to flourish.

The tropical climate in Sri Lanka is also perfect for coconuts, which are used fresh and can be grated into *sambols*, wonderful accompaniments to rice and curry. I love that Sri Lankans refer to 'rice and curry' always in that order, denoting the importance of rice. A simple meal might be rice and *sambol*, pickles or chutney to liven up the flavour with at least one vegetable curry or dhal. Depending on the occasion, there may be even more dishes – meat curries, seafood curries, endless *sambols* and accompaniments, and even spicy scrambled eggs, which our local goddess of Asian food, Charmaine Solomon, made for me when she shared her tried-and-true chicken curry recipe. After this I can never eat plain scrambled eggs again – hers were creamy and full of fresh herbs and mellow spices.

At many special banquets you'll be served lovely little pancakes that have the sweet name of hoppers (*appam*). They're made in a deep, circular pan and the rice-flour mixture is rolled around the pan so it comes right up the sides. Crispy on the bottom, these pancakes are broken into pieces to scoop up curries – similar to how you'd use Lebanese bread. If you're even luckier you'll also discover their unusual cousin the stringhopper (*idiyappam*), which are made from fine rice-flour strings that have been squeezed through a sieve onto a little circular mat and steamed – they are a little nest of noodle-like strands and a feature of banquets for special occasions. Trying to eat these fiddly but delicious things with curry sauces running up your arm is quite an art – but very yummy!

Chutneys, Pickles and Sambols

It would be unthinkable to have a meal in Sri Lanka without these accompaniments. They serve to enhance the flavours of curries and awaken the tastebuds. There are many different types, ranging from savoury eggplant and tomato pickles, tangy lime and date chutneys, to fiery *sambols* based on salt, lime, maldive fish, chilli and shallots.

COCONUT AND COCONUT OIL

The coconut palm is referred to in Sinhalese as a gift of the gods. Every part of the tree is used – in building, for utensils, right down to the milk, the oil and of course the flesh. Finely grated in *sambols* and *mallungs*, added to curries and baked into sweet delights, it is the quintessential Sri Lankan ingredient. Coconut oil is traditionally used for cooking and is beautifully fragrant, but use it sparingly due to its high saturated-fat content.

CURRY LEAVES

Picked from a tree related to the citrus family, curry leaves are often fried in oil before being used in curries and chutneys. Although also available in dried or powdered form, they are at their aromatic best when fresh. You can use fresh leaves still attached to the stem for extra flavour.

CURRY POWDERS

Sri Lankan curry powders get their dark colour, aroma and distinctive flavour from roasting the spices – which might include coriander, cumin, fennel, fenugreek and cardamom. As well as the classic dark roasted powder, special blends such as fish curry powder and meat powders are commonly used.

FENUGREEK

No Sri Lankan curry is complete without these small, brown, square-shaped seeds which add a slight bitterness and have a thickening effect on sauces. They must be heated slowly to prevent becoming too bitter.

GORAKA

A souring and thickening agent unique to Sri Lanka is this fluted orange fruit whose segments are dried, turning black. It can be soaked in hot water and ground to a paste or added whole and removed after cooking.

MALDIVE FISH

Dried, smoked and finely shaved, maldive fish is the shrimp paste or fish sauce equivalent for Sri Lankan cuisine. It is a key ingredient in *sambols* and is also sparingly used as a thickening agent in curries. Store in a screw-top glass jar as it's quite pungent!

PANDAN LEAF

Most Sri Lankan households grow the pandan plant, whose long green leaves are used to perfume curries and rice. Pandan is often referred to as the vanilla of Asia, such is its beautiful aroma.

'Nothing tastes as good
as when it's cooked over
a wood-fired stove.'

Pol Sambol
Coconut *Sambol*

from Paul Van Reyk

Sambols are fresh or cooked relishes that
enliven Sri Lankan meals of rice and curry.
This version, made from chilli, maldive fish
and fresh coconut, will give your tastebuds
a warm but mellow tingle.

1 coconut, cracked and peeled
1 tablespoon maldive fish
2 teaspoons chilli powder
2 shallots, finely chopped
juice of ½ lime
salt

Finely grate the coconut flesh with a hand grater
or in a food processor. Grind the maldive fish to
a powder in a mortar. Mix the coconut, maldive
fish and chilli powder until the coconut turns
orange. Add the shallots, lime juice and a small
sprinkle of salt. Mix well and taste, adding more
lime or salt if desired.

Makes 3 cups

Leafy Vegetable *Mallung*

from Paul Van Reyk

The word *mallung* means literally 'to mix up'
and this delightful dish can feature any number
of different vegetables. In this recipe it is a
combination of shredded leafy greens, maldive
fish, green chilli and coconut. For the greens,
Paul says you could use almost anything:
spinach, silverbeet, chicory, chrysanthemum
leaves, beetroot or turnip leaves or mustard
greens. Mix a few kinds together if you like –
say, mild spinach with peppery turnip leaves.

oil
1 teaspoon black mustard seeds
handful of curry leaves
1 teaspoon turmeric
pinch of salt
1 tablespoon maldive fish, finely ground (optional)
1 bunch leafy vegetables, shredded
1 green chilli, finely chopped
1 cup grated fresh coconut

Heat a little oil in a wok or large frying pan and
add the mustard seeds. Fry until they begin to
pop, then add the curry leaves, turmeric, salt and
maldive fish if using, stirring constantly to prevent the curry leaves burning. Immediately add
the shredded leaves and stir rapidly. When the
leaves have darkened and become limp, add the
green chilli and coconut and stir for another
1–2 minutes. Remove from the heat and serve.

Serves 6

Prawn Curry

from Peter Kuravita

A creamy, velvety dish with delicious depth of flavour. This is achieved by including prawn pieces in the curry sauce (to be strained out with the aromatics later) and pureeing and straining a few heads just like in a French bisque. The recipe includes Paul's impressive serving suggestion of nestling pairs of prawns into each other to create a seafood version of the yin–yang symbol, all stacked up and served in a moat of sauce. It's a perfect dinner party dish as you can make the sauce in advance then cook the prawns in it very quickly just before serving. Serve with rice and pickles.

CURRY SAUCE

10 green prawns

2 tablespoons coconut oil or clarified butter (ghee)

30 curry leaves

10 shallots, sliced

12 garlic cloves, sliced

3 cm piece of ginger, finely chopped

1 tablespoon fenugreek seeds

5 cardamom pods

2 cinnamon sticks

5 cloves

2 tablespoons ground cumin

4 tablespoons ground coriander

¾ tablespoon chilli powder

1 tablespoon turmeric

2 tablespoons sweet paprika

½ tablespoon fish curry powder

2 long green chillies, sliced

1 piece of *goraka*

1 pandan leaf, cut in a few pieces

1 litre coconut milk

salt

TO SERVE

24 large shelled green prawns

juice of ½ lemon

coriander leaves

Remove the heads from the prawns, reserving half of them. Cut the bodies into pieces through the shells.

Heat some oil or ghee in a saucepan and add the curry leaves, shallots, garlic and ginger. Fry until the shallots are translucent. Add the prawn pieces, spices, green chilli, *goraka* and pandan leaf. Stir briefly to coat the prawns, then add half the coconut milk and salt to taste. Simmer for 8–10 minutes.

Meanwhile, puree the reserved prawn heads in a food processor. Strain through a fine sieve, discarding the solids. Mix the strained puree with the remaining coconut milk. Add to the curry and bring back to a simmer without boiling. Remove from the heat.

To serve, fit pairs of shelled prawns into each other by laying them flat, facing them towards each other and sliding them together to form circle shapes. Arrange the pairs in the base of a frying pan (as they cook, they stick together a little). Strain the curry sauce over the prawns until just covered. Cover the pan with a lid and bring to a simmer, cooking until the prawns turn opaque. Add the lemon juice.

Stack the prawn circles up on serving plates, spoon over the sauce and garnish with coriander.

Serves 4

Chicken Curry

from Charmaine Solomon

A classic chicken curry that's full of flavour and best made with chicken on the bone. Charmaine has made this dish for decades – it's always a marvellous meal. Serve with stringhoppers if you can (or otherwise rice) and with coconut *sambol* (see page 230).

2 tablespoons clarified butter (ghee) or vegetable oil (or a combination)

¼ teaspoon fenugreek seeds

10 curry leaves on the stem

2 large onions, finely chopped

4–5 garlic cloves, finely chopped

2 teaspoons grated ginger

1 teaspoon turmeric

1 teaspoon chilli powder

1 tablespoon ground coriander

½ teaspoon ground fennel

1 teaspoon ground cumin

2 teaspoons sweet paprika

2 teaspoons salt

2 tablespoons vinegar

2 tomatoes, peeled and chopped

6 cardamom pods, cracked

1 cinnamon stick

1 lemongrass stalk, bruised

1 pandan leaf, folded

1.5 kg chicken thighs on the bone

250 ml thick coconut milk

lemon juice (optional)

Heat the ghee or oil and fry the fenugreek seeds and curry leaves until the leaves start to brown. Add the onion, garlic and ginger and fry gently until the onion is soft and translucent. Add the ground spices, salt and vinegar and stir well. Add the tomato, whole spices, lemongrass and pandan leaf, then add the chicken. Stir to coat the chicken pieces in the spices, then cover and cook over low heat for 40–50 minutes. The curry will look dry at first but liquid will be released from the chicken.

Stir in the coconut milk and taste for salt. Add a squeeze of lemon juice if desired.

Serves 6

'When peeling jackfruit and cashews, cover your hands in palm oil – the jackfruit has a sticky sap and the cashew contains an acid that will burn your skin.'

Wattaka Kalu Pol
Pumpkin Curry
from Sunil Ranasinghe

A simple but delicious vegetable curry that uses Sri Lanka's dark roasted curry powder and is thickened and flavoured with toasted rice and desiccated coconut. A glorious dish.

2 tablespoons vegetable oil

2 medium red onions, finely sliced

2 sprigs of curry leaves

4 garlic cloves, finely sliced

3 long green chillies, sliced

½ teaspoon black mustard seeds, ground

½ teaspoon fenugreek seeds

1 kg pumpkin, cut into cubes, skin left on

1 teaspoon seeded mustard

2 tablespoons dark roasted curry powder

1 teaspoon chilli powder

1 teaspoon turmeric

1–2 teaspoons salt

500 ml coconut milk

2 tablespoons short-grain rice

⅓ cup desiccated coconut

Heat the oil in a large saucepan and add the onion, curry leaves, garlic and green chilli. Fry briefly then add the mustard and fenugreek seeds and continue frying.

Quickly toss the pumpkin in a bowl with the seeded mustard, ground spices and salt and add to the pan along with the coconut milk. Bring to the boil and cook over high heat until the pumpkin is tender.

Meanwhile, heat a small frying pan and dry-fry the rice and coconut until brown and fragrant. Grind to a powder in a mortar or blender.

Add the rice and coconut powder to the curry and cook for a few more minutes.

Serves 6

Wattalappam
from Deborah Solomon

A beautiful, dense, spiced custard that makes a perfect finish to a meal. It can be served warm or chilled, in which case you can make it a day in advance. Make a little extra syrup to spoon on top if desired.

175 g jaggery or dark palm sugar, roughly chopped

100 ml water

375 ml coconut milk (homemade, or use a good-quality brand like Kara)

½ teaspoon ground cardamom

¼ teaspoon ground mace

pinch of ground cloves

1 tablespoon rosewater

200 ml cream

4 large eggs, lightly beaten

Put the jaggery or palm sugar and water in a saucepan and heat, stirring, until the sugar dissolves. Leave to cool.

Preheat the oven to 140°C. Whisk the coconut milk with the spices and rosewater. Strain in the syrup, whisking to combine, then add the cream followed by the eggs. Pour into 8 small ramekins and place in a baking dish. Pour hot water to come halfway up the ramekins and bake in the oven for 50–60 minutes, or until the custards are just set.

Makes 8 custards

SYRIA

Syrian cuisine is full of delights – you'll find the freshest, most delicious salads and inventive dips, as well as main courses that sing with exotic spices and desserts and sweets that are legendary throughout the Middle East. While many dishes are similar to food from neighbouring Lebanon, a couple stand apart as distinctly Syrian and they are simply wonderful.

One of my favourites is the national dish *kibbeh*. It is made from very fresh, finely minced lamb or beef that's seasoned, spiced and mixed with burghul (cracked wheat), and it comes in many varieties – raw, baked or fried. The taste and texture are superb whichever way you have it. Other popular dishes are based on Mediterranean vegetables such as zucchini and eggplant, which are often hollowed out and stuffed with meat and rice. *Ma a'loube* is a delicious Syrian meal of eggplant that is stacked and layered with rice and lamb.

The Syrian palate adores salty, tangy and sour flavours. Along with a generous use of salt in cooking, cheeses like *labneh*, *shankleesh* and *jibne baida* satisfy some of their salt cravings. Lemon juice is used liberally for its sour tang, as are generous pinches of sumac, a deep-red spice that adds a lemony taste to salads and meats. Another slightly tangy flavour comes from the fresh herb *baqli* (or purslane as it's called in English).

One ingredient found commonly in Syria and its neighbours is freekeh, a young wheat that is harvested then roasted to give it a smoky flavour. Freekeh has a chewy texture like brown rice and is delicious served with meat or poultry. Syria also boasts truffles, which are found in the desert and have a wonderful earthy flavour and aroma – although they are nowhere near as strong as those found in France. The combination of freekeh, truffles and perfectly poached chicken is simply lovely.

One of the highlights of Syrian food is *mezza*, the tapas of the Middle East. *Mezza* is a generous spread of small dishes, mostly eaten without cutlery, using flatbread, lettuce or vine leaves instead to scoop up dips or wrap up morsels and colourful salads. Many who are new to the concept of *mezza* mistake the endless array of dishes as the meal itself rather than the prelude to even more food! Amid the social bustle and conversations of family and friends, Syrian meals are to be enjoyed for more than an hour or two. This reflects their culture of hospitality and generosity, where everything to do with food is presented on a large scale.

Essential flavours

BAHARAT

This is a spice mix that blends allspice, white and black pepper, lots of cinnamon, cloves, nutmeg, coriander and caraway. Syrian *baharat is* sometimes known as seven-spice mix and it's often used in meat dishes like baked *kibbeh* and freekeh with chicken.

FREEKEH

A roasted wheat grain very popular in Syria, which is cooked in a similar way to risotto rice. Freekeh is harvested from wheat while the seeds are still young and green – the wheat is set alight, which burns the dry straw and bran but not the seeds. These are then left to dry in the sun. The resulting grain has a nutty, smoky flavour.

NUTS

Syrians love to cook with almonds, walnuts and pine nuts. These nuts are often toasted in butter and used as garnish to add flavour and crunch to rice dishes. Pistachios are also much loved. The pistachio trees of Aleppo are famous, providing bountiful produce that is used particularly in sweet dishes like *baklawa*, *halwa* and *ma'moul* (date pastries).

POMEGRANATE MOLASSES

Made from pomegranate juice, lemon juice and sugar that are reduced over a low heat for a couple of hours to create a thick caramelised syrup with a tangy, piquant taste. It is a condiment readily found in Middle Eastern grocery stores and increasingly in major supermarkets as well. It is used in cooking to give a tart flavour to dishes and is a good tenderiser for meat.

PURSLANE

Generally considered a weed by those unfamiliar with its use as a leaf vegetable, purslane has long been valued by Lebanese and Syrians for its slightly sour and salty taste.

SHANKLEESH

A sharp-tasting cheese made from *labneh* that is formed into balls and rolled in oregano. It is often served broken up into a rough crumble with chopped tomato and onion and drizzled with extra-virgin olive oil.

SUMAC

Made from dried, powdered berries that grow around the Mediterranean, sumac gives a nice sour tang to dishes. It is sprinkled on kebabs and *pilav* and used in the spice mixture *za'atar*.

TAHINI

A creamy paste made from sesame seeds that have been soaked, crushed, soaked again in highly salted water to remove their husk, toasted and then ground. It is used as the basis of many dips, sauces and in some sweets like *halwa*.

Smoky baba ghanouj and creamy hoummus, both well known in the West, are key elements of a traditional *mezza* feast. Another favourite in Syria is *muhammara*, a spicy capsicum and walnut dip made with pomegranate molasses. Popular salads include tabbouleh, the well-known parsley and burghul salad that is often served with baby cos lettuce leaves to eat it with; and *fattoush*, which includes toasted or fried pieces of bread in a crunchy mixture of fresh cucumber, radish, tomato and herbs. *Fateh* is a favourite comfort food – a warm bowl of chickpeas, yoghurt, tahini and garlic. Tasty finger foods include *sambusic*, golden pastries filled with minced meat and spices; and *sfeeha*, baked lamb pies. And those are just for starters!

The sweet makers of Damascus are famous, as are their creations. They use wonderful seasonal fruit such as sour cherries and dried fruit such as apricots to make *qamar al-deen* (thin sheets of sweetened 'apricot leather'); use delicious nutty tahini to make *halwa* (halva, a sweet based on tahini, sugar and often pistachios); and have perfected a luscious clotted cream called *ashta*. Being a lover of sweets, one of my Syrian favourites is Damascus rose, which features baked rounds of filo pastry that are sandwiched with *ashta* then drizzled with syrup and crushed nuts. Exquisite!

'Never lift a boiling saucepan without saying "Isem Allah" (In God's name) – this will protect you from dropping the pot and burning yourself.'

Baklawa

from Amal Malouf

The sound of the hot syrup as it's poured onto the hot pastry is one of the best things, only surpassed by the sound of your first crunchy bite into this golden delicacy. Yum!

2–3 cups walnuts or pistachios

2 tablespoons sugar

2 teaspoons orange-blossom water

1 teaspoon rosewater

350 g clarified butter (ghee)
or unsalted butter, melted

375 g filo pastry

SYRUP

440 g (2 cups) sugar

250 ml water

½ teaspoon orange-blossom water

½ teaspoon rosewater

squeeze of lemon juice

Lightly crush the nuts in a food processor. Tip into a bowl and mix with the sugar, orange-blossom water and rosewater.

Preheat the oven to 180°C. Brush a baking tray measuring 20 × 30 cm with melted ghee or butter. Add a layer of filo in the base of the tray and brush with more butter. Keep layering with buttered filo until you have used half the filo. Spread the nuts in an even layer on top. Continue layering with the remaining filo.

Carefully cut the *baklawa* into diamond shapes. Pour a little melted butter over the top and bake for about 55 minutes, or until golden brown.

Meanwhile, prepare the syrup. Combine the sugar and water in a saucepan and bring to the boil. Simmer for 15 minutes, until slightly thickened, then remove from the heat and add the orange-blossom water, rosewater and lemon juice. Pour the hot syrup over the hot pastry. Cool before serving.

Makes approximately 20 pieces

Fattoush

from Sharon Salloum

After tabbouleh, *fattoush* is the most well-known salad of Syria and for many it's the favourite too. The sharp flavour of sumac in the dressing, the chunky tomato pieces, the crisp cucumber and radish, and the thin, baked pieces of bread that soak up the dressing are all delicious. Syrians often eat *fattoush* by spooning a manageable amount into a lettuce or vine leaf, wrapping it up into a little parcel and eating it with their fingers.

DRESSING

3 garlic cloves, crushed

1 teaspoon salt

2 teaspoons sweet paprika

2 teaspoons sumac

2 tablespoons olive oil

2 tablespoons lemon juice

1 pita bread

2 Lebanese cucumbers, halved lengthwise, cut into 1 cm slices

2 medium tomatoes, cut into chunky pieces

4–5 radishes, halved and thinly sliced

½ red capsicum, cut into 2 cm cubes

½ green capsicum, cut into 2 cm cubes

4 iceberg lettuce leaves, torn

handful of purslane leaves

½ cup chopped mint

½ cup chopped flat-leaf parsley

3 spring onions, sliced

Mix the dressing ingredients in a small bowl. If desired you can add more sumac or lemon juice.

Crisp the pita bread in a moderate oven or under a grill.

Place all the vegetables and herbs in a large bowl. Break the bread into small, rough pieces into the bowl. Add the dressing and toss well with your hands.

Serves 4

"*Sallem hal eid*" is the phrase spoken to protect the hand that prepared the food (the hand is symbolic of the person).'

Freekeh with Chicken

from *Ayman Abbassi*

Similar to the popular dish *riz a'djaj* (poached chicken served on rice), this recipe uses toasted freekeh wheat with its distinctive nutty taste. The wheat is cooked slowly like a risotto with chicken stock, minced meat, spices and onion until it is soft and flavoursome. The dish is then piled high onto a serving platter and served with poached chicken pieces, Syrian truffle (if available), pine nuts and almonds.

2 cups freekeh

1 medium free-range chicken (about 1.5 kg)

½ brown onion, quartered

3 cinnamon sticks

4 bay leaves

6 cardamom pods

salt

2 tablespoons clarified butter (ghee) or olive oil

1 red onion, finely chopped

300 g minced lamb or beef (optional)

1 teaspoon *baharat*

butter

½ cup almonds

½ cup pine nuts

4–6 small Syrian truffles, peeled and sliced (optional)

1 teaspoon ground cinnamon

Wash the freekeh and remove any burnt grains or stones.

Put the chicken in a pot and cover with water. Add the brown onion, cinnamon sticks, bay leaves, cardamom and 1 teaspoon of salt. Cover with a lid and bring to the boil. Simmer for 30 minutes or until cooked through. Remove the chicken from the pot (leaving a light stock) and set aside until cool enough to handle. Remove the skin and break the meat into large pieces, removing the bones.

Bring the chicken stock back to a slow simmer. Heat the ghee or olive oil in a large saucepan and add the red onion. Fry until beginning to soften, then add the lamb or beef, if using, and cook until browned. Stir in the freekeh. Add the *baharat* and 1 heaped teaspoon of salt and stir through.

Add 1 litre of hot chicken stock and bring to the boil. Lower the heat, cover and simmer for 40 minutes.

Melt a little butter in a large frying pan over medium heat. Add the almonds and cook until lightly toasted. Remove from the pan and repeat with the pine nuts. Remove from the pan and add another knob of butter. When it melts, add the truffles, if using, and coat with butter. Add the chicken pieces, ground cinnamon and 500 ml of hot stock. Bring to the boil, reheating the chicken.

Spoon the freekeh onto a large serving plate. Place the chicken and truffles on top and scatter with the nuts.

Serves 6

Kibbeh bil Sanieh
from Najla Atmaja

Syria's national dish of minced meat and burghul is so deeply loved that over the years its fans have found many different ways to prepare it. The secret is using fresh, very finely minced meat. This is carefully spiced then served raw, baked or fried in endlessly varying shapes, often with delicious fillings (that often include more minced meat). This recipe is for a kind of *kibbeh* sandwich: a layer of cooked, spiced meat and pine nuts is pressed between two layers of fine *kibbeh*, then baked and served in wedges like pieces of cake. Serve with salad and drained yoghurt (natural yoghurt that has been drained in muslin until thick).

FILLING

3 tablespoons olive oil

800 g minced lamb or beef

4 large onions, finely chopped

1 teaspoon *baharat*

½ teaspoon cinnamon (optional)

1 teaspoon salt

1½ teaspoons freshly ground black pepper

1 tablespoon butter

3 tablespoons pine nuts

KIBBEH

1½ cups fine burghul, soaked overnight in 250 ml water, drained well

800 g lean, finely minced lamb or beef (ask your butcher to mince it twice)

2 large onions, finely grated

1 teaspoon *baharat*

2 teaspoons salt

3 teaspoons freshly ground black pepper

1 tablespoon olive oil

To make the filling, heat the oil in a frying pan over low heat and add the meat. Cook, stirring constantly to break up the grains of meat. When the meat is browned and separated and the moisture is starting to evaporate, stir in the onion, spices, salt and pepper and keep cooking until the onion is soft.

Meanwhile, melt the butter in a small frying pan and add the pine nuts. Fry until they start to brown, then stir into the meat mixture. Remove from the heat and set aside to cool.

To make the *kibbeh*, combine the burghul, meat, onion, *baharat*, salt and pepper in a bowl and mix well by hand until it forms a paste. You may need a little water to keep the mixture soft. Cover and leave to rest for 30 minutes.

Preheat the oven to 180°C and oil a round baking tray with deep sides (around 2 cm). Dampen your hands and layer the tray with half of the *kibbeh* by forming small balls of the mixture then flattening them over the tray. Smooth the surface and make sure there are no gaps. Spread the cooled meat filling on top, pressing it down a little to keep the layers tight. Top with the rest of the *kibbeh* using the same technique. When the surface is smooth, push a small hole through the centre of the *kibbeh* with your finger. Slice into wedges fanning around the hole. Brush with the olive oil and bake in the oven for 25 minutes.

Serves 6

THAILAND

The world's love affair with Thai food has been long and satisfying, and the number of Thai restaurants now in big cities and small towns is a tribute to our desire for these fresh flavours. We can all recognise great tom yum soup, green chicken curry and pad thai noodles – at their best, Thai dishes perfectly balance sweet, sour, salty, spicy and bitter flavours to make your tastebuds tingle.

One thing I have discovered is the distinction Thai people make between foods they cook at home and ones they eat in restaurants. The famous chicken and holy basil stir-fry (*gai pad graprow*) is a great example. When the many pounded chillies hit the hot oil, the fumes must be like a good dose of capsicum spray – intense and choking. The stir-fry is delicious but it's no wonder Thai people prefer to eat this dish in restaurants – it is so pungent that 'all the neighbours know what you're having for dinner!'

There are usually a couple of different types of chilli used in every recipe, both fresh and dried, and roasted chilli powder is sometimes added as well. This is one of the world's really hot cuisines! One useful piece of kitchen equipment that will help you get the best out of chillies (and other ingredients) is a deep mortar and pestle, which is in constant use in Thai kitchens. Some cooks also use a blender to mix up curry pastes or to chop fresh coconut with a little warm water ready for squeezing through a fine sieve to make really fresh coconut milk.

Eating Thai-style is to be served all the dishes at the same time in the centre of the table – there is no separation into entree/main course. It's a great way to eat as the cook gets to sit down and not be ferrying food backwards and forwards. Rice is an integral part of every meal, along with soup, a couple of curries and side dishes. Thai people generally eat with a spoon and fork and use the fork to push the food onto the spoon – the fork is never actually eaten from.

In the northeast, the way of eating is different – the Isaan style of cooking prefers sticky rice that is served in bamboo baskets and eaten by rolling the rice into a ball to scoop up the fiery curries and salads.

I've always been interested in how people from different cultures serve their food and I love the way Thai people use banana leaves as a backdrop to whatever they serve – sometimes the leaf is carefully cut to fit the serving plate exactly. It all adds to the sense that food is a form of art and it's all beautiful, aromatic and delicious – a totally sensual feast. Even some of the desserts are created like artworks. One popular dessert is called *luk chup*, which are moulded fruit shapes made from mung bean paste that are coloured and dipped in agar agar jelly to glaze. Some find these sweets too gorgeous to eat!

Essential flavours

BASIL
Thai basil, with dark green leaves and purple stems, has a mild aniseed smell and sweet flavour. Holy (or hot) basil has a minty, peppery flavour. Both are freshly torn into salads or cooked dishes.

CHILLI
Many different types of chillies are used in Thai cooking, both fresh and dried. Fresh chillies include long chillies and small, fiery birdseyes (also known as 'scuds'). Dried chillies (long or small) are usually softened in water before using – dried long chillies aren't too spicy but add warmth and colour to dishes such as red curries. Many recipes also call for roasted chilli powder.

FISH SAUCE
Known as '*nam pla*', this fishy-smelling fermented sauce is clear, pale and salty. The most popular is the Squid brand.

GALANGAL
This root has a distinctive flavour that is similar to ginger but sharper – it gives tom yum soup its special taste. Galangal has a woody texture and is harder to cut than ginger.

KAFFIR LIME

Similar in size to a normal lime but with a bumpy skin. Both the leaves and grated skin are used to flavour stir-fries and curries. When grating the skin, make sure that you only use the coloured surface. The flesh of the fruit is not used at all and the fruit yields very little juice (instead the juice from regular limes is used to add tang to salad dressings). The leaves, which are easily recognised by their unique double leaf, are often shredded very finely and added to salads.

LEMONGRASS

A woody, aromatic herb that is used to flavour many Thai dishes. The tough outer layers need to be removed to expose the more tender, white and purple-edged centre.

THAI EGGPLANTS

'Apple eggplants', are about the size of a golf ball and can be either white or green – the white type is used in curries and the green, which is more crunchy, is used in salads. Also commonly used is a very small pea eggplant, which is eaten whole and bursts in your mouth.

THAI SEASONING SAUCE

A Thai-style soybean sauce that has a different flavour to Chinese soy sauce. Popular brands include Golden Mountain or Maggi.

245

Banana Flower Salad

from Rachda Mahamontchir

This is a wonderful dish that combines the deliciously rich and creamy texture of banana flower with crunchy cashews and chicken and prawns spiked with roasted chilli and lime juice. Banana flowers resemble large bell-shaped buds and they're not difficult to find fresh, although they're also available preserved from Asian grocery stores – soak preserved buds in cold water for 10 minutes and rinse before use.

100 g chicken breast fillet, sliced

200 g green king prawns, shelled and de-veined

2 tablespoons lime juice

1 banana flower (about 200 g)

50 g dried shrimp, finely chopped

1 tablespoon sliced shallots

2 tablespoons cashews, roasted and crushed

finely sliced long red chilli

fried shallots

handful of coriander leaves

DRESSING

2 tablespoons fish sauce

3 tablespoons lime juice

1 tablespoon grated palm sugar

1 tablespoon roasted chilli paste

2 teaspoons Thai roasted chilli powder

3 tablespoons coconut milk

Bring 500 ml of water to the boil. Add the chicken, reduce the heat to a simmer and poach for 5 minutes. Add the prawns and continue poaching for 3 minutes, until cooked through. Drain and set aside.

Pour the lime juice and 500 ml of water into a bowl. Cut the banana flower in half and remove the soft, pale heart from each half, discarding the outer leaves. Finely slice on the diagonal and add to the bowl. Soak for 5 minutes; the lime will prevent discolouration.

Combine the dressing ingredients in a large bowl, stirring until the palm sugar dissolves. Drain the banana flower, gently squeeze out the excess water, and add to the dressing along with the poached chicken and prawns, dried shrimp, sliced shallots and cashews. Mix well.

Serve sprinkled with fresh chilli, fried shallots and coriander.

Serves 4

'Always leave a little food on your plate after you have eaten to show you are satisfied, but never leave rice on your plate as it is considered wasteful.'

Pad Thai

from Jay Phao-Chinda

Once you've seen this popular dish made in a Thai kitchen, you realise how easy it is if you know how! It is a wonderful combination of noodles, prawns, crunchy fresh veggies and that distinctive sweet and tangy sauce. A little dried shrimp and preserved radish, with its soft but chewy texture and unique flavour, are two of the essential ingredients. You can adjust the amount of sauce you add to the noodles according to how strong a flavour you like. This quantity of sauce is about right for four people but you can keep any unused sauce in a jar in the refrigerator for next time.

SAUCE

100 g tamarind pulp

300 ml warm water

200 g palm sugar

50 g caster sugar

150 ml Thai seasoning sauce

oil

6 large shelled green prawns

10 g dried shrimp

¼ red onion, sliced

40 g firm tofu, sliced

40 g shredded preserved radish

2 eggs

200 g flat rice noodles, soaked in warm water for 30 minutes, drained

garlic chives (some chopped and some left whole to garnish)

bean sprouts

fried shallots

chopped roasted peanuts

roasted chilli powder

lime wedges

Combine the tamarind and warm water in a bowl. Break up the pulp with your fingers until it is dissolving into the water. Strain the water into a saucepan, squeezing all the liquid from the pulp. Add the palm sugar, caster sugar and seasoning sauce. Bring to the boil, then simmer until reduced and slightly syrupy.

Heat a little oil in a wok and when hot, add the prawns. Fry until they curl and change colour then add the dried shrimp, onion, tofu and radish. Stir-fry briefly then push the ingredients to one side and crack in the eggs, breaking them up just a little. Without letting them cook completely, add the noodles, 2 tablespoons of water, a few scoops of tamarind sauce (or to taste) and some chopped garlic chives, bean sprouts, fried shallots, peanuts and chilli powder to taste. Stir briefly then serve garnished with whole garlic chives, more bean sprouts, fried shallots, peanuts and wedges of lime.

Serves 2

'To tell a cook their food is delicious you must screw up your face with intense emotion and say *"Aroi mahk"* with great determination!'

Kaeng Ped Pett Yang
Red Duck Curry
from Sujet Saengkham

My friend Air swears by making fresh coconut milk every day! If this sounds a bit extreme, you can always do what Sujet does before he starts this recipe, which is to boil tinned coconut milk for 5 minutes to rid it of the 'tinned taste'. The curry is finished with Thai basil, which you should always add after you've turned off the heat to stop the leaves turning black.

RED CURRY PASTE

10 dried long chillies, softened in warm water for 10 minutes, drained

2–3 fresh small red chillies

1 lemongrass stalk, white part only, sliced

2 cm piece of galangal, sliced

1 cm piece of fresh turmeric, sliced

7 garlic cloves

1 shallot, sliced

rind of 1 kaffir lime

1 tablespoon shrimp paste

125 ml water

vegetable oil

400 ml coconut milk

300 g roasted duck meat, skin removed, broken into large bite-sized pieces

1 tablespoon fish sauce

4 tinned lychees and 1 tablespoon juice from the tin

4 bite-sized chunks of fresh pineapple

100 g apple eggplants, cut into wedges

100 g pea eggplants

1 long red chilli, diagonally sliced

6 kaffir lime leaves, torn

50 g Thai basil leaves, torn

Put the curry paste ingredients other than the oil in a blender and process to a smooth paste.

Heat a little oil in a small frying pan and fry the paste for 10 minutes to remove the raw taste. Spoon into a jar.

Heat half of the coconut milk in a saucepan over medium heat. Add 3 tablespoons of curry paste (store the rest in the refrigerator) and stir well to combine. Cook for about 5 minutes, until the oil starts to come to the surface. Add the duck, fish sauce, lychees, lychee juice, pineapple and remaining coconut milk. Bring to the boil and add the eggplants and chilli. Cook for a few minutes, until the eggplants are just tender. Stir in the lime leaves, then remove from the heat and stir in the basil. Serve with steamed rice.

Serves 4

Gai Pad Graprow
Chicken and Holy Basil Stir-fry

from Rachda Mahamontchir

One of the favourite dishes among Thai people, often ordered for breakfast with a deep-fried egg, sunny-side up, on top.

10–12 garlic cloves, sliced

10 long red chillies, sliced

2–3 tablespoons vegetable oil

500 g chicken thigh fillets, finely sliced

1 tablespoon oyster sauce

1 teaspoon soy sauce

1 teaspoon fish sauce

pinch of white pepper

1 small onion, sliced

2 spring onions, cut into 3 cm lengths

extra 1–2 long red chillies, finely sliced

2–3 tablespoons chicken stock

½ bunch holy basil, leaves picked

FRIED EGGS

125 ml vegetable oil

4 eggs, cracked into a bowl

Put the garlic and chillies in a mortar and pound to a rough paste. Heat a wok until smoking hot then add the oil and swirl to coat the surface. Add the pounded chilli and garlic and stir-fry for 15–20 seconds. Add the chicken and stir-fry for 1–2 minutes, or until most of the chicken has changed colour. Stir in the oyster, soy and fish sauces and add the pepper, onion, spring onion and extra chilli. Keep stir-frying and when the chicken is just cooked, add the chicken stock. Turn off the heat and toss through the basil leaves. Transfer to a serving plate.

To fry the eggs, wipe out the wok and add the oil. When hot, gently pour in the eggs. Be careful as they crackle and pop. Fry the eggs until golden (they should stick together), then lift out with a slotted spoon and place on top of the chicken stir-fry.

Serves 4

Black Sticky Rice Pudding

from Pacharin Jantrakool

A lovely dessert and an impressive one to make at home. Try to grate your own fresh coconut for the true Thai flavour!

2 cups black glutinous rice, soaked overnight

1.25 litres water

440 g (2 cups) sugar

SWEET COCONUT CREAM

250 ml coconut cream

2 teaspoons rice flour

½ teaspoon salt

pinch of sugar

CARAMELISED COCONUT

2 cups freshly grated coconut
(or dried shredded coconut)

200 g (1 cup) brown sugar

Rinse the rice and place in a saucepan with the water. Bring to the boil over medium heat and cook until the grains are soft and split and most of the water has been absorbed. Add the sugar and continue cooking until dissolved.

Meanwhile, make the sweet coconut cream. Combine the ingredients in a saucepan and gently bring to the boil, then remove from the heat. The rice flour should thicken the cream.

To make the caramelised coconut, put the grated coconut and sugar in a saucepan with a little water and stir constantly over medium heat until thick.

Spoon the black sticky rice into serving bowls and top with the coconut cream and caramelised coconut.

Serves 4–6

TURKEY

For lovers of food, there's nothing like that first taste of something that fires up all your senses and makes your heart beat faster. With Turkish food my magical moment was from a single spoonful of thick, creamy yoghurt topped with sour cherries in syrup, which I tasted in a little village on the Turkish coast. That was it – from that first picturesque breakfast under grape vines at a table full of delights, I've sought out Turkish food and learned as much as I can about it.

Because Turkey stretches from the Mediterranean to the Middle East there's a huge range of ingredients and culinary styles throughout the country. Some food is beautifully rustic while other is highly developed having been fostered by the Ottoman Empire, which capitalised on Turkey's place at the centre of spice routes. These highly travelled routes brought exotic ingredients to Turkey from all around the world.

There would have been no better place to be than in the Ottoman Empire at the apex of this golden age of food – provided you were part of the upper classes. It's said that Turkish delight (*lokum*) was created by order of Sultan Abdul Hamid who wanted to please his legions of mistresses who revelled in new, delicious flavours and textures.

Turkish food in Australia has gradually evolved beyond kebabs and dips. More bakeries are turning out basic pide – the paddle-shaped bread that is a central part of many meals and essential fare at Ramadan – as well as alluring versions stuffed with white cheese and spinach, or spicy lamb or beef with an egg cracked on top. More butchers are making *sucuk* (a spicy sausage) and *bastourma* (spice-coated, air-dried beef), and there are now many Turkish sweets palaces, restaurants and cafes.

You shouldn't discount the kebabs however – Turkish know-how is a wonderful thing. Whether beef, lamb or chicken kebabs or spiced minced lamb on skewers with long chillies and tomatoes, this is some of the best simply cooked food you can find.

If you're lucky enough to spend time in a Turkish home, you'll be overwhelmed with offers of food and drink. These might start with freshly roasted nuts and move onto endless dishes, including a range of vegetable dips that are all colours of the rainbow. The feast might finish with sweet flaky pastries and rich Turkish coffee served in little cups.

Turkish coffee is renowned the world over – and deservedly so. It is made in a long-handled pot (*jezve*) with the special pulverised coffee beloved by Turks. The coffee is sweetened and stirred then allowed to gently boil up the sides of the pot a couple of times so a thick, dark crema appears on top. The art is then to carefully pour the coffee into cups, making sure each cup has a layer of smooth crema. Hot, strong and wickedly sweet!

CHILLI

Biber dövme are hot red chilli flakes made from semi-dried chillies. Look for one that is slightly oily. *Biber Salçasi* is a chilli paste that can be hot or mild.

NIGELLA SEEDS

Small black seeds also known (incorrectly) as black cumin. These are commonly sprinkled over bread such as pide before it's baked.

SUCUK

A paprika and garlic sausage sometimes used to fill pide bread, very similar to chorizo sausage.

SUMAC

A dark red spice made from the sumac berry, which has a tangy, lemony flavour. Used in marinades and salads.

YOGHURT

Used in dips and desserts as well as served with grilled meats and vegetable dishes. It is also used to make the cold drink *ayran*, which is often thinned with either milk or water and flavoured with salt – it is traditionally served with kebabs.

'At the start of a meal say to the cook, *"Eline sağlik!"* (Health to your hands!)'

Yoğurtlu Havuc
Carrot Dip

from Esma Koroglu

Easy, colourful and great to serve as part of a spread of dips.

6–7 carrots, grated
olive oil
200 g Greek-style yoghurt
1 garlic clove, crushed
pinch of salt
black olives

Cook the carrots in a frying pan with ½ tablespoon of olive oil until just softened. Remove from the pan and leave to cool.

Combine the yoghurt, garlic and salt and mix well. Stir in the cooled carrot. Scoop into a serving bowl, decorate with olives and drizzle with a little olive oil.

Makes 2 cups

Kiz Güzeli
Beetroot Dip

from Esma Koroglu

Unsurprisingly the hero of this dip is beetroot at its sweet, deep-red best, mixed with creamy yoghurt.

3 beetroots
200 g Greek-style yoghurt
1 garlic clove, crushed
pinch of salt
olive oil

Parboil the beetroots, then bake them until soft. Peel and cut into quarters. Finely chop in a food processor or blender.

Combine the yoghurt, garlic and salt and mix well. Stir in the beetroot. Scoop into a serving bowl and drizzle with olive oil.

Makes 3 cups

'You shouldn't put water
in a meal already cooked.'
(Don't meddle.)

Burghul *Pilav*
from Ishil Itiyar

This *pilav* is described as a 'no-stir risotto', with
the red of the tomato and chilli paste adding
colour and flavour.

3 tablespoons olive oil

2 small onions, chopped

1 teaspoon Turkish chilli paste (*biber salçasi*)

3 tomatoes, diced

salt and pepper

2 cups coarse burghul, rinsed

1 litre chicken stock

Heat the oil in a saucepan and add the onion,
chilli paste and tomatoes and season with salt
and pepper. Cook for a few minutes until the
onion and tomato are starting to soften. Stir in
the burghul, add the stock and bring to the boil.
Reduce the heat to a simmer, cover and cook for
15–20 minutes, or until the stock has been
absorbed.

Serves 6–8

Lamb *Kofte*
from Serif Kaya

Kofte is perfect for the barbecue, the pan or
the oven, says Serif. I couldn't agree more – this
recipe is simple and delicious. All it needs is a
salad.

500 g minced lamb

1 medium onion, grated

2 garlic cloves, crushed

pinch of allspice

pinch of freshly ground black pepper

pinch of chilli flakes

pinch of sweet paprika

pinch of ground cumin

1 teaspoon salt

1 egg

Mix the ingredients together with your hands,
kneading until smooth. Wet your hands and roll
walnut-sized pieces of mixture into balls. Flatten
them slightly. Fry the *kofte* on a lightly oiled barbecue grill, or in a chargrill pan, for about 1
minute on each side.

Serves 6

Burghul *Pilav*

'Problems will arise if one
eats and the other watches.'

Dolma
Stuffed Vegetables
from Bulent Pektuzun

A colourful, fresh and clever dish. Try to use a
range of vegetables with this rice and pine nut
stuffing as they'll look so pretty together on a
serving platter.

185 ml olive oil
4 medium onions, finely chopped
100 g pine nuts
salt
500 g medium-grain rice, rinsed
400 g tin diced tomatoes
100 g currants
1 teaspoon chilli flakes (or to taste)
pepper
½ bunch dill, finely chopped
¼ bunch mint, leaves picked and finely chopped
½ bunch flat-leaf parsley, finely chopped
2 small tomatoes, sliced

TO STUFF

6 small eggplants
6 Lebanese zucchini
6 small red capsicums
6 medium tomatoes

Heat all but 2 tablespoons of the olive oil in a
large saucepan. Add the onions, pine nuts and
some salt and fry over medium heat for 5 minutes, stirring frequently, until the onion softens.
Add the rice and continue to stir for a few minutes. Add the diced tomato, currants, chilli and
extra salt and pepper and cook for a few more
minutes. Add enough boiling water to cover the
rice, then stir in the herbs. Reduce the heat to a
simmer, cover and cook for about 10 minutes,
until the water has been absorbed. The rice
should be al dente. Leave to cool a little.

Cut the stems from the eggplants and hollow
out the flesh using a small melon baller or teaspoon, leaving a shell about 5 mm thick. Slice
through the zucchini one-third to halfway down
from the stem (so the opening is not too narrow)
and scoop out the flesh as for the eggplants.
Slice the tops off the capsicums without cutting
all the way through, so the tops stay attached
like lids. Remove the seeds. Slice the tops off
the tomatoes as for the capsicums and scoop
out the flesh.

Fill the vegetables with the rice and arrange
in the base of a wide saucepan or frying pan. Fit
them in snugly so they stay upright. Decorate
the tops of the eggplants and zucchini with
slices of tomato. Drizzle over the remaining olive
oil and enough warm water to come 2–3 cm up
the sides of the vegetables. Cover with a lid and
simmer on medium heat for around 20 minutes.
Serves 6–8

'Life comes from the throat.'
(That is, eating is life.)

Ravani
Semolina Orange Cakes
from Gulbahar Kaya

With the Turkish diaspora spread throughout Greece, Cyprus, Syria, Iraq and the Balkans, it's no wonder many countries in the region also lay claim to this lovely light cake.

5 medium eggs, separated

1 tablespoon sugar, plus 1 pinch extra

grated zest of 1 orange

50 g fine semolina

50 g plain flour

100 g ground pistachios

SYRUP

600 ml fresh orange juice

grated zest of 1 orange

500 g sugar

TO SERVE

300 ml cream

300 ml Greek-style yoghurt

2 oranges

Preheat the oven to 180°C. Butter a muffin tray that has 6 large moulds.

In a large bowl beat the egg whites with a pinch of sugar until stiff. In a separate bowl, beat the egg yolks with 1 tablespoon of sugar and the orange zest until pale. Add the semolina, flour and pistachios to the egg whites and partly mix through. Add the egg yolks and fold through until combined. Spoon into the muffin tray and bake for 30 minutes.

Meanwhile, make the syrup. Put the orange juice, zest and sugar in a saucepan and bring to the boil over medium heat, stirring until the sugar dissolves. Simmer for 10 minutes or until syrupy and reduced by half. Leave to cool.

Whip the cream until thick and stir in the yoghurt.

Segment the oranges by cutting off the peel with a small sharp knife, making sure you remove all the white pith. Cut on either side of each segment, removing wedges of flesh but leaving the membranes.

When the cakes are cooked, ladle over some of the cooled syrup and leave to soak for at least 10 minutes (or longer if you prefer the cakes softer). Serve the cakes with the whipped cream and yoghurt, orange segments and a little extra syrup.

Makes 6 cakes

UNITED STATES

Ask any American expatriate about food from home and they'll start listing numerous dishes that quickly show you that what's on offer is a far cry from hot dogs, burgers and fries. Among other things, they'll speak lovingly of Thanksgiving feasts and special foods from different regions. From the wonderfully fresh foods grown in sunny California to the plentiful seafood of Maryland's Chesapeake Bay, this is a country rich in produce and know-how. Given this abundance and variety, food from the United States is complex, from delicate crab cakes to the more hearty fare of the Deep South. American-Indian cooking traditions have fused with those brought by early settlers and waves of immigrants and a sophisticated cuisine has developed that is distinctly 'American'.

The Mississippi Delta captures this blending of cultures perfectly. New Orleans is the heart of Creole and Cajun food, which were influenced by the French, Spanish, Irish and Italians and the huge population of African-Americans in the South. This city has given us many culinary delights such as jambalaya, gumbo, fried chicken, collard greens and grits.

The African black-eyed pea is an important ingredient in southern 'soul food'. As well as introducing this staple, African slaves were resourceful – chickens were easy to keep, catching a fish was free and collard greens grew like weeds. Further north, the food couldn't be more different and the New England region is renowned for its maple syrup, baked beans, brown bread, clam chowder and clambakes.

Almost every kind of cooking can be found in New York City while in the other parts of the mid-Atlantic, Dutch influences are prominent – particularly among the Amish community of Pennsylvania.

Two feasts are always mentioned in discussions of American food. The first is Thanksgiving, which is a reminder of the first harvest feast the new settlers celebrated with the local Indians. Americans still celebrate this holiday with some of the same food – cranberries, pecans and turkey.

The other feast is the all-American 'cookout'. In these extravagant barbecues, cooks use many different types of wood to achieve a wonderful smoky flavour, enhanced by combinations of dry spices used to make rubs and marinades.

As a sweets lover, I have to also mention those lovely high wedges of all-American pies. Each region uses local produce to make wonders such as key lime pie, shoofly pie (made with molasses), lemon meringue pie and pecan pie. Oh yeah!

Essential flavours

BARBECUE SAUCE
The preferred flavours of this accompaniment to barbecued meat varies around the country, but most draw on a tomato base that is sometimes mixed with vinegar, capsicum, chilli or sugar. Tastes range from sweet to smoky or spicy.

BEEF
The New York steak and the ubiquitous hamburger made from minced beef are America's most popular exports and have colonised tastebuds around the world. The name 'hamburger' comes from the German city of Hamburg, where this pounded style of meat is common – not from the word 'ham'.

CLAMS
Clam chowder is a very popular dish and there are a number of different versions, for example with the clams cooked in milk or cooked in a stock broth with tomato.

CORN
A staple vegetable that is native to the Americas. It's thought that the American-Indians taught early settlers how to grow and eat corn, thereby saving their lives. Whether eaten straight off the cob or processed into cornmeal it can be used in endless ways. Cornbread and grits, made from ground corn, are southern favourites.

CRAB
Beloved up and down the American seaboard, blue crabs and king crabs are the most common varieties. On the West Coast dungeness crab is also popular, while in Alaska it's the red king crab. On the East Coast, the crab season in Chesapeake Bay marks the start of summer.

GRITS

Similar to polenta, grits is made from hominy, which is corn that has been soaked in lye water to remove the outside shell of the corn kernel. The hominy is then dried and ground to a slightly coarser texture than polenta.

It is commonly cooked like porridge and eaten for breakfast with butter and sugar, or with cheese for a savoury version, but it can be flavoured with anything – garlic, chilli, meat, vegetables and so on.

PECANS

Native to the United States, the pecan tree is a type of hickory that produces the edible pecan nut. Pecans hold a special place in the American heart, the most famous recipe being the much-celebrated pecan pie.

PUMPKIN

The orange pumpkin that is famously used as a jack-o-lantern at Halloween is the only member of the pumpkin family that is called a 'pumpkin' in the United States. Other varieties with golden or green outer skins are generally referred to as squashes.

TABASCO SAUCE

The brand Tabasco has become synonymous with this hot chilli sauce made from tabasco peppers, vinegar and salt. It can be used to spice up many sauces and dishes.

TOMATOES

Native to South America, tomatoes are a popular accompaniment to grilled or barbecued meat. Fried green tomatoes or other green tomato recipes put unripe late-season tomatoes to good use and tomato-based salsas employ tomatoes in a way inspired by neighbouring Latin America.

'When making jambalaya, let it simmer like a man's heart so that it develops full flavour and always wants more!'

Jambalaya

from Victor Kimble

A classic Creole dish from New Orleans and a true one-pot wonder blending French, African, Spanish and American influences. Make sure you use parboiled or 'converted' rice. Serve with cornbread muffins (see page 264).

½ tablespoon sweet paprika

1 teaspoon cayenne pepper

½ tablespoon dried oregano

½ tablespoon dried thyme

olive oil

1 red onion, diced

4 celery stalks, diced

1 red capsicum, diced

2 teaspoons crushed garlic (or garlic powder)

500 g *andouille* or chorizo sausage, diced

1 kg chicken breast fillets, diced

6–8 large tomatoes, diced

2 tablespoons tomato paste

1 kg parboiled rice

750 ml chicken stock

1 teaspoon salt

Mix the spices with the dried herbs. Heat some olive oil in a pot and add the onion, celery and capsicum. Fry for a few minutes then add the garlic and 2 teaspoons of the spices and herbs. Stir well. Add the sausage, chicken, tomatoes, tomato paste, rice, stock, salt and the remaining spices and herbs. Mix well and bring to the boil. Boil for 3–5 minutes then reduce the heat and simmer for 20–25 minutes. Keep stirring to prevent the rice from sticking to the bottom of the pot. Add a little water if needed.

Serves 6–8

'The roux is the most important ingredient to a good gumbo. Be sure not to burn it – take your time or it can ruin the gumbo!'

Chesapeake Bay Crab Cakes with Cajun Remoulade

from George Francisco

This dish is traditionally made from blue crab in the Chesapeake Bay region of Maryland, but crab cakes are also popular along all of America's coasts. They are sometimes served with a sauce such as this remoulade, or with tartare sauce, mustard or ketchup.

The recipe uses Old Bay Seasoning, a traditional spice blend for crab cakes, 'crab boils' and other favourite American shellfish dishes, but if you can't find it add a large pinch of ground celery seeds, smaller pinches of pepper and ground cardamom, and extra paprika and cayenne pepper.

CRAB CAKES

500 g crab meat (blue swimmer crab if possible)

40 g breadcrumbs

2 tablespoons Old Bay Seasoning

2 tablespoons dijon mustard

pinch of sweet paprika

pinch of cayenne pepper

salt

1 egg plus 1 egg yolk

2 tablespoons chopped tarragon

2 tablespoons chopped flat-leaf parsley

plain flour

vegetable oil

REMOULADE

2 egg yolks

50 g cornichons (or gherkins), finely chopped, plus ½ tablespoon liquid from the jar

juice of 1 lemon

250 ml vegetable oil

1½ teaspoons salted capers, rinsed and chopped

¼ bunch chives, finely chopped

¼ bunch chervil, finely chopped

¼ bunch flat-leaf parsley, finely chopped

¼ bunch tarragon, finely chopped

pinch of Spanish smoked paprika

cayenne pepper

salt

Combine the crab cake ingredients except the flour and oil and mix well. Form into 6 cakes. Refrigerate for 15 minutes to help the cakes bind.

To make the remoulade, beat the egg yolks in a bowl and add the liquid from the cornichons, then the lemon juice. Gradually beat in the vegetable oil; the mixture should thicken like mayonnaise. Stir in the cornichons, capers and herbs and add paprika and cayenne to taste (it is supposed to be spicy). Season with salt.

Dust the crab cakes in flour and fry in generous oil over medium heat until golden. Serve with the remoulade.

Serves 6

Cornbread Muffins

from Victor Kimble

Oh, yum! Cornbread muffins are made every day in the South. Victor's grandmother would have pounded the corn kernels by hand but he says tinned creamed corn is really handy and much easier! These muffins are lovely by themselves or served with collard greens, gumbo or jambalaya.

90 g (½ cup) polenta

225 g (1½ cups) self-raising flour

110 g (½ cup) caster sugar

pinch of salt

150 g butter, melted

3 eggs

1 cup creamed corn

250 ml full-cream milk

Preheat the oven to 180°C and butter a muffin tray. Mix the polenta, flour, sugar, salt, butter and eggs until well combined. Stir in the creamed corn and milk. Spoon the mixture into the muffin tray and bake for 15–20 minutes or until golden brown.

Makes 12 muffins

Southern Fried Chicken

from Ashley Sheridan

Fried chicken is the traditional Sunday lunch of the southern states. Thought to have evolved during slavery as most slaves were permitted to keep poultry, the dish has become mainstream and travelled the world. This lovely recipe is from Ashley's beloved black nanny, Blanchie, and contains her clever tip to tenderise the chicken in buttermilk. Serve with grits (see page 268) and southern greens (see page 268).

1 medium chicken (about 1.5 kg), chopped into pieces

600 ml buttermilk, to cover the chicken

225 g (1½ cups) plain flour

1 tablespoon Creole seasoning

1 tablespoon onion powder

½ tablespoon garlic powder

½ tablespoon Old Bay Seasoning (or use ½ teaspoon cayenne pepper and 1½ teaspoons sweet paprika)

1 tablespoon dried tarragon

1 tablespoon dried dill

salt and pepper

1 large egg, beaten

vegetable oil or lard

Marinate the chicken pieces in buttermilk in the refrigerator overnight.

The next day, combine the dry ingredients in a wide bowl. Drain the chicken pieces of excess buttermilk and dip them into the beaten egg, then coat them evenly in the flour mixture. Place the pieces on a sheet of baking paper to rest for about 15 minutes.

Add enough oil or lard to a large frying pan to come halfway up the chicken pieces. Heat over high heat until almost smoking. Add the chicken and cook for 10–12 minutes or until golden brown on the first side. Turn and cook the other side for 8–10 minutes. Drain on a wire rack.

Serves 6

Cornbread Muffins

'Never buy dandelion greens when you can pick them in the front yard.'

Barbecued Ribs

from Victor Pisapia

A finger-lickin' good recipe with layers of flavour from the spice rub, the homemade *chipotle* barbecue sauce and the final sizzle on the barbecue. Delicious! The sauce can be made a day in advance and stored in the refrigerator.

CHIPOTLE BARBECUE SAUCE

25 g butter

1 large onion, chopped

1 fresh or pickled jalapeño chilli, chopped

400 ml tomato puree

1 dried *chipotle* chilli

1 tablespoon molasses

1 tablespoon dark brown sugar

2 garlic cloves, chopped

3 tablespoons white-wine vinegar

80 ml Worcestershire sauce

80 ml Tabasco sauce

½ tablespoon tomato paste

RIBS

2 tablespoons sweet paprika

2 tablespoons salt

2 tablespoons garlic powder

1 tablespoon onion powder

1 tablespoon pepper

1 tablespoon cayenne pepper

1 tablespoon dried thyme

1 tablespoon dried oregano

4 racks of baby pork back ribs (about 3–4 kg)

1–2 bottles dark beer

To make the sauce, heat the butter in a saucepan and sauté the onion and jalapeño chilli. Put in a blender with the tomato puree, *chipotle* chilli, molasses, sugar and garlic and blend to a puree. Return to the saucepan, add the remaining ingredients and bring to the boil over medium heat. Simmer until reduced to a thick sauce consistency.

Combine the dry ingredients for the ribs. Rub 2–3 tablespoons of the spice mixture into the ribs, coating them on both sides. (Store the remaining spices in a jar for next time.) Place the ribs in a large dish and pour over the beer. Marinate in the refrigerator for 1–2 hours.

Bring the ribs to room temperature. Preheat the oven to 160°C. Place a large piece of foil over a large baking sheet and put the ribs on top, removing them from the beer. Wrap tightly in the foil and bake for 2 hours.

Preheat a barbecue grill to medium heat. Take the ribs out of the foil and place on the grill. Brush with barbecue sauce and cook for 6–8 minutes on each side. The sauce should caramelise a little on the surface.

Break the ribs into pieces and serve with extra barbecue sauce.

Serves 6–8

Southern Greens

from Ashley Sheridan

This dish is typically made from collard, which has leaves that look a bit like pale silverbeet and have a slightly bitter taste. Turnip leaves, mustard greens, kale, dandelion or Australia's native spinach (otherwise known as warrigal greens) also work well.

1 litre water

1 cup chopped onion

2 small–medium smoked ham hocks

1 kg greens, leaves picked

Tabasco sauce (optional)

malt vinegar (optional)

Put the water, onion and ham hocks in a pot and bring to the boil. Add the greens, reduce the heat, cover and simmer for 2 hours.

Remove the ham hocks from the pot and take the meat off the bone. Cut or break into bite-sized pieces and return to the pot. Add dashes of Tabasco and malt vinegar to your liking.

Serves 4

Grits

from Ashley Sheridan

This is a very popular dish in the South, traditionally cheap and readily available. It is delicious served with fried chicken or other Southern dishes.

Everyone has their favourite recipe, savoury or sweet, and it can be boiled, baked or fried. This recipe is a tasty, savoury porridge that is flavoured with cheese, but a mixture of goat's cheese and semi-dried tomatoes would also work wonders.

500–750 ml water

2 cups grits (or instant polenta if you can't find the real thing)

2 tablespoons butter

salt and pepper

dash of buttermilk

3 tablespoons grated extra-tasty cheese

dash of sweet paprika (optional)

Heat the water in a saucepan until almost boiling then add the grits, butter and salt and pepper to taste. Bring to the boil then reduce the heat and cook for about 30 minutes or until the grits are the consistency of mashed potatoes. Stir in the buttermilk, cheese and paprika (if using).

Serves 6–8

'The ultimate compliment to an African-American is, "That gumbo was screamin!".'

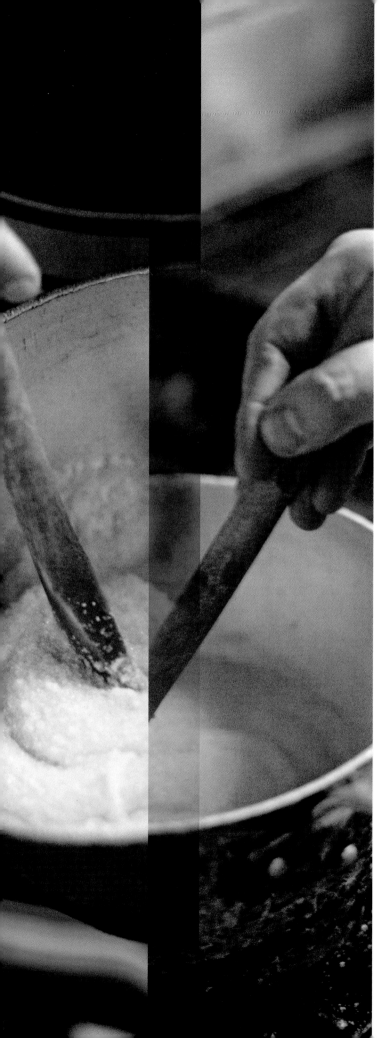

Pecan Pie

from Norma Barne

My friend Norma whips up this easy and delicious pie in just over 10 minutes. It makes wonderful use of America's native nut, which is ground and used in the pie crust as well as the filling.

CRUST

10 pecans, roasted

225 g (1½ cups) plain flour

½ tablespoon butter

pinch of salt

3 tablespoons water

FILLING

3 eggs

110 g (½ cup) caster sugar

3 tablespoons butter, melted

250 ml dark corn syrup

2 cups pecans, roasted

130 g (1 cup) cornflour

To make the crust, grind the pecans in a food processor. Add the flour, butter and salt and blend until combined. Slowly add the water while the machine is running until the mixture comes together in a ball. Remove from the food processor, cover in plastic wrap and refrigerate for 30 minutes.

Preheat the oven to 200°C and butter a medium pie tin. Roll the pastry out on a lightly floured surface and line the tin, trimming off the excess pastry. Prick the pastry to stop it puffing up and bake for 15 minutes.

Reduce the oven temperature to 180°C. Whisk the eggs with the sugar, butter and corn syrup. Stir in the pecans and cornflour. Pour into the pie crust and bake for about 1 hour. Leave to cool before serving with scoops of ice cream.

Serves 10–12

VIETNAM

Vietnamese food is dangerously seductive … its lightness and freshness make it very healthy and its depth of flavour and variety of textures will always have you coming back for more. The magic starts working from your very first fragrant bowl of pho, with its clear star anise-scented broth, thin slices of beef, noodles and many aromatic herbs. I've been lucky enough to have spent a lot of time in Vietnam and I have to say that after ten days of Vietnamese food, I feel like a new person. My chef friend Angie calls pho the Vietnamese equivalent of Jewish chicken soup – it's good for both the body and soul.

While a bowl of pho will soothe you back to health with its gentle fresh flavours, a few mouthfuls of green papaya salad is instant zing and terrific when you and your palate are feeling jaded! It's crunchy, fresh and chilli hot.

More than any other cuisine, Vietnamese food centres on herbs and uses an amazing array in many dishes, along with plenty of salad greens. These herbs are eaten for their healing properties as well as for their taste. And the way they're used makes the token garnish of curly parsley in Anglo cooking look positively pathetic – in Vietnam they're used by the bunchful for salads and accompaniments, and piled on as a garnish. Each herby mouthful is different, fresh and exciting and may include purple-stemmed basil and coriander, fresh cumin leaves, lemon verbena and Vietnamese mint.

Vietnamese cuisine is such an interesting and delicious blend of age-old flavours and techniques with the food of colonial visitors. One such example is the combination of crisp golden baguette (a legacy of French colonial times) that is brushed with the classic Vietnamese *nuoc cham* (a mixture of fish sauce, garlic and chilli) then topped with shredded chicken or pork meatballs, lots of crisp salad and herbs. This taste sensation now has people lining up at the many Vietnamese sandwich shops of our big cities!

The best news is that most Vietnamese dishes are very easy and quick to cook. Most Vietnamese homes I've visited in Vietnam only cook using one or two gas burners and never for less than eight people at a time, so dishes have to be simple to prepare. Other than the stock for pho, which simmers for a long time, most dishes are quickly whipped together and served with easy salads or shredded vegetables. With such beautiful flavours so readily prepared, it's no surprise this food does such good things for people!

Essential flavours

ANCHOVY SAUCE
Widely used as a condiment in central and southern Vietnamese food, this sauce is made from fermented, salted anchovies and is sold in a bottle. It is very strong in taste and smell and is normally diluted when used.

CASSIA
This spice is the bark of the cassia tree and it also comes in powdered form. It is used in marinades for roasted chicken or duck, beef braises and pho.

FISH SAUCE
The essence of Vietnamese food and a source of flavour as well as protein. *Nuoc mam nhi* is the first pressing – the equivalent of extra-virgin olive oil. Use this clear, clean sauce for dipping sauces and salads. The second pressing is less expensive and is used for cooking. The famous sauce made from fish sauce is called nuoc cham.

SESAME SEEDS
Used every day in Vietnamese cooking. Toasted and crushed sesame seeds are used to flavour dipping sauces and marinades or to coat sweets and other foods. After toasting they lose flavour rapidly, so be sure to toast them as close to serving as possible.

SHRIMP SAUCE
This mash of marinated shrimp is widely used as a dipping sauce in the north. It has a very strong smell but is an excellent marinade for fish and meat. Many people also like to use it as a condiment on its own.

STAR ANISE
A six-to-eight pointed star, this spice is as beautiful as it is fragrant. Its flavour resembles cinnamon and cloves and it's used in soups and stews as well as marinades. It is one of the vital ingredients in pho.

Herbs

Herbs (rau) are essential to Vietnamese cuisine where they are used not only for flavour and aroma but also for their medicinal qualities. When purchasing herbs, choose the freshest bunch you can find, handle them delicately and wash them only when you are ready to use them. These are the most widely used Vietnamese herbs:

Betel Leaf

This glossy, dark-green, heart-shaped leaf has a slightly bitter taste and is mostly used as a wrapper for grilled meats.

Coriander

A very popular widely used herb – the leaves, stems and roots of the plant are all used. They enhance the flavour of sour fish soup and crab soup and are fabulous in salads and for garnishing.

Dill

These very fine leaves are often used in fish soups or with shellfish in northern Vietnamese cuisine. Dill can also be mixed with shrimp paste or fried fish.

Fish Herb

Considered by some as an acquired taste, this herb has a definite fishy smell and flavour. Often used in soups.

Garlic Chives

Dark-green, flat chives with a garlic flavour and aroma.

Mint

Both spearmint and peppermint are used in salads and served with the famous pho soup. Vietnamese mint has long, pointed leaves that are green or crimson-brown in colour. It has a hot and spicy flavour, which combines well in salads and some shellfish dishes. Also called laksa leaf, it is said to help lower cholesterol and increase the libido.

Perilla

Large leaves that are purple on one side and dark green on the other. The leaves are shredded and used in eggplant dishes and rice-paper rolls. Also known as *shiso* in Japanese cookery.

Sawtooth Herb

A long, dark-green leaf with serrated edges and a fragrance similar to coriander but stronger. It enhances the flavour of fresh bamboo shoots and can be added to soups and salads.

Thai Basil

This fragrant, purple-stemmed herb is used in salads, especially with marinated grilled meats wrapped in lettuce leaves. It is also an essential accompaniment to pho, arriving in sprigs to be torn into the soup.

Tropical Fruits

Carambola or Star Fruit

Either yellow, orange or green, this fruit reveals its star shape when cut into cross sections. Eaten raw and finely sliced, the young star fruit has an acidic taste and is often served on a Vietnamese vegetable platter along with sliced unripe banana.

Dragon Fruit

There are two varieites of dragon fruit: one with bright red flesh and the other with white; both have tiny black seeds. Although it can be bland in flavour it makes a striking addition to a fruit platter.

Durian

This has a very strong odour but the taste is lush and tropical. Thought by many to have aphrodisiac qualities.

Jackfruit

A large, green fruit with a tough, knobbly skin that reveals yellow segmented flesh when opened. It is naturally sweet when ripe but the young jackfruit is used like a vegetable in cooking or in salads.

Longan

A small, brown-skinned fruit that grows in the Mekong Delta and in the north. The inside is a juicy cream colour with seeds.

Lychee

Exquisite tropical fruit encased in red–brown skin that is peeled to reveal white, juicy flesh. The lychee tree is cultivated in the humid tropical regions for its fruit and wood.

Mangosteen

A fruit with thick purple skin and creamy white segments inside. Discard the skin and enjoy the delicious flavour of the flesh.

Rambutan

The fiery red, spiky skins give the rambutan the look of tiny suns. They have tender white flesh and a cool, sweet flavour.

Green Papaya Salad
from Hanh Nguyen

A delicious, crunchy, fresh-tasting salad that is easy to make. The texture is fantastic when the papaya and carrot are grated as finely as possible – a mandolin with a grater attachment is ideal. I love Hanh's suggestion of serving the salad on Vietnamese rice crackers – traditionally they're cooked over a flame but Hanh's brother Peter found it works incredibly well in the microwave.

3 tablespoons fish sauce

3 tablespoons white vinegar

3 tablespoons light soy sauce

3 tablespoons water

110 g (½ cup) sugar

1 green papaya, peeled, halved, seeded and finely grated

2 carrots, finely grated

8 cooked prawns, sliced in half crosswise

16 thin slices of cooked pork belly

⅓ cup shredded Vietnamese mint

3 tablespoons fried shallots

TO SERVE

4 large sesame rice crackers

finely sliced red chilli

beef jerky, broken into small pieces

crushed roasted peanuts or cashews

To make the dressing, combine the fish sauce, vinegar, soy sauce, water and sugar in a bowl, stirring until the sugar dissolves. Combine the papaya, carrot, prawns, pork, mint and fried shallots in a separate bowl. Pour a liberal amount of dressing over the salad and toss well.

Cook the rice crackers on high in the microwave for 1 minute, or until puffed. Use them as plates, spooning the green papaya salad on top. Garnish with chilli, beef jerky and crushed nuts. To eat, break off pieces of rice cracker and use them to scoop up mouthfuls of salad.

Serves 4

Nuoc Cham
from Hanh Nguyen

Nuoc cham is Vietnam's key dipping sauce and accompanies salads and many other dishes.

1 garlic clove

3 small red chillies

140 ml first-grade fish sauce (*nuoc mam nhi*)

130 g sugar

2 tablespoons water

juice of 1 lemon

Pound the garlic and chillies to a paste in a mortar. Combine the fish sauce, sugar, water and lemon juice in a bowl. Stir thoroughly until the sugar has dissolved. Stir in the garlic and chilli paste; the chilli should float on the surface.

Makes 1½ cups

'The rite of passage for young Vietnamese girls is to learn how to mix the *nuoc cham* dipping sauce – if the chilli doesn't float on the surface, their chances of impressing a future mother-in-law are very slim.'

Bun Bo Xao

from Luke Nguyen

Luke grew up on this very authentic southern dish, which makes a perfect light lunch. 'Bun' is the vermicelli noodles, 'bo' is the beef and 'xao' means to stir-fry – the beef is quickly marinated and charred in a hot wok and served on top of cold noodles, cucumber, bean sprouts and herbs. You simply add *nuoc cham* (see page 273) and garnish to taste.

500 g rump steak, finely sliced

2 tablespoons fish sauce, plus 1 teaspoon extra

½ tablespoon crushed garlic

1 lemongrass stalk, white part only, finely sliced

500 g rice vermicelli, cooked and cooled

handful of bean sprouts

1 cucumber, halved lengthwise and sliced

10 perilla leaves, finely shredded

10 mint leaves, finely shredded

10 Vietnamese mint leaves, finely shredded

2 tablespoons vegetable oil

1 small onion, sliced

pickled vegetables (from Asian food stores)

crushed roasted peanuts

fried shallots

nuoc cham (see page 273)

Combine the beef with 2 tablespoons of fish sauce, half the garlic and a little of the lemongrass. Marinate for 10 minutes.

Put the noodles into bowls and top with the bean sprouts, cucumber and most of the herbs.

Heat the oil in a wok over high heat and add the onion and remaining lemongrass. Stir briefly then throw in the beef, allowing it to char and develop a smoky flavour. Add the extra fish sauce and remove from the heat. Add the beef to the bowls and sprinkle with the remaining herbs. Garnish with pickled vegetables, peanuts and fried shallots and dress with *nuoc cham*.

Serves 4

Caramelised Fish in a Clay Pot

from Lanna Tran

Fish cooked in caramel sauce may not sound appetising and yet it's one of the yummiest things. Take your time to get the caramel right and it will be a sure success.

CARAMEL

1 tablespoon sugar

3 tablespoons water

3 tablespoons vegetable oil

1 garlic clove, crushed

500 g firm white fish cutlets such as blue eye, cut into large pieces

1 tablespoon first-grade fish sauce (*nuoc mam nhi*)

3 tablespoons water

3 spring onions, white part only, sliced

1 teaspoon salt

½ tablespoon potato starch, mixed to a smooth paste with a little water

3 tablespoons chopped garlic chives

3 tablespoons chopped coriander

¼ teaspoon pepper

To make the caramel, put the sugar in a small saucepan and melt over medium heat. Cook until it turns dark brown. Add the water, reduce the heat to low and cook until the sugar blends into the water and the mixture becomes syrupy. Remove from the heat.

Heat the oil in a clay pot (or saucepan) and add the garlic. Fry until golden then add the fish. Stir in the caramel and cook for about 5 minutes until the fish changes colour.

Add the fish sauce, water, spring onion and salt. Bring to the boil then reduce the heat and simmer for 5 minutes. Add the potato starch and cook until the sauce has thickened. Remove from the heat and add the chives, coriander and pepper. Serve with steamed rice.

Serves 4

Pho

from Angie Hong

Pho (pronounced 'fahr') is a light, fragrant soup eaten for breakfast and all through the day. It is one of the Vietnamese's most loved dishes. The secret lies in the quality of the stock – along with the beautiful spices. Delicious!

STOCK

2 onions

10 cm piece of ginger

2½ kg beef soup bones

5 star anise

6 garlic cloves

8 cm piece cassia bark

450 g beef brisket or chuck steak

1½ tablespoons salt

80 ml fish sauce

1 tablespoon palm sugar

FOR BOWLS

1 kg dried or fresh pho noodles (rice sticks)

225 g beef sirloin, finely sliced across the grain

1 onion, finely sliced

4 spring onions, green part only, finely sliced

⅓ cup chopped coriander

black pepper

GARNISHES

lime wedges

sliced chillies

Thai basil or Vietnamese mint sprigs

bean sprouts

To prepare the stock, sear the onion and ginger over a naked flame or under a grill for about 15 minutes. Remove any charred skin and set aside.

Place the bones in a large pot and cover with cold water. Bring to the boil and cook vigorously for 3 minutes. Discard the water and rinse the bones in warm water. Wipe out the pot, return the bones to it and add 6 litres of water. Bring to the boil then reduce the heat to a gentle simmer. Skim off any scum. Add the onion, ginger and remaining ingredients and cook for 1½ hours. When the meat is cooked (slightly chewy but not tough), remove it and set aside in a bowl of cold water for 10 minutes. Remove from the water and refrigerate. Leave the broth to cook for a further 1½ hours. Strain and refrigerate. Skim off the fat when cold.

To serve, reheat the stock. Thinly slice the cold meat. Soak dried noodles (if using) in hot water for 15–20 minutes, until soft. If using fresh noodles, briefly heat them in boiling water. Arrange the noodles in the bottom of deep serving bowls and add slices of cooked meat and raw sirloin on top. Garnish with onion, spring onion and coriander. Season with pepper. Ladle over the hot stock.

To eat pho, taste the broth first, then add lime juice and chilli to taste followed by generous amounts of basil or mint and bean sprouts.

Serves 6

'How Vietnamese women don't get fat: food is shared communally and everyone has to wait for the eldest to start and to ask permission to finish the last morsel, so one tends to eat only as much as one needs.'

Pork Braised in Coconut Juice with Eggs

from Nhut Huynh

For Nhut and his seven brothers and sisters, this dish was looked forward to all year – his beloved mother used to prepare it for Vietnamese New Year. He says, 'In the years when we were farmers and very poor in the Vietnamese countryside, meat was hard to get so this dish was so good ... And now I love watching the silence as people discover the rich flavours of this great regional Vietnamese dish in my restaurant.'

Coconut juice – the clear water from the centre of the coconut rather than the milk or cream that is extracted from the flesh – imparts a sweet, mellow coconut flavour to the dish and is available frozen from Asian supermarkets.

1 kg pork belly (not too fatty), cut into 5 cm cubes

2 garlic cloves, finely chopped

4 shallots, finely chopped

2 spring onions, bruised and finely chopped (roots included)

3 tablespoons fish sauce

3 tablespoons light soy sauce

1½ tablespoons dark soy sauce

½ teaspoon freshly ground black pepper

2 tablespoons grated palm sugar or dark brown sugar

4 star anise

1 tablespoon vegetable oil

½ onion, finely chopped

750 ml young coconut juice

375 ml water

8 eggs, hard-boiled and peeled

coriander

Combine the pork, garlic, shallots, spring onion, fish sauce, soy sauces, pepper, sugar and star anise in a bowl, stirring to coat the pork. Marinate in the refrigerator for at least 3 hours or ideally overnight.

Heat the oil in a large, heavy-based saucepan and add the onion. Fry until golden then remove the pork from the marinade and add to the pan. Seal over high heat. Add the marinade, coconut juice and water. Bring to the boil and skim off any scum that rises to the surface. Gently simmer for 1 hour, skimming occasionally. Add the eggs and simmer for a further hour. Garnish with coriander and serve with jasmine rice.

Serves 6–8

'Never waste a grain of rice or in the next life that grain will become a maggot you have to eat in hell!'

Acknowledgements

This book is the result of the work of lots of people who have shared their recipes and culture. They are the soul of this book and Australia is a richer place for them being here. Their names appear with their recipes and many of their voices are heard in the wisdom that peppers each chapter – the sort of things you hear as you spend time in kitchens – after all, that's where the best lessons are learned – about food and life.

Other friends across many cuisines contributed gems – among them Mona Charabati, Aurora Charabati, Clare Horikawa, Eric Moschietto, Liz Kaydos, Sam Cosentino, David Kim, Russoul Sajadi, Jinan Ammourh, Jorge Chacon and Margie Burke. And to the conduits to some great thoughts – Aisha Cooper for tapping into the wisdom of Guillaume Brahimi; Rosie Adesua for getting the best from Kunle; Meera Joshi for some great words from Ajoy; Shinji Halim from Rohanna; Masako Fuukui from Kei and Edna Barzel for battling ancient technology to send emails from the wilds of Brazil. I must also mention the unquenchable force that is Stephen (Istvan) Oroszvari who gathered a cracking list that ran to pages of great Hungarian sayings about food and eating … all of which were fabulous.

We have tried so hard to make sure that nothing is lost in translation – from the measurement of spices to how a dish is served. That has meant a lot of painstaking explanations of how something comes together, often on top of a barrage of late night emails and phone calls – thank you so much. To Hardie Grant's hardworking publisher Pam Brewster for helping to shape this beautiful book and to photographer Sharyn Cairns, many thanks.

The faces that smile from these pages are all largely from small family businesses who work so hard to make what they do so delicious … we took photos at Arzum Markets, Auburn; Azuma Japanese Restaurant, Sydney; Baalbek Bakery, Canterbury; Billu's Indian Eatery, Harris Park; Bluefire Churrascaria Grill, Docklands; Casa Iberica, Fitzroy; Chat Thai Restaurant, Haymarket; Dalmatino Restaurant, Port Melbourne; Dench Bakers, North Fitzroy; Eilat at Hadassa, Bondi; Frank's Fruit Market, Haberfield; Gato's Pastizzi, Carramar; Grand China Restaurant, Haymarket; Hellas Cake Shop, Richmond; Hellenic Bakery, Marrickville; Janani Restaurant, Homebush; Jasmine One Lebanese Restaurant, Punchbowl; Kam Fook Restaurant, Chatswood; Illawarra Meat Market, Marrickville; Los Amatas Mexican Kitchen, Fitzroy; Madang Restaurant, Sydney; Mado Café, Auburn; Mamak Restaurant, Haymarket; Margarita's Cecinas Butchery, Fairfield; Mesnoy Injera Retail Shop, Footscray; MGM Spices, Surry Hills; La Bergerie, Canterbury; La Patisserie, Petersham; Paesanella, Haberfield; Pal-do Kim-Chi Pty Ltd, Canterbury; Portuguese Butchery, Petersham; Portuguese Style Chicken, Petersham; Sulfaro Paticceria, Haberfield; Real Turkish Delight, Auburn; Rob's British & Irish Butchery, Dandenong; Souk in the City Restaurant, Surry Hills; Tierra's Latinas, Fairfield; Vatan Restaurant, Auburn; Wellington Cake Shop, Bondi … plus at Yum Yum Pizza in Punchbowl.

Special thanks to our tiny but wonderfully talented crew from Kismet Productions who helped breathe life into such a gorgeous looking TV show (on which this book is based) and many thanks also to SBS where I've worked since 1990, a rich source of invaluable contacts and warm food-loving people. To Margaret Murphy for her wisdom and eternal support and to Matt Campbell and management for loving the whole food concept and going with it.

Sincere thanks to my Gourmet Safaris family – our wonderful energetic guides who open up their worlds to the public and who have been such an inspiration and support and source of knowledge; to the unflappable, supremely organised Suzy Brien, Georgie Neal and Jinan Ammourh, who run the safaris office; and of course to my partner-in-crime Toufic Charabati for his clear-headed direction and support.

Index

Published in 2009 by
Hardie Grant Books
85 High Street
Prahran, Victoria 3181, Australia
www.hardiegrant.com.au

Cataloguing-in-Publication data is available from the
National Library of Australia.

ISBN 978 1 74066 761 6

Cover and text design by Pfisterer + Freeman
Photography by Sharyn Cairns
Styling by Glen Proebstel
Food styling by Georgia Young
Colour reproduction by Splitting Image Colour Studio
Printed and bound in China by C & C Offset Printing

The publisher would like to thank the following for their
generosity in supplying props for the book: Brunschwig &
Fils for Fawkes Cotton Print fabric in Chocolate on page 131;
Carnfields 2 for silver cake stand on page 66 and silver tray
on page 153; Husk for black dish on page 17, Nanouche
tagine on page 179 and copper bowl on page 237; Izzi and
Popo for copper dish on page 85 and terracotta bowl on
page 163; Kasbah for terracotta bowls on page 168 and bowl
on page 258; Minimax for black ceramic dish on page 211
and green plate on page 228; Mokum Textiles for Matterhorn
fabric in Graphite on page 17; Radford Furnishings for
Greenwich Floral fabric in Onyx by Ralph Lauren on page 79
and Island Key Floral fabric in Indigo from Coastal Harbour
Collection on page 228; Seneca Textiles for Society Linen
on page 242.